Praise for *Woman*

"If someone were to ask me 'What do you hope for in a feminist book?' I would say: 'A book which demands of us activity, not passivity; which enlarges our sense of female presence in the world; a book which uses language and sensual imagery to impart a new vision of reality, from a woman-centered location; a book which expands our sense of the connections among us in the bonds of history; a book which drives us wild, that is, helps us break out from tameness and repetition into new trajectories of our own.' *Woman and Nature* is such a book." —Adrienne Rich, *New Woman's Times Feminist Review*

"*Woman and Nature* is feminist philosophy written in poetic prose. Susan Griffin explores woman's traditional identification with the earth—both as sustenance for humanity and victim of male ravage. The book is cultural anthropology, visionary prediction, literary indictment and personal claim."
—*San Francisco Examiner & Chronicle*

"Griffin's work suggests that it is exactly the naturalization and justification by Western science of the domination of matter, the human body, sensations, feelings, emotions, and "subjective" experience—and its failure to examine critically the theories and social practices producing this metaphysics or epistemology—that directs the arrogant relation to 'others' visible in our contemporary ecological havoc and social injustice." —*Isis*

"A powerful exposition of how women and the natural world have been seen as versions of each other, and violated in strangely similar ways."
—*Utne Reader* "The Canon: 150 Great Works to Set Your Imagination on Fire"

"For those inured to a steady diet of mainstream psychology, Susan Griffin's book will probably seem unpalatable. The ingredients will seem unfamiliar and their processing will seem incomplete. But for radical feminists and for those craving the sharp spice of poetic prose, *Woman and Nature* is a gourmet item."
—*Contemporary Sociology*

"Occasionally a book so fine appears that I want to shout, 'Go buy it immediately!' Such is this brilliantly provocative feminist revisioning of just about everything: history, philosophy, science, women, men, nature . . . Though not precisely history or philosophy, the book is clearly poetry. The most exciting book on feminine experience that I have yet encountered. Clearly it is not a book for everyone: those who demand officially sanctioned revelation should stay away—this book is for mature thinkers only." —*Horizons*

Also by Susan Griffin

LIKE THE IRIS OF AN EYE
RAPE
A CHORUS OF STONES
THE EROS OF EVERYDAY LIFE
WHAT HER BODY THOUGHT

Woman and Nature

WOMAN AND NATURE

THE ROARING INSIDE HER

Susan Griffin

Sierra Club Books • San Francisco

Copyright © 1978 by Susan Griffin

A hardcover edition of this book was first published by Harper & Row, Publishers.

Grateful acknowledgment is made for permission to reprint:
Excerpt from *The Dream of a Common Language, Poems 1974–1977,* by Adrienne Rich,
with the permission of W. W. Norton & Company, Inc. Copyright © 1978 by W. W. Nor-
ton & Company, Inc.
Lines from "On a Night of the Full Moon" reprinted from *Coal,* by Audre Lorde, with
the permission of W. W. Norton & Company, Inc. Copyright © 1968, 1970, 1976 by
Audre Lorde.
Quotation from *Lady of the Beasts,* by Robin Morgan. Copyright © 1976 by Robin Mor-
gan. Reprinted by permission of Random House, Inc.
Quotation from "Under the Oak" reprinted from *The Complete Poems of D. H. Lawrence.*
Copyright © 1964, 1971 by Angelo Ravagli and C. M. Weekly, Executors of The Estate of
Frieda Lawrence Ravagli. Reprinted by permission of The Viking Press Inc.
Quotation from "I Felt a Cleaving in My Mind" reprinted from *The Poems of Emily
Dickinson,* edited by Thomas H. Johnson. Reprinted by permission of the publishers and
Trustees of Amherst College. Cambridge, Mass.: The Belknap Press. Copyright © 1951,
1955 by the President and Fellows of Harvard College.
Quotation from "A Woman Is Talking to Death" from *A Woman Is Talking to Death* by
Judy Grahn. Copyright © 1974 by Judy Grahn. The Diana Press, Oakland California.
Portions of this work originally appeared in *Chrysalis* magazine.

Published by Sierra Club Books

Library of Congress Cataloging-in-Publication Data
Griffin, Susan.
Woman and nature: the roaring inside her/Susan Griffin.
    p.   cm.
Previous ed.: New York: Harper & Row. 1978.
Includes bibliographical references.
ISBN 1-57805-047-2 (alk. paper)
1. Women.   2. Nature.   3. Sex role.   4. Feminism.   I. Title.
HQ1150.G75   2000   305.3—dc21   99-37881

These words are written for those of us
whose language is not heard, whose words
have been stolen or erased, those robbed
of language, who are called voiceless or
mute, even the earthworms, even the shellfish and the sponges, for those of us who
speak our own language, and

this book is dedicated in love
to Adrienne Rich
for her friendship and for
her words

PREFACE TO THE SECOND EDITION

Two decades have passed since I wrote *Woman and Nature: The Roaring Inside Her*. Measured against the scale of evolution, the time it took, for instance, for the first living cells to become trees or animals or human beings, twenty years seems like a very short period of time. Yet the book was written in the midst of a crisis that has deepened in the intervening years. When life as we know it hangs in the balance, even the smallest moments in time take on a greater weight.

The fate of the earth was on my mind twenty years ago. But I was more sanguine about it than I am now. The times were generally more hopeful then—not because the world was a better place but because the atmosphere was charged with vision. In 1974, as I began writing this book, many women and men in my generation were thinking about the manner in which we live and about how we might create a more just world. We were asking probing and insightful questions about race and sexuality, about violence and power, and in the process scrutinized the culture we had inherited for clues to how we might see differently and thus change.

In the mid-seventies, while teaching and writing, I became interested in an old, stereotypical notion about women. Woven everywhere into the tapestry of European art and literature and seemingly an inseparable part of most philosophical and scientific texts—even embedded in the structure of European languages—is the assumption that women are closer to nature than men are. The notion is not intended as a compliment. In the hierarchical geography of European tradition, not only are human beings elevated above the rest of nature, but men are closer to heaven than women. In short, the idea that women are close to nature is an argument for the dominion of men.

During the most heady days of feminism, there were some who turned this idea on its head and argued that indeed women are closer to nature, a proximity making us *superior* to men. By the same token, the taxonomy of virtues through which men dominate—the capacity for reason and cool-headedness—was also reversed. Rationality itself became suspect, and passionate sensuality was enshrined.

I do not agree with the idea that women are closer to nature than are men in either its traditional or inverted form. Everything that exists on Earth, including rational thought, is part of nature. Thus, that one element would be closer to nature than another seems implausible to me. What does, however, seem very possible to me is that one gender may be more aware of being part of nature than another. And yet this difference in awareness must also be treated with subtlety. Today, largely due to the feminist movement, many more women are abandoning traditional feminine roles altogether and in some cases have become as divided from an awareness of natural process than any man. But even women who have a more direct knowledge of the stuff of earthly existence because they play traditional domestic roles are not born with this proclivity. They are shaped to it by society. As Simone de Beauvoir wrote in the mid–twentieth century, "A woman is not born she is made." And the same can be said for the tendency of some men not only to think of themselves as apart from nature but to place themselves at a distance from actual life processes. This behavior has less to do with genetics than with another tendency. When civilizations come to embody certain ideas through the influence of art, science, and institution, we who are the citizens of those civilizations come to resemble those ideas. As Oscar Wilde has written, "Life imitates art."

If society has succeeded in making men and women after a set of ideas that in the end diminishes human nature, we are now perilously close to making the earth after a philosophy that not only limits but even erases nature. As logical as the arguments for controlling women and nature appear to be, they veil a profound illogic, a heated fear, indeed a terror, that serve as the engines for a civilization in retreat from natural processes that must and do include change and loss, vulnerability, the rise and then ebb of powers, mortality. The association between women and nature has not only served to oppress women, it has also acted as a device for denial, a means to evade the simple truth that human existence is immersed in nature, dependent on nature, inseparable from it. By imagining women as closer to nature, it becomes possible to imagine men as farther away from nature. And in this way, both men and women can indulge in the fantasy that the human condition can be free of mortality, as well as the exigencies and needs of natural limitation.

It is popular now to speak in glowing terms of free markets, as if the marketplace had no relationship to earthly necessity but were instead entirely conceptual and could thus grow as numbers grow, without boundaries and without end. This is the latest fantasy of dominion over the earth, as if through the power of will human beings can make natural resources multiply on demand. But loving freedom as we do, we are ignoring another kind of freedom—liberation from a limiting philosophy, from a habit of self-deception that prevents us from treasuring what we actually possess: life.

At the heart of what I discovered as I wrote *Woman and Nature* is a vision of freedom from an imprisoning state of mind. The book is written in poetic prose, a style that allowed me to move underneath the seemingly logical propositions of our culture, not only to discover the machinery of our fear but to find evidence for a wisdom that is at once old and new, forgotten and yet still alive.

If the next twenty years are crucial in the history of the planet, so is the future of this wisdom—logical and sensual, realistic and imaginative—that is in us all and is indispensable to our survival. Read this book playfully, read it to the edges of the pages and then over the margins into other books, other worlds, other possibilities.

SUSAN GRIFFIN
Berkeley
July 1999

PREFACE

This is an unconventional book and so, it was felt, needed some preface. I began writing this book roughly three years ago, after I was asked to deliver a lecture on women and ecology. I was concerned that the ecological movement had often placed the burden for solving its problems, those that this civilization has with nature, on women. I said in that lecture that women were always being asked to clean up, and to this I added the observation that men consider women to be more material than themselves, or more a part of nature. The fact that man does not consider himself a part of nature, but indeed considers himself superior to matter, seemed to me to gain significance when placed against man's attitude that woman is both inferior to him and closer to nature. Hence this book called *Woman and Nature* grew.

In the process of writing I found that I could best discover my insights about the logic of civilized man by going underneath logic, that is by writing associatively, and thus enlisting my intuition, or uncivilized self. Thus my prose in this book is like poetry, and like poetry always begins with feeling. One of the loudest complaints which this book makes about patriarchal thought (or the thought of civilized man) is that it claims to be objective, and separated from emotion, and so it is appropriate that the style of this book does not make that separation.

Since patriarchal thought does, however, represent itself as emotionless (objective, detached and bodiless), the dicta of Western civilization° and science on the subjects of woman and nature in this book are written in a parody of a voice with such presumptions. This voice rarely uses a personal pronoun, never speaks as "I" or "we," and almost always

---

°I have purposely limited the scope of this book to Western civilization.

implies that it has found absolute truth, or at least has the authority to do so. In writing this book, this paternal voice became quite real to me, and I was afraid of it. It sprang out at me in the form of recognized opinion and told me that the reactions I experienced in my female body to its declarations were ridiculous (unfounded, hysterical, biased). You will recognize that voice from its use of such phrases as "it is decided" or "the discovery was made." Much research went into the reconstruction of this voice: I tried to preserve its style and tone accurately.

The other voice in the book began as my voice but was quickly joined by the voices of other women, and voices from nature, with which I felt more and more strongly identified, particularly as I read the opinions of men about us. This is an embodied voice, and an impassioned one. These two voices (though you will find more than two in the text) are set in different type styles; thus a dialogue is implied throughout the book.

I begin the book by tracing a history of patriarchy's judgments about the nature of matter, or the nature of nature, and place these judgments side by side, chronologically, with men's opinions about the nature of women throughout history. From this philosophical beginning the book becomes more actual, treating of the effect of patriarchal logic on material beings. And so the first book, "Matter," continues the analogy drawn between woman and nature into explorations of the earth, trees, cows, show horses and women's bodies as we all exist in patriarchy.

The second book is entitled "Separation," and beginning with the separation of a womb from a woman's body, lists and protests against all those separations which are part of the civilized male's thinking and living—mind from emotion, body from soul—and reveals that separation which patriarchy requires us to make from ourselves. The third book, called "Passage," finally separates our consciousness from the consciousness of patriarchy, and thus the fourth book is called "Her Vision: Now She Sees Through Her Own Eyes."

In "Her Vision," all that we have seen in the first two books from the eye of patriarchy is now reseen. Thus the book is not so much utopian as a description of a different way of seeing. And so the section called "The Zoological Garden" is reflected in "Her Vision" as "The Lion in the Den of the Prophets." I had thought, in writing "Her Vision," that this book would be like a mirror, and hence tried to put the sections in the same order (except backward) as they appeared in the first two books. But this proved impossible. "Her Vision" would not be so constricted.

While I was writing *Woman and Nature: The Roaring Inside Her,* the spaces I created within it began to be real for me; passing over into work on "Her Vision," I would feel as if I had entered a free zone, and breathe a sigh of relief.

I hope the reader will enter these spaces as I entered them, moving through these ways of seeing with passion, and will hear the voices as I hear them, especially the great chorus of woman and nature, which will swell with time. And I hope the reader will know, too, though this is just a book and thus just a fiction, that the feelings which enter these words are very real, and that in this matter of woman and nature, *we have cause to feel deeply.*

SUSAN GRIFFIN
Berkeley
November 1977

ACKNOWLEDGMENTS

The ways of thought are never simple to trace; all along, my thinking has been part of the thinking of other women. (And in this I use "think" as it is constructed in Chinese calligraphy: "brain" and "heart" together.)* What I learned of the necessities of daily life from the women of my family, the work necessary to keep house together and raise children—all that women know of naming feeling while we live in a culture that misnames and mistakes what we experience—goes into this book. In particular this book was generated in the midst of a time and space defined by the words and images of other women and this as part of a feminist movement which has made such a time and space possible. This book could not have been written otherwise. And so my greatest debt is to women who are part of this movement, now and a hundred or many hundred years ago.

I will name a few who helped me with this writing. My editor, Fran McCullogh, has been wise and supportive throughout this writing and I am deeply grateful for her brilliance and her grace; Adrienne Rich, through her work and her profoundly generous friendship and her insight, has been present in all this writing, and these two women in the sometimes very difficult years of writing the book truly sustained this effort. Let me also thank Kirsten Grimstad and Susan Rennie for their warm friendship and constant encouragement, and their continually inspiring turns of mind. This must be said also for Frances Jaffe and Mark Linenthal and Beverly Dahlen. June Jordan has been deeply understanding and supportive. Tillie Olsen, Kathleen Barry, Kathleen

---

*I owe this observation to Diane Wolff, *Chinese Writing* (New York: Holt, Rinehart and Winston, 1975).

Fraser, Rena Rosenwasser, Pat Loomes, Karen Petersen, J. J. Wilson, Thalia Kitrilakis, Barbara Christian, Gloria Bowles, Carol Murray, Valerie Miner, Mary Mackey, Kate Millett, Alta, Ruth Rosen, Nancy Scott, Helene Wenzel, Joan Levinson, Harriet Whitehead, Sandy Boucher, Barbara McClandish, Nancy Snow, Judith Van Allen and Eve Merriam all read parts of the manuscript, and gave me both encouraging and helpful critical response. I want especially to thank Michelle Cliff for her understanding of this work and her close readings of it, and for her continual kind support. Carol Smith Rosenberg has also been deeply supportive and her scholarship and writing on the history of women has been illuminating; she directed me to important sources, as did Robin Morgan. Conversations with Claire Fischer and with Florence Rush were very helpful to me. Both Nancy Reeves and Mary Felstiner spoke with me about the history of science. Carolyn Iltis, a science historian with brilliant insights, shared some of her knowledge with me and gave me courage by the example of her work. This book could not exist had I not read Mary Daly's *Beyond God the Father*, which opened ways of thinking for me. And I thank her for her reading of my manuscript and for wonderful and amazing dialogues. Audre Lorde's essay "Poems Are Not Luxuries," published in *Chrysalis* magazine, had a deep influence, as did conversations with Susan Sherman. Monique Wittig aided me with a translation, and through her own work and thought. Let me thank Ellen Lewin for her help with medical research and Charlene Spretnak for providing me with clippings and references. Wendell and Tanya Berry discussed this question of woman and nature with me and generously helped me in my efforts to observe the effects of strip mines in Kentucky. The editors of the *Mountain Eagle* showed me some of the damage from the strip mines in the Cumberland Mountains. Joan Medlin helped me with preparing the footnotes and bibliography for this work. I wish also to thank Fanchon Lewis for her fine typing of the manuscript, and her patience. And I must thank the instructors for "Environmental Issues," a course in the Department of Agriculture at the University of California at Berkeley, for asking me, almost four years ago, to deliver a lecture on women and ecology, thus beginning my thinking in this direction. And I thank the National Endowment for the Arts for a grant which allowed me the time and space to do much of this writing.

Finally, there is much work and writing by women that is not mentioned directly in these pages but has shaped these words. I think especially of the paintings of Georgia O'Keeffe, the novels of Virginia Woolf, the poetry of Josephine Miles, so often bearing on these concerns; of Diane di Prima, Joanna Griffin, the writing of Annie Dillard. There is so much that is not visible from others in this book that still is here, and I thank those spirits.

CONTENTS

ix   *Preface to the Second Edition*

xiii   *Preface*

xvii   *Acknowledgments*

3   PROLOGUE

5   BOOK ONE: *MATTER*

           How man regards and makes use of woman and nature

7   MATTER

           Wherein man's ideas about nature and his attitudes toward women are revealed side by side and in historical order

49   LAND (*Her Changing Face*)

           In which he shapes this earth to his use

58   TIMBER (*What Was There for Them*)

           In which he makes the trees his own

67   WIND

           In which he harnesses the elements

69   COWS (*The Way We Yield*)

           In which he domesticates the animals

76   MULES

           And the domesticated speak

78   THE SHOW HORSE

> And the domesticated learn to please

85   HER BODY

> And he makes her body over to his liking

95   BOOK TWO: *SEPARATION*

> The separations in his vision and under his rule (*wherein our voice rises*)

97   WHERE HE BEGINS

> *Separation* wherein he separates himself from woman and nature, and *The Image* wherein he makes woman and nature the object of his art, and *Marriage* wherein he makes woman and nature a part of himself

105   HIS POWER (*He Tames What Is Wild*)

> *The Hunt* whereby he captures her wildness, and *The Zoological Garden* in which she paces in her cage, and *The Garden* wherein he civilizes wilderness

109   HIS VIGILANCE (*How He Must Keep Watch*)

> *Space Divided* and *Time Divided* by which he guards time and space, and *Silence* which is recognized as her silence

115   HIS KNOWLEDGE (*He Determines What Is Real*)

> *What He Sees* (The Art of It) wherein the method of his vision is examined, and *The Anatomy Lesson* wherein she has difficulty with his method, and *Acoustics* where the quality of his hearing is exposed, and *Reason* in which he calls her unreasonable, and *The Argument* wherein we see the separations in his argument

122   HIS CONTROL (*How He Becomes Invulnerable*)

> Childish Fear *in which we remember his fear of the dark,* and *Speed* wherein he speeds past what women and children fear, and *Burial* wherein he buries himself in her

127   HIS CERTAINTY (*How He Rules the Universe*)

> *Quantity* in which he calculates existence, and *Probability* in which he determines the future, and *Gravity* in which the laws of the universe determine his fate

134   HIS CATACLYSM (*The Universe Shudders*)

> Prophets *in which they warn us of the corruption of this earth, and* Plutonium *in which we accept their judgment, and* Pollution *wherein he poisons the world*

138   HIS SECRETS *(What Is Sleeping Within)*

> *Dream Life* where his right hand and his left hand never meet, and *Nightmares* where we glimpse another future

150   TERROR

> In which he warns her with his vision of the universe

155   BOOK THREE: *PASSAGE*

> Her journey through the *Labyrinth* to the *Cave* where she has Her Vision

165   BOOK FOUR: *HER VISION*

> Now she sees through her own eyes (wherein the world is no longer his)

THE SEPARATE REJOINED

169   MYSTERY *(How the Divided Come Together Again)*

> What had terrified him

171   THE OPENING

> *We enter a new space. We enter a new time* (The territory beyond his vigilance)

177   OUR DREAMS *(What Lies Under Our Stillness)*

> *Our* Flying, *our* Deviling, *our* Dancing, *our* Animals Familiar (What was kept secret from him)

184   OUR ANCIENT RAGES

> *We allow* Turbulence *and* Cataclysm *cannot be denied, and we say there are always* Consequences (The universe he tried to deny)

189   THE LION IN THE DEN OF THE PROPHETS

> The power he could not tame

190   POSSIBILITY

> Gravity, *what we have had to do, and* Numbers, *what we will not do, and* Naming, *all that we cannot say, and* The Possible, *what the universe reveals* (Of what no one can be certain)

195   TRANSFORMATION

> We Visit Our Fears, *we are transformed, and* Erosion, *we transform* (What he failed to control)

198 CLARITY

Vision *to know the being of another, and* One from Another (*The Knowledge*) *what passes between us, and* Acoustics *how we listen for signs* (*What he would not acknowledge*), *and* Our Labor *by which we continue*

MATTER REVISITED

209 THE YEARS (*Her Body Awakens*)

and The Anatomy Lesson *her body reclaimed, and* History *what her hair tells us, and* Memory *what we know from her breasts, and* Archives *what is hidden in her vulva, and* Letters *what her clitoris says, and* Records *what is part of her womb*

219 OUR NATURE (*What Is Still Wild in Us*)

221 THIS EARTH (*What She Is to Me*) *Where we are*

222 FOREST (*The Way We Stand*) *Why we are here*

224 THE WIND (*How everything changes*), *and*

225 MATTER (*How We Know*)

231 *Notes*

261 *Bibliography*

Woman and Nature

PROLOGUE

He says that woman speaks with nature. That she hears voices from under the earth. That wind blows in her ears and trees whisper to her. That the dead sing through her mouth and the cries of infants are clear to her. But for him this dialogue is over. He says he is not part of this world, that he was set on this world as a stranger. He sets himself apart from woman and nature.

And so it is Goldilocks who goes to the home of the three bears, Little Red Riding Hood who converses with the wolf, Dorothy who befriends a lion, Snow White who talks to the birds, Cinderella with mice as her allies, the Mermaid who is half fish, Thumbelina courted by a mole. *(And when we hear in the Navaho chant of the mountain that a grown man sits and smokes with bears and follows directions given to him by squirrels, we are surprised. We had thought only little girls spoke with animals.)*

We are the bird's eggs. Bird's eggs, flowers, butterflies, rabbits, cows, sheep; we are caterpillars; we are leaves of ivy and sprigs of wallflower. We are women. We rise from the wave. We are gazelle and doe, elephant and whale, lilies and roses and peach, we are air, we are flame, we are oyster and pearl, we are girls. We are woman and nature. And he says he cannot hear us speak.

But we hear.

BOOK
ONE

MATTER

How Man Regards

and Makes Use of

Woman and Nature

So this was how it looked, the determining, the crucial sky, and this was how man moved through it, remote above the dwindled earth, the concealed human life. Vulnerable life, that could scar.

TILLIE OLSEN,
Tell Me a Riddle

MATTER

It is decided that matter is transitory and illusory like the shadows on a wall cast by firelight; that we dwell in a cave, in the cave of our flesh, which is also matter, also illusory; it is decided that what is real is outside the cave, in a light brighter than we can imagine, that matter traps us in darkness. That the idea of matter existed before matter and is more perfect, ideal.

Sic transit, how quickly pass, *gloria mundi,* the glories of this world, it is said.

Matter is transitory and illusory, it is said. This world is an allegory for the next. The moon is an image of the Church, which reflects Divine Light. The wind is an image of the Spirit. The sapphire resembles the number eleven, which has transgressed ten, the number of the commandments. Therefore the number eleven stands for sin.

It is decided that matter is passive and inert, and that all motion originates from outside matter.

That the soul is the cause of all movement in matter and that the soul was created by God: that all other movement proceeds from violent contact with other moving matter, which was first moved by God. That the spheres in perpetual movement are moved by the winds of heaven, which are moved by God, that all movement proceeds from God.

That matter is only a potential for form or a potential for movement.

It is decided that the nature of woman is passive, that she is a vessel waiting to be filled.

It is decided that the existence of God can be proved by reason and that reason exists to apprehend God and Nature.

God is unchangeable, it is said. *Logos* is a quality of God created in man by God and it is eternal. The soul existed before the body and will live after it.

"And I do not know how long anything I touch by a bodily sense will exist," the words of a saint read, "as, for instance, this sky and this land, and whatever other bodies I perceive in them. But seven and three are ten and not only now but always . . . therefore . . . this incorruptible truth of numbers is common to me and anyone at all who reasons."

And it is stated elsewhere that Genesis cannot be understood without a mastery of mathematics.

"He who does not know mathematics cannot know any of the other sciences," it is said again, and it is decided that all truth can be found in mathematics, that the true explanation is mathematics and fact merely evidence.

That there are three degrees of abstraction, each leading to higher truths. The scientist peels away uniqueness, revealing category; the mathematician peels away sensual fact, revealing number; the metaphysician peels away even number and reveals the fruit of pure being.

It is put forward that science might be able to prolong life for longer periods than might be accomplished by nature. And it is predicted:

> that machines for navigation can
> be made without rowers so that the
> largest ships on rivers or seas will
> by a single man be propelled with
> greater velocity than if they were
> full of men
> that cars can be made to move with
> out the aid of animals at an un
> believable rapidity
> that flying machines can be con
> structed
> that such things can be
> made without limit

It is decided that vision takes place because of a ray of light emanating from the eye to the thing perceived.

It is decided that God is primordial light, shining in the darkness of first matter, giving it substantial being. It is decided that geometrical optics holds the key to all understanding.

It is said that the waters of the firmament separate the corporeal from the spiritual creation.

That the space above is infinite, indivisible, immutable, and is the immensity of God.

That the earth is a central sphere surrounded by concentric zones, perfect circles of air, ether and fire, containing the stars, the sun and the planets, all kept in motion by the winds of heaven. That heaven is beyond the zone of fire and that Hell is within the sphere of the earth. That Hell is beneath our feet.

It is stated that all bodies have a natural place, the heavy bodies tending toward the earth, the lighter toward the heavens.

And what is sublunary is decaying and corruptible. The earth "is so depraved and broken in all kinds of vice and abominations that it seemeth to be a place that hath received all the filthiness and purgings of all other worlds and ages," it is said.

And the air below the moon is thick and dirty, while the air above "shineth night and day of resplendour perpetual," it is said.

And it is decided that the angels live above the moon and aid God in the movement of celestial spheres. "The good angels," it is said, "hold cheap all the knowledge of material and temporal matters which inflates the demon with pride."

And the demon resides in the earth, it is decided, in Hell, under our feet.

It is observed that women are closer to the earth.

That women lead to man's corruption. Women are "the Devil's Gateway," it is said.

That regarding the understanding of spiritual things, women have a different nature than men, it is observed, and it is stated that women are "intellectually like children." That women are feebler of body and mind than men, it is said: "Frailty, thy name is woman."

And it is stated that "the word woman is used to mean the lust of the flesh."

That men are moved to carnal lust when they hear or see woman, whose face is a burning wind, whose voice is a hissing serpent.

It is decided that in birth the female provides the matter (the menstruum, the yolk) and that the male provides the form which is immaterial, and that out of this union is born the embryo.

And it is written in the scripture that out of Adam who was the first man was taken Eve, and because she was born of man he also named her: "She shall be called Woman."

And it is written in the bestiary that the cubs of the Lioness are born dead but on the third day the Lion breathes between their eyes and they wake to life.

It is decided that Vital Heat is the source of all vital activity, that this heat emanates from God to the male of the species, and that this vital heat informs the form of the species with maleness, whereas the female is too cold to effect this change.

It is decided also that all monstrosities of birth come from a defect in the matter provided by the female, which resists the male effort to determine form.

It is decided that Vital Heat is included in semen, that it is the natural principle in the spirit and is analogous to that element in the stars.

It is decided that the Vital Heat of the sun causes spontaneous generation.

The discovery is made that the sun and not the earth is the center of the universe. And the one who discovers this writes:

"In the middle of all sits Sun enthroned. In this most beautiful temple could we place this luminary in any better position from which he can illuminate the whole at once? He is rightly called the Lamp, the Mind, the Ruler of the Universe; Hermes Trismegistus names him the visible God, Sophocles' Electra calls him the All-Seeing. So the Sun sits as upon a royal throne ruling his children the planets which circle round him. . . . Meanwhile the earth conceives by the Sun, and becomes pregnant with an annual rebirth."

And it is decided that the Sun is God the Father, the stars God the Son, and the ethereal medium the Holy Ghost.

Mutability on the earth, it is said, came to the Garden of Eden after the Fall. That before the Fall there was immortal bliss on earth, but that after the Fall "all things decay in time and to their end do draw."

That the face of the earth is a record of man's sin. That the height of mountains, the depth of valleys, the sites of great boulders, craters, seas, bodies of land, lakes and rivers, the shapes of rocks, cliffs, all were formed by the deluge, which was God's punishment for sin.

"The world is the Devil and the Devil is the world," it is said.

And of the fact that women are the Devil's Gateway it is observed that sin and afterward death came into the world because Eve consorted with the devil in the body of a serpent.

That the power of the devil lies in the privy parts of men.

That women act as the devil's agent and use flesh as bait.

That women under the power of the devil meet with him secretly, in the woods (in the wilderness), at night. That they kiss him on the anus. That they offer him pitch-black candles, which he lights with a fart. That they anoint themselves with his urine. That they dance back to back together and feast on food that would nauseate "the most ravenously hungry stomach." That a mass is held, with a naked woman's body as an altar, feces, urine and menstrual blood upon her ass. That the devil copulates with all the women in this orgy, in this ritual.

That these women are witches.

That "Lucifer before his Fall, as an archangel, was a clear body, composed of the purest and brightest air, but that after his Fall he was veiled with a grosser substance and took a new form of dark and thick air."

That "Virgin's urine is quite unclouded, bright and thin, and almost lemon color," whereas "the urine of the woman who has lost her virginity is very muddy and never bright or clear. . . ."

And that though it is written that there is no wickedness to compare to the wickedness of a woman, it is also written that good women have brought "beatitude to men, saved nations, lands and cities," and that "Blessed is the man who has a virtuous wife, for the number of his days shall be doubled."

And that a virtuous wife is one who obeys her husband, as the Church obeys Christ.

And it is said that there are certain woods which exist free from the "penalty of Adam," where there are "tongues in trees, books in running brooks, sermons in stones and good in everything."

It is now discovered that the celestial substance, like the substance of the earth, is mutable.

And it is decided that though the celestial substance is mutable, yet immutable laws govern all mutability, and that the invariability of God's will can be deduced from the perfection of His laws which rule the natural world.

It is posited that the spaces between the planetary orbits each correspond to Euclid's five perfect solids: that from Saturn to Mercury each corresponds to a cube, a tetrahedron, a dodecahedron, an icosahedron and an octahedron.

For this reason it is said that there are only six planets and that there could be only six planets (no more and no less).

It is announced that the music of the spheres may be discovered through mathematical laws.

The cause of the universe, it is said, lies in mathematical harmony, which exists in the mind of the creator.

It is said that all shapes, celestial and terrestrial, are in reality geometrical shapes.

A compass is devised and a set of rules drawn for reducing the irregular to the regular and for simplifying a combination of regular shapes to a single figure.

It is argued that the heliocentric system, since it requires only thirty-four epicycles (as opposed to the eighty required by the geocentric system), is more simple and that therefore it must be true.

It is said, "Nature doth not that by many things which can be done by a few."

That "Nature is not redundant."

That "Nature is pleased with simplicity and affects not the pomp of superfluous causes."

"Vain pomp and glory of this world, I hate ye," it is said.

(And extravagance and excess are seen to be apparent in women: women have the defect of "inordinate affections and passions" it is written and women's sorrows are "either too extreme or not to be believed" it is said and "women being moved to anger" are "more envious than a serpent, more malicious than a tyrant, more deceitful than the devil," and of women's wrath it is said they "are made of blood," and of women's mind it is said that it "shifts oft like the inconstant wind," and it is said that "all witchcraft comes from carnal lust which is in women insatiable.")

And it is said that all sin originated in the flesh of the body of a woman and lives in her body. (And the old text reads that Christ was born of a Virgin in order that the disobedience caused by the serpent might be destroyed in the same manner in which it had originated.)

And we are reminded that we have brought death into the world.

Now it is disputed and then it is made clear that angels do not possess bodies but only assume them. That they do not occupy any point in space but are virtually present and operating at that point.

And from this some suppose that angels are thin.

And it is wondered how thin angels are (and how many angels could occupy, at one time, the space on the head of a pin).

And it is said that nature can be understood only by reduction, that only by reducing her to numbers does she become clear.

That without mathematics "one wanders in vain through a dark labyrinth."

It is decided that that which cannot be measured and reduced to number is not real.

It is questioned whether or not motion is real.

It is discovered that motion can be measured by measuring the space through which movement moves and the time in which the moving takes place.

It is decided that motion is real.

(But it is said again that all motion came originally from God and that God has given the universe a fixed quantity of movement.)

It is decided that all motion results from bodies acting directly on other bodies, that one body cannot affect another at a distance.

And it is stated that all matter is made up of smaller particles of matter, whose motions determine the appearance of the universe. That God alone sees things as they are, that He sees the particles directly. That if anyone were to know the position of all the particles at any given time he could predict the future.

It is said that the sensation of color is produced by the action of these particles on the retina of the eye. That the particles are real but that the sensation they produce is not.

That color is not real. Odor is not real. Dreams not real. Pleasure and pain not real. Nor nightmares. Nor chamber music.

And of the difference of women from men it is said that women are more sensual than they.

It is said that women exist for pleasure.

"How fair and pleasant art thou, O love, for thy delights," it is written.

The human mind, it is written, was made by God to understand "not whatever you please, but quantity."

"For what is there in the human mind besides figures and magnitudes?" it is asked.

And it is seen that the senses are deceptive. And the ancient texts reveal that of understanding there are two kinds: one authentic and the other bastard, and sight, hearing, smell, taste and touch are all bastard understandings.

And it is said that women are the fountain, the flood and the very root of deception, falsity and lies.

Woman, for instance, was formed from a defective rib of man's breast, it is said, which was bent contrary to him, and so therefore it is in woman's nature to deceive.

And it is advised that if one would follow a woman to her dressing room one might discover the truth. Beneath her paint, her wigs, her jewels, her robes, is a monstrous creature so odious and ugly that one finds there "Serpents rather than saints."

It is ascertained that sensations are confused thoughts and that imagination and memory because they derive from sensation should be distrusted.

The word "hysterical" is taken from the word *hyster,* meaning womb, because it is observed that the womb is the seat of the emotions (and women are more emotional than men).

That crying is womanish, it is observed, and that dramatic poetry, since it causes crying, ought to be avoided, that it "has a most formidable power of corrupting even men of high character."

And it is written that women have the defect of "inordinate affections and passions" and overlively imaginations, and for this reason young girls should not be taught Italian and Spanish, since books written in both those languages have a "dangerous effect" on women.

And it is cautioned that husbands should not counsel with their wives nor allow them to see their accounting books.

Those

> "Who, moving others are themselves as stone
> Unmoved, cold and to temptation slow:
> They rightly do inherit heaven's graces
> And husband nature's riches from expense"

it is written.

And it is also written that woman "is not fully the master of herself" and that "only one woman in thousands has been endowed with the God-given aptitude to live in chastity and virginity."

And the old texts read that where there is death there too is sexual coupling and where there is no death there is no sexual coupling either.

And it is decided that God does not die.

It is decided that God is the maker but that he has no hands. It is decided that He created Harmony and Beauty but that He has no ears, no eyes. That He is not corporeal nor is He matter, but He is ultimate reality. That he exists absolutely and infinitely. That he is dependent on no other being. That He was not born. That He has no mother. He is the Father. He will not die.

And it is said that God is a mathematician. That the human mind understands some propositions in geometry and arithmetic but that in "these the Divine Wisdom knows infinitely more propositions because It knows them all."

That God has allowed us to see "by creating us after His own image so that we could share in his own thoughts."

Cogito, I think, *ergo,* therefore, *sum,* I am, it is said.

And it is written that "not the woman but the man is the image of God."

And that "the image of God is in man and it is one." That "Women were drawn from man, who has God's jurisdiction as if he were God's vicar, because he has the image of the one God."

That as God is the principle of the universe so is man, in likeness to God, the principle of the human race.

It is decided that the minds of women are defective. That the fibers of the brain are weak. That because women menstruate regularly the supply of blood to the brain is weakened.

All abstract knowledge, all knowledge which is dry, it is cautioned, must be abandoned to the laborious and solid mind of man. "For this reason," it is further reasoned, "women will never learn geometry."

There is a controversy over whether or not women should be taught arithmetic.

To a woman who owns a telescope it is suggested that she rid herself of it, that she "stop trying to find out what's happening on the moon."

It is decided that matter cannot know matter.

That matter "is but a brute thing and only capable of local motion."

That matter has no intellect and no perception.

And it is stated that nature should be approached only through reason.

1382 Thomas Brawardine in *Treatise on the Proportions of Velocities in Moving Bodies* proposes a mathematical law of dynamics universally valid for all changes in velocity.

1431 Joan of Arc, aged 22, "placed high on the fire so the flames would reach her slowly," dies.

(She is asked why she wears male costume.)

1468 The Pope defines witchcraft as *crimen exceptum,* removing all legal limit to torture.

1482 Leonardo da Vinci moves to Milan, and begins his notebooks on hydraulics, mechanics, anatomy; he paints *Madonna of the Rocks.*

(Does she see the body of St. Michael, they ask her? Did he come to her naked?)

1523 One thousand witches burn in a single year in the diocese of Como.

1543 Vesalius publishes *De Humani Corporis Fabrica.*

1543 Copernicus publishes *De Revolutionibus Orbium Coelestium.*

(She is asked if she is in a state of grace. She is asked if St. Margaret speaks English.)

1571 Johannes Kepler born.

1572 Augustus the Pious issues *Consultationes Saxionicae,* stating that a good witch must be burned because she has made a pact with the devil.

(She confesses that she falsely pretended to have revelations from God and his angels, from St. Catherine and St. Margaret.)

1585 Witch burnings in two villages leave one female inhabitant each.

1589 Francis Bacon is made clerk of the Star Chamber.

(He says that nature herself must be examined.)

1581–1591 Nine hundred burned in Lorraine.

(That nature must be bound into service, he persuades.)

1600   Gilbert's *De Magnete* published.
1603   William Harvey assists at the examination of the witches.
1609   Galileo, on hearing a rumor of the invention of a glass magnify-
        ing distant objects, constructs a telescope.

        (It is urged that nature must be hounded in her wanderings
        before one can lead her and drive her.)

1609   Kepler publishes *Astronomia Nova.*
1609   The whole population of Navarre is declared witches.

        (He says that the earth should be put on the rack and tor-
        tured for her secrets.)

1615   William Harvey lectures on the circulation of the blood at the
        Royal College of Physicians.
1619   Kepler publishes his third law, *De Harmonice Mundi.*
1619   The first black slaves are introduced in America.

        (She is asked if she signed the devil's book.
        She is asked if the devil had a body.
        She is asked whom she chose to be an incubus.)

1622   Francis Bacon publishes *Natural and Experimental History for
        the Foundation of Philosophy.*
1622–1623   Johann George II, Prince Bishop, builds a house for the
        trying of witches at Bamberg, where six hundred burn.
1628   One hundred fifty-eight burned at Würzburg.
1637   Descartes publishes *Discours de la Méthóde.*

        (She is asked what oath she made. What finger she was
        forced to raise. Where she made a union with her incubus.
        What food she ate at the sabbat. What music was played, what
        dances were danced. What devil's marks were on her body.
        Who were the children on whom she cast spells; what animals
        she bewitched. How she was able to fly through the air.)

1638   Galileo publishes *Two New Sciences.*
1640   Carbon dioxide obtained by Helmont.
1644   Descartes publishes *Principia Philosophiae.*
1670   Rouen witch trials.
1687   Newton publishes *Principia.*

(She confesses that every Monday the devil lay with her for fornication. She confesses that when he copulated with her she felt intense pain.)

(She confesses that after having intercourse with the devil she married her daughter to him.)

1666 Newton procures "a triangular glass prism to try the celebrated phenomena of colors."

1704 Newton publishes *Opticks*.

1717 Halley reveals that the world is adrift in a star swirl.

1738 Dean of Faculty of Law at Rostock demands that witches be extirpated by fire and sword.

1745 Witch trial at Lyon, five sentenced to death.

1749 Sister Maria Renata executed and burned.

1775 Anna Maria Schnagel executed for witchcraft.

(She confesses she passed through the keyhole of a door. That she became a cat and then a horse. She confesses she made a pact with the devil, that she asked for the devil's help.)

(We confess we were carried through the air in a moment.)

And it is stated that the rational soul, which is immaterial, bears the image of its divine maker, has will, is endowed with intellect and is more noble and more valuable of being than "the whole corporeal world."

That Adam is soul and Eve is flesh.

It is argued now that animals do not think. That animals move automatically like machines. That passion in animals is more violent because it is not accompanied by thought. That our own bodies are distinguished from machines only by "a mind which thinks without reference to any passion."

And it is further argued that if animals could think, they might have immortal souls.

But it becomes obvious that animals do not have immortal souls (and cannot think), since if one animal had an immortal soul, all might, and that "there are many of them too imperfect to make it possible to believe it of them, such as oysters, sponges, etc."

And it is said that the souls of women are small.

It is decided that matter is dead.

That the universe acts as a machine which can be described by describing the actions of particles of matter upon other particles according to immutable mechanical laws.

That the secret of the universe may be revealed only through understanding how it works. That behind the material "how" may lie the first cause, which is immaterial.

That the particular (like the parts of a machine) may be understood without reference to the whole.

That the "celestial machine is to be likened not to a divine organism but rather to clockwork."

And it is discovered:

That the weights of two bodies are proportional to their masses.

That every body perseveres in its state of rest or uniform motion in a straight line, except as compelled to change that state by impressed forces.

That change of motion is proportional to the moving force impressed and takes place in the direction of the straight line in which such force is impressed.

That reaction is always equal and opposite to action.

Inertia is named.

And it is said that the maker of the universe was skilled in mechanics.

And it is discovered of light that the sines of the angles of refraction and incidence bear a true ratio and it is argued "was the eye contrived without skill in optics?"

And it is discovered that the heart circulates the blood through the body like a hydraulic pump.

And it is said that just as a king is the foundation of a kingdom, so the "heart of animals is the foundation of their life, the sovereign of everything within them, the sun of their microcosm, that upon which all growth depends, from which all power proceeds."

And it is decided that the moment of death occurs at the moment when the heart stops beating.

And it is determined that air has weight. That its volume is proportional inversely to its pressure.

That a heavy weight and a light weight falling reach the ground simultaneously.

That God is skilled in gravity.

And the parabola is discovered as a result of continuous horizontal movement and inexorable gravity.

And the ellipse is discovered to be the path of the planets.

Everything in the universe, it is perceived, moves according to the same laws: the earth, the moon, the wind, the rain, blood, atoms.

And it is asserted that God constructed his clock to run autonomously. And it is argued whether or not God fixes his clock.

And it is stated that God does not learn. That God knows everything. That God made the laws of the universe and that there is nothing He cannot do. That He created natural law but that He is above natural law and need not obey it.

Yet it is finally agreed that God does not speak to us. (God has no mouth.) That God does not respond to our prayers. (He has no ears.) That God knows everything but He does not choose to respond.

And it is decided that what makes God divine is his power.

That "a God without dominion . . . is nothing but Fate and Nature."

That we adore God for his power.

And Eve is said to have said to Adam:

> My author and Disposer, what thou bidst
> Unargu'd I obey; so God ordains
> God is thy law, thou mine: to know no more
> Is woman's happiest knowledge and her praise.

And it is written in the law that "Women should be subject to their men."

And we learn

And it is advised that women not be allowed to teach nor should they baptize. That "even the Virgin Mary" was not allowed to baptize.

that our speech is unholy

And it is stated that nature should be approached only through reason, that one should be taught by nature "not in the character of a pupil who agrees to everything the master likes, but as an appointed judge, who compels the witness to answer the question which he himself proposes."

(And it is written that women, on discovering that they have ovaries, are liable to become arrogant through this knowledge.)

And we seek dumbness

And it is decided that human knowledge and human power are one. That "in the womb of nature" are "many secrets of excellent use."

And it is written that "it is annoying and impossible to suffer proud women, because in general Nature has given men proud and high spirits, while it has made women humble in character and submissive. . . ."

We practice muteness

And it is written that in the inferior world of brutes and vegetables man was created to act as the viceroy of the great God of heaven and earth, and that he should then name the brutes and the vegetables. For there is power in words, it is said, and it is put forward that by knowing the names of natural things, man can command them, that he who calls the creatures by their true names has power over them.

(Thus it is decided that earth shall be called land; trees, timber; animals to be called hunted, to be called domesticated; her body to be named hair, to be named skin, to be called breast, vulva, clitoris, to be named womb.)

And it is pointed out that man fell at one and the same time from both innocence and dominion, and it is promised that while faith will restore innocence, science can restore dominion.

By "knowing the force and action of fire, water, air, the stars, the heavens and all other bodies that surround us," it is declared, "men can be the masters and possessors of nature."

And so then it is predicted that life will be prolonged, youth restored, age retarded, and incurable disease cured, and pain mitigated, and one body transformed to another, new species created, new instruments of destruction, such as poisons, invented, the time of germination accelerated, composts for the earth fabricated, new foods fabricated, new threads made, paper, glass, artificial minerals and cements, and that there will be means to convey sounds great distances over lines, stronger and more violent engines of war, and that men will fly in the air, and go under water in great ships.

And now the nature of time and of space is wondered at, and it is said that there are two spaces, one vulgar, changeable, relative, the other absolute, changeless, eternal. And that absolute space is the mind of God, it is suggested. (And it is cautioned that the vulgar know only vulgar space.)

Such a thing, therefore, as absolute motion is said to exist in absolute space. And time flows universally, it is said, and always will.

But "Man has been but a few years dweller on the earth," it is reflected, and it is put forward that the life of the earth like the life of man is short.

The changes to be seen on the surface of the earth, it is stated, took place swiftly and violently. That this earth was formed not by one cataclysm, but by cataclysm following cataclysm, each the sign of God's will, each marking the end of one age and the beginning of another.

And the marks of these ages can be traced in the strata of rocks holding imprints from the bodies of perished animals and perished plants, it is shown, and it is declared that all the boulders, even enormous fragments from the Alps, were rolled by the sea in one great tidal wave which spread over the splintered valleys. And the chains of mountains, it is said, were made by violent upheavals of the earth, sand, stone. That because of this violence, no life persisted from one age to another. (And the only link between the species is in the mind of God.)

And the sun will soon burn itself out.

It is decided that man is the last of a series of species made according to a plan by which the whole animal kingdom was constructed.

(Yet it is said that the appearance of man was "a geological event of vast importance . . . utterly unaccounted for by . . . the laws of nature.")

"There is in this universe a stair," it is declared.

And woman is "the idlest part of God's Creation," it is said.

(And it is sung that only slaves love women, for the love of women is dangerous, and to drudge in "fair Aurelia's womb" is to find death.)

(And the theory is held that savage races have fallen through sin from civilization, that the further removed from the Garden of Eden, the more animalized is a race of people.)

All nature, it is said, has been designed to benefit man. That coal has been placed closer to the surface of the earth for his use. That animals run on four feet because it makes them better beasts of burden. That teeth were created for chewing, and that women "exist solely for the propagation of the race."

That nature has made it natural for a woman to seek only to be a good wife and mother, and "nature's darling" woman stays at home, it is pointed out. (Yet the woman who neglects her home is unnatural, it is observed, "a monster more horrible than Frankenstein." That since nature has closed the avenues of intellectual distinction to women, it is reasoned, education for the female is unnatural.)

"Nature is the art of God," it is declared.

(And it is decided to name all the species. That in naming, man is given a glimpse into the secret cabinet of God. And so all the species are named according to their sexual parts.)

And we are assured that we have no reason to fear being overlooked or neglected by this artful creator since he takes extreme care even in so small and insignificant a detail of creation as the hinges of an earwig.

But still, the motives of the creator are questioned regarding the creation of rudimentary organs, and it is debated whether or not any malevolence came to play in the making of parasites.

And now there is doubt. For it is postulated that in the rocks of the earth, it is discovered that there is no evidence for a beginning or an end to time here. And it is slowly realized that not cataclysms but wind shaped stone, that water drops indeed wear granite away, that water can carry soil and make mountains, that water passes from land to sea to land, that as the earth is worn away it is built again, and finally it is agreed that "nature lives in motion."

And now in the "traces of vanished limbs, soldered wing cases and buried teeth," secrets are revealed and facts discovered which "undermine the stability of the species."

And that God made each living thing is questioned.

For instance, it is observed that teeth appear in situations where they do not bite, wings where they do not fly. (That ducks use wings as paddles, penguins as fins, and the ostrich spreads its plumes like sails to the breeze.) And the passage by which nature joins the lizard to the snake is now observed.

That each species was not fashioned separately by God, it is concluded, and the species are not immutable.

(And of this, it is put forward that "it is derogatory that the Creator . . . should have created each of the myriad of creeping parasites and slimy worms which have swarmed . . . this globe.")

That animals originated not from the ark but in the environment in which they live now by modification from earlier forms, it is now clear, and it is said that species form species and nature makes nature.

Thus it is implied that there are species which once existed and exist no longer, which are extinct, and the bones of animals no longer living in the pampas are said to be akin to the bones of llamas now alive there.

(And in 1852 the last spectacled cormorant is seen.)

Still, it is testified that this evolution reveals an "immanent purpose to perfect the creation" and that animals are diverted from reaching perfection by the mutability of the world.

(And it is wondered if the orang-utan might have been diverted from perfection by the wilderness.)

Yet the possibility is entertained that nature evolves species without design, and there are those who reason that the forces of nature are blind, that they are blind will, without reflection or morality. That this will is a will to live and infects all natural forms, from the growth of plants to the drive for mating, and the hunger for food in animals and man.

Yes, nature is merciless and insatiable, it is said, red in tooth and claw, it is written.

(And it is also written that nature lives and breathes by crime. Hungers at her pores for bloodshed. Aches in her nerves for sin. Yearns for cruelty. That she kindles death out of life, and feeds with fresh blood the innumerable and insatiable mouths suckled at her milkless breast. That she takes pain to sharpen her pleasure. That she stabs, poisons, crushes and corrodes. That nature is weary of life. That her eyes are sick of seeing, her ears heavy with hearing. That she is burned up with creation. That she labors in the desire for death.)

And it is stated that woman's nature is more natural than man's, that she is genuine with the "cunning suppleness of a beast of prey," the tiger's claw under the glove, the naïveté of her egoism, her uneducability and inner wildness.

And the scope and movement of her desires and virtues are said to be incomprehensible.

And we learn to be afraid

("Woman! The very name's a crime," it is written.)

of our nature

That opposed to the will is idea. That idea negates nature.

And it is made clear that the evolution of the brain and hence the ability to reason set man apart from the other animals, and gave him the control over his own evolution.

That only through reason can one refuse to be a slave to nature.

And it is stated that "the genitals are the real focus of the will and consequently, the opposite pole of the brain."

And that the organs compete with one another for a supply of blood.

It is recorded that woman's generative organs exercise a strange power over her heart, her mind and her soul.

That woman is what she is in character, charm, body, mind and soul because of her womb alone. (That after menopause a woman is "degraded to the level of a being who has no further duty to perform in this world.") That woman is a natal mechanism.

Thus it is advised that too much mental activity can cause an "ovarian neuralgia," during which neither the brain nor the womb receives enough blood.

That the thinking woman, by "deflecting blood to the brain from the generative organs . . . lost touch with the sacred primitive rhythms that bound her to the deepest law of the cosmos."

(And the young man who would develop his intellect and his physique is cautioned to avoid as far as possible all loss of sexual fluid.)

For the good of the human race it is prescribed that girls complete their education by the age of sixteen or seventeen and then marry. Higher education, it is said, will render a defective development of the sexual organs.

(And it is suggested that higher education had already caused the reduced size of the pelvis in women.)

Woman's greatest achievement, it is declared, is to be the mother of a great man.

1735, Linnaeus names the plants and animals in *Systema Naturae*. 1762, Rousseau publishes *Contrat Social* and *Émile*. 1792, Mary Wollstonecraft publishes *A Vindication of the Rights of Woman*. 1798, Victor, the wild child of Aveyron, an uncivilized boy with the behavior of an animal, is captured by three sportsmen in the woods of Caune. 1812, Cuvier publishes *Recherches sur les Ossements Fossiles de Quadrupèdes*. 1835, the *Beagle* reaches the Galapagos archipelago. 1845, Dr. Sims invents the speculum. 1848, Revolution in France. 1848, Karl Marx and Friedrich Engels distribute the *Communist Manifesto*. 1848, Woman's Rights Convention at Seneca Falls. 1853, Dr. L. P. Burnham performs the first successful hysterectomy in America. 1856, Bessemer turns out the first ton of cast iron steel from his converter.

Through evolution, "All corporeal and mental endowments will tend to progress toward perfection," it is written.

"The brain stands vertically poised on the summit of the backbone. Beyond there is no further progress."

And it is observed that woman is less evolved than man. Men and women differ as much, it is observed, as plants and animals do. And men and animals correspond just as women and plants correspond, for women develop more placidly, like plants, and have an "indeterminant unity of feeling."

That her evolution resulted in a higher and shriller voice, a smaller larynx, fewer red corpuscles and a less complex nervous system.

Our voices diminish

(That the later development of the abbreviated foot in women must have been a throwback, since the short foot is clearly "unworthy of a noble animal.")

We become less

And it is observed that the woman's brain mass is smaller.

We become less

That lacking in reason and morality, women are a kind of middle step between the child and the man, who is the true human being.

And they say that muteness is natural in us

(That in the womb the fetus goes through all the stages of human evolution.)

That mentally women are prostrate before the male sex.

That indeed the thoughts of women (and "the inferior races") are said to be filled with special and personal experience but not with general truths. And it is pointed out that neither women, nor those of the "lower races," are able to abstract ideas from concrete cases.

"Science offends the modesty of all real women," it is written. "It makes them feel as if one wanted to peep under their skin—yet, worse, under their dress and finery."

And it is stated that abstract thought causes physical pain in women, that their incapacity for intellectual thought is a secondary sexual characteristic.

(That the female organism transmits instincts, habits and intuition, and those features of the species established by heredity, to her offspring.)

(That "the male of the species has centralized in himself most of the activities independent of the sexual motor.")

That men "undergo . . . a severe struggle in order to maintain themselves and their families" and that this struggle may increase their intelligence and hence "an inequality between the sexes," it is written.

1859, Charles Darwin publishes *The Origin of Species.* 1864, Navaho tribe forced from the Canyon de Chelly by the U.S. military and marched to a reservation. 1864, Contagious Disease Act in England requires all women suspected of prostitution to register as such. 1872, Married Women's Property Act, giving married women the right to own property, repealed. 1872, Alexandre de Lodyguine makes lamps with short, straight carbon filaments. 1872, Battey performs the first clitoridectomy in America. 1894, at the official academy of art in

London, women are finally admitted to life drawing classes, but only when the model is partially draped. 1913, Emmeline Pankhurst's first hunger and thirst strike at Holloway Prison.

And it is said that without the male, "civilization would be impossible"

That mankind has evolved away from the bestial and closer to the angel

> Arise and fly
> The reeling fawn, the sensual feast

It is declared

> move upward, working out the beast
> And let the ape and tiger die.

That all animals are merely fetal stages of man, it is decided.

> And *striving* to be man, the worm
> Mounts through all the spires of form

it is sung.

It is declared then that man is an animal, and he is the most perfect animal.

That according to the laws of survival, a creature *wills* himself and his species to perfection.

("What was her womanhood," it is written, "that it could stand against the energy of his manly will.")

That "the stronger and the better equipped . . . eat the weaker and . . . the larger species devour the smaller."

And it is stated that if women were not meant to be dominated by men, they would not have been created weaker.

(That woman is as far from man as man is from the forest monkeys, it is reflected.)

That the able survive

As for instance the wolf who is the swiftest and the slimmest.

That nature has selected this wolf and his offspring to live.

That stags have horns and cocks spurs

Because among males it is always the victor who is allowed to breed. That the species are shaped by death.

It is said that the world (outside the home) is a "vast wilderness." And that man goes naked and alone into this world, where he is surrounded by savages.
That he is subjected to "a rage of competitive battle."
That the whirl and contact with the world is the inheritance of his sex.

(And therefore it is suggested that sons be raised with bodily constitutions possessing extraordinary powers of endurance. That the young man must be constantly seeking manly thoughts to feed his mind. That in his education he must sacrifice some of the delights of culture in order to fit himself for competition.)

On the other hand, it is said that woman's place is in the home.
That in evolution woman missed the powerful intellectual stimulus competition creates among men.
(That as the male brain became increasingly larger than that of the female, so men began to dominate human society.)

Women are the weaker sex, it is said, and therefore those women have survived who best succeeded in pleasing men.
And that because of this weakness, nature has made woman a better liar, "For, as nature has endowed the lion with claw and fang, elephant and boar with tusks, the bull with horns and the jellyfish with obscuring liquid—in the same way she has endowed women with deceit."
(That those women who betrayed anger at ill treatment from the male were less likely to survive than those who could conceal their anger.)
(That indeed nature has provided men with beards so that they might conceal their emotions, but that women, being naturally deceptive, have no beards.)
And it is postulated that those women skilled in intuition survived, since a woman able to detect instantly a rising passion in her savage husband would be more likely to escape danger from him.
(That girls should emphasize culture in their educations, it is suggested.)

And it is said that nature endows woman with a superabundant beauty so that she might attract a male, but that this beauty vanishes after she has bred one or two children, just as the ant loses her wings after fertilization.

And it is warned that men do not like and would not seek to mate with an independent factor.

That society can be thankful that neither the emancipated woman nor the prostitute propagates her own kind.

It is decided that the ovum is passive and the sperm is adventurous.

That in sperm is the concentrated power of man's perfect being.

Totus homo semen est, it is said.

That runts, feeble infants and girls are produced by debilitated sperm.

That the sperm functions to vitalize the ovum.

That the ovum transmits instinct, habits, intuition and laws of conduct.

And that the sperm is the means by which the newer variations of nature are implanted in the conservative ovum.

We are nature, we are told

(That the male mind, just as the male organism creates variation, has the power of discovering new experience, and new laws of nature, which become, in their turn, new laws of action.)

We are nature, we are told, without intelligence

"All organic beings are exposed to severe competition," it is written.

And it is observed that all creatures are pressed into a struggle for existence

That all the plants of a given country are at war with one another

That it is the tendency of all beings to multiply faster than their source of nourishment

(Indeed, it is written that the human race tends to outrun subsistence and is kept in bounds only by famine, pestilence or war.)

And this struggle is called a natural government, and this warfare is said to lead to perfection.

(And it is suggested that war serves "for the real health of humanity and the building of strong races.")

(And it is declared that the history of human society is the history of class struggle. That the collisions between the classes will end in the victory of the proletariat.)

(And the development of large corporations, it is pointed out, is also merely the survival of the fittest, merely the working out of a law of nature and a law of God.)

And it is postulated that each organism is a product of a struggle for existence among the molecules.

That the human body is a product of warfare among its parts.

Woman is "a milk-white lamb that bleats/For man's protection," it is sung.

And it is written that "every woman is always more or less an invalid."

That during menses women suffer a languor and depression which disqualifies them for thought or action.

And it is said that pity is the offspring of weakness and that women and animals, being weaker, feel more pity.

And the poets are said to have learned pity from women.

And the scientist observes that women appear to be more tender and less selfish than men.

(But pity is said to be an emotion closer to the state of nature; that pity depends on the ability to identify with another creature; but that a rational state of mind gives birth to isolation through reflection; that the rational man on seeing suffering can say, "Die, if you will. I am safe.")

But it is also written that "the sick are the greatest danger for the sound," the "great danger of man . . . sick women especially."

That a man whose house is infested with a woman is weaker for it.

For men must work and women must weep, it is sung.

That woman elicits pity

But that those who would sympathize with women will have the same fate as the zookeeper who sympathized with the lioness as she defended her cubs. He was eaten, it is written.

It is decided that man evolved from the great apes.

That under the surface of the earth one finds the first inhabitants of the land

Whose protruding jaws and low forehead betray a savage animal, and that this skull resembles that of the Negro, the Mongol, the Hottentot and the Australian.

That all the stages of the evolution of men and of human society still exist.

That the struggle for existence continues still among the different races.

And that "the white man is improving off the face of the earth even races nearly his equal."

Of the men who live in the gloom of the forest, it is whispered, one might as easily pass "for an Orang-Utang as a man."

(Hottentots are brutal, it is said, and their speech is a farrago of bestial sounds like the chatter of apes.)

(There are tribes in South America, it is told, whose language is so deficient they cannot converse in the dark.)

(Negroes, it is reported, like orang-utans and chimpanzees, are difficult to teach after puberty.)

(And among the lower races, it is observed, the pendulous abdomen, want of calves, flatness of the thighs, all features of the ape, are common.)

And woman, it is observed, like the Negro, is flat-footed, with a prominent inclination of the pelvis making her appear less erect, and her gait less steady.

That as regards his intellectual faculties, the Negro partakes of the nature of the child or the female or the senile white.

That woman's brain is smaller and the shape of her head closer to that of infants and those of the "lower races."

And it is put forward that "wherever one sees an approach to the animal type the female is nearer to it than the male." That in the *female* Hottentot one can see the monkey more clearly.

(From voyages about the globe, it is whispered, one hears stories of women mating with monkeys or bears and bearing progeny.)

Slavery is said to be a condition of every higher civilization.

A woman should be an enthusiastic slave to the man to whom she has given her heart, it is declared.

"I am a woman again—a woman, at your feet," a woman is said to have said.

And both the emancipated woman and the Negro freedman are said to exhibit symptoms of insanity or nervousness.

Finally, it is declared that "the generous sentiments of slaveholders are sufficient guarantee of the rights of women the world over."

But as to women and men, it is noticed that the existence of two parents enlarges the possibility for variation.

And it is observed that the struggle for existence leads not only to extinction but also to a diversity of form, that it "enlarges nature's domain."

The gene is discovered.

It is said that the progeny does *not* inherit the habit of the parent.

(That the gene is isolated and impenetrable by either will or design,

That the mutations which create new species are spontaneous and cannot be calculated, it is admitted.)

Still, it is hoped that the theory of mutation may make it possible to discover the exact moment when men became immortal.

(*Yet we read the words* "animals our fellow brethren in pain, disease, suffering and famine" *and we hear that they may share our origins, that* "we may all be melted together.")

1892 Artificial silk is produced from wood pulp.

1884 The steam turbine is developed.

1884 The first steel-frame skyscraper is built.

The redder blood of sailors in the tropics and the warmth of water in a storm are observed.

Heat and motion are said to be the same. It is said that energy can be neither created nor destroyed.

The engineer discovers work.

Heat, energy and work are measured.

1884 Cocaine is discovered.

1883 The high-speed gasoline engine is developed.

> "Where are the limits," it is written, "before which human power will come to stop? Commonplace individuals can never imagine them beyond their own horizon but nevertheless

every day that horizon is widened. Every day its limits are put back. . . ."

1882 A central power station is built in New York City.

1876 Barbed wire is manufactured on a large scale.

1865 The first oil pipeline laid.

"The enjoyment, the commodities of life which had been reserved only for men of fortune are now enjoyed by artisans . . . In a few more years they will be shared equally with all classes. . . ."

1860 A gas engine is invented.

1846 The electric arc is patented.

1839 The electric telegraph is patented.

"And just where the direct force of material power has shown itself insufficient to accomplish its work and to persevere in progress; where his will seems to be broken against insurmountable obstacles . . ."

1838 A steamship first crosses the Atlantic in fifteen days.

"just then a drop of water turned into steam acts to supplement this weakness, to create for him a power of which we cannot now, nor yet for a long time to come, measure the extent . . ."

1829 Stephenson's "Rocket" locomotive railway carriage achieves the speed of thirty miles per hour.

"By means of that same steam, rivers, seas are navigated. It transports us with inconceivable speed to all the extremities of the world in floating palaces which shelter the poor man, the rich man . . ."

1769 James Watt patents the steam engine.

". . . in our own valleys and across our hills wind and spread long ribbons of iron, along which rush, rapid as thought, those formidable machines which seem to eat up space with a spontaneous impatience and which seem almost alive in their breathing and in their movement."

The energy of a man is said to be like the power of the iron horse. (And the train to the track is said to be like the man to his wife.)

It is discovered that animal heat results from the combustion of nutriment. (And it is calculated that if both the sexes were given one pound of bread to convert to vital energy, the male would produce more energy.)

Rules for mobilizing and multiplying personal energy are published.

Men "are naturally and practically indolent and . . . need powerful stimulants and heavy pressure to awaken their powers and call forth exertions," it is said.

Cures are invented to quicken "torpid energies" and prevent the "current of mental life from becoming utterly stagnant."

(Women are not good candidates for these cures, it is said.)

It is put forward that men should concentrate their energies on a particular point.

Under proper control the body becomes obedient to the potent sway of the mind, it is said, but he who indulges in lascivious thoughts is in danger of letting his body become his master.

(And it is said of men who lose control that all their energy is concentrated in their sexual organs.)

Entropy is discovered.

And it is decided that entropy, the amount of energy no longer available for work, always increases. That energy always decreases.

(That therefore the earth cannot be more than two hundred million years old. That the sun will burn itself out.)

"The energies of our system will decay," it is written. "Man will go down into the pit, and his thoughts will perish."

It is said that promiscuous intercourse with women leads to seminal weakness.

That the "generative energy . . . when we are loose, dissipates and makes us unclean," but that "when we are continent," we are invigorated.

And it is said that the young man who would best develop his energies should avoid all loss of sexual fluid.

> Through those two great black eyes
> the events of your soul
> O pitiless demon! Pour me less
> Flame . . .

Sturdy manhood, it is said, loses its energy and bends under the too frequent expenditure of this "important secretion."

> Alas and dissolute Megaera
> I cannot become Proserpine
> in the hell of your bed . . .

The victim of masturbation, it is said, passes from one degree of imbecility to another . . .

> to break your courage and reduce you
> to desperation . . .

. . . until all the powers of the system, mental, physical, moral, are blotted out forever.

> I shall go . . .

And it is said also that the practice of building castles in the air . . .

> to the land where trees and men full of sap
> slowly swoon

. . . of allowing the thoughts to wander when alone . . .

> . . . beneath the passionate heat of the climate;
> strong locks be the swell that carries me away!
> O ebony sea, you hold a dazzling dream . . .

. . . is dangerous and leads to dissipation.

> I shall plunge my head, which loves intoxication
> into this dark ocean . . . O fertile idleness!
> Infinite rocking of scented leisure!

It is observed that no nation has ever existed on the face of the earth which did not crumble under the use of its perverted energies when the gospel reached it.

Only lust creates semen, it is said, pure love never any.

("Prostitution," it is sung, "moves in the bosom of the filthy city like a worm stealing man's food.")

And the soldier on a campaign is warned to save his energy for the honor of his country, to stay away from the temptation of wine and beware the temptation of women.

"Only science," it is now written, "exact science about human nature . . . will deliver man from his present gloom, and will purge him from his contemporary shame in the sphere of interhuman relationships."

The behavior of dogs is said to be affected by "associations." (At the sight and smell of food, it is discovered, a dog will salivate. If a bell is rung when the food is presented, it is further ascertained, the dog will soon salivate when he hears the bell ring.)

Of charges of electricity, it is said that the space around them is conditioned. That space which has the condition of the possibility of force is called a field.

(When a change occurs in an electric field, there is said to be created a magnetic field, and when a change occurs in a magnetic field an electric field appears.)

Electromagnetism is discovered.

(And it is said that electromagnetic waves travel with the speed of light.)

And the electromagnetic field is said to have a structure and a history that can be determined.

All kinds of stimuli can be associated with food, it is determined: noises, colors, shapes, touches to various parts of the body, electric shock.

This association is called a "conditioned reflex."

(And it is put forward that human nature can be explained as a series of conditioned reflexes.)

And it is said of us that we have no understanding.

1851   Herbert Spencer publishes *Social Statics.*
1884   Smokeless powder is developed.

1905   Bernard Sachs, author of *A Treatise on the Nervous Diseases of Children,* recommends that masturbation in children be treated by cautery to the spine and to the genitals.

All matter, it is declared now, can be reduced to ninety-one elements.

For each of these elements there is an atom, it is said, and these ninety-one atoms are the building blocks of the universe: hard, impenetrable, unchanging, irreducible, revealed, under the scrutiny of science, to be ultimate reality.

(Movements of molecules are detected in the paths of pollen dancing in stilled water. Inanimate matter moves.)

It is said that there is nothing in this world one can be so certain of as oneself, that one knows oneself ultimately.

X-rays are discovered. (X, it is explained, is a symbol for the unknown.)

Radium is isolated. (It is observed that one gram of radium creates one hundred calories of heat in one hour: the sun radiates light; it will burn itself out much more slowly.)

Radioactivity is explained as the disintegration of the atom. The atom, it is agreed finally, is not immutable.

The unconscious is discovered.

(And the unconscious, it is explained, is that part of the self unknown to the conscious self, at any given moment.)

From the phosphorescent effects on the glass walls of a charged tube, a particle of energy is discovered. This particle is smaller than the atom, it is said, and it is *in* the atom, it is suggested, and this particle is called the electron.

(The atom is not inanimate.)

The energy of the self is hidden, it is revealed, in a "dark and inaccessible" region of the mind, filled with sexual longings. This region of the mind can be detected in dreams, in slips of the tongue, concealed memories, in associations, accidental falls, words misspelled, names forgotten, in the idle humming of melodies, scribblings, in loss. (That all these are symptoms. That the paralyzed limb is a symptom of this energy.) This energy of the mind is named the libido.

(It is revealed that women have a weaker libido.)

The geography of the atom is explored. Its parts are named the electron, the proton and the neutron. It is thought that the atom might resemble the solar system, smaller particles circling a larger center.

The self is made up of three parts, it is said, the superego, the ego and the id.

And that although women have less libido, it is said, their animal instincts are less subject to control; they have less superego also. That women also have less ego, that (like children and primitive peoples) they are less aware of the necessities of life.

That women have less of a sense of justice, that their thoughts are more colored by feelings than those of men.

(That women are less objective.)

That men are responsible for civilization, it is stated.

Activity is the share of the man, it is said. Small boys build vertical, outward shapes, it is reasoned, and as men they move into the outside world to shape reality.

Passivity is the share of the women, it is pointed out, and small girls build enclosures, direct their energies inward. That they feel abandoned by the outward movement of the man, that they resent civilization, that in the wake of its progress they cause discord.

That to be female is to cling to the home, to sameness, to tradition.

And as we lift our heads we are reminded again and again of tradition

It is noted that man is confined to this earth.

And that confinement, it is said, shapes our perceptions. (A group of scientists performs a set of experiments inside an elevator. It is an ideal elevator, without air resistance or friction.)

It is realized now that the electromagnetic field is real and thus the truth of mechanical law is called into question.

And the understanding that because we move with the velocity of the earth turning, time moves differently for us, is arrived at, and it is said

That a single event is different to different observers if they move at different speeds.

That near the speed of light, a moving clock changes its rhythm and a measuring rod its length.

(The elevator breaks loose from its cable. It falls in a gravitational field. But the scientists do not know of any gravity. Their world is confined to the space inside the elevator.)

Time and space have no meaning unless it is first determined where one is.

(Since all bodies in a gravitational field fall at the same rate of acceleration, all bodies in the elevator move uniformly, at rest or in motion. "Sooner or later," it is said, "the elevator will collide with the earth, destroying the observers and their experiments.")

And now it is revealed that time slows down at higher speeds. And one can imagine that the heartbeat of a man speeding near the velocity of light would slow down and he would grow old more slowly and he would die later.

(The scientists conclude that they are in a system in which the mechanical laws of inertial systems are true, and that their measurements are true absolutely.)

And one hears that what is simultaneous to some observers may not be to others. That the laws of natural processes cannot be known independently of any real reference point.

(But observers outside the elevator see the elevator is accelerating in a gravitational field. And it is impossible to say that either conclusion is absolutely true.)

"The two frightening ghosts," it is written, "absolute time and an inertial system, have disappeared."

The idea of time, it is said, originates in the ego. But in the id, there is no time (and the id itself is not changed by time).

(A young woman suffering from great thirst cannot swallow water. At each attempt to drink, her throat closes.)

In the dream, it is told, the child continues his existence in the man.

(Thinking of her attempts to drink water, she is made to remember her past.)

That one may take a trip backward in time, into the territory of the id.

(She remembers the picture of a dog drinking from her nurse's water glass. She is disgusted, and these words having been spoken, she is free to drink.)

That in the id all wishes and memories still exist, unchanged, "immortal." That the past lives in the mind.

Space and time are forms of intuition, it is now said, which cannot be separated.

Gravity, it is stated, is a curve in space-time. Space-time, it is conceived, curves around matter. And the universe is shaped by its content: stars, moon, earth, galaxies, shape the space around them.

And there is no such thing, it is agreed, as empty space, or time without change.

(The universe is curved back on itself, it is said. The Euclidean propositions are not true.)

We are shaped by what we see, it is said, there is no objectivity, what we see is shaped by what we are, by our past, and our past has shaped us.

Matter, it is now seen, is an event.

(Mass changes at greater speeds; energy has weight.)

It is articulated that matter is a form of energy. That there is no difference in kind between matter and energy, except that matter stores greater energy, and energy has a smaller mass.

(From the formula mass equals energy divided by the speed of light squared, it is said that one can calculate the mass of energy.)

(From the formula energy is equal to mass multiplied by the speed of light squared, it is said that one can calculate the energy in matter.)

The distinction between matter and energy is temporary, it is stated, and no real surface can be found between matter and the field of energy around it.

Between the id, the ego and the superego, it is said that no firm boundaries can be drawn. That the three parts of the self merge into one another.

It is said that boys and girls, before the emergence of the ego, are similar. But after this emergence, the girl is more passive, it is said,

that she seeks to merge her image with the man,
that she seeks identity in love.

And it is said that the thoughts of women are formless and wandering; that the female in her mind bends back upon herself, is self-absorbed and narcissistic.

"and it was like leap year now yes 16 years ago my God after that long kiss I near lost my breath yes he said I was a flower of the mountain yes so we are flowers all a woman's body yes that was one true thing he said in his life and the sun shines for you today yes that was why I liked him because I saw he understood or felt what a woman is . . ."

And it is said that it is impossible to picture the subatomic world, and that the electron cannot be described.

(It is said that women show a bias for the mysterious.)

Discontinuity is discovered and it is said that light moves in particles.

And yet it is said light also moves in waves.

And the electron, too, is discovered to be both a wave and a particle.

A duality pervades nature, it is decided.

(As to how much space an electron takes up, or where it is at any given time, it is said, those questions are "as meaningless as . . . how much room a fear, an anxiety, or an uncertainty take up.")

And it is written that psychology is unable to solve "the riddle of femininity."

Häupter in Hieroglyphenmützen,
Heads in hieroglyphic bonnets

(That the behavior of the ovum and the sperm are models for the behavior of man and woman in love, it is decided.)

Häupter in Turban und schwarzem Barett,
Heads in turbans and black berets

(That the nature of woman is determined by her biology.)

Perückenhaupter und tausend andere
Heads in wigs and a thousand other

(That the female must undergo a second birth and renounce her clitoris for her vagina, and renounce activity for passivity.)

(That passivity now has the upper hand, it is written.)

Arme schwitzende Menschenhäupter
Wretched, sweaty hands of humans.

It is confessed that what a woman wants is unknown.

It is said that from what is known of the nature of matter, there is no way to make a picture, no image is possible.

And it is written that the idiosyncrasies of a mental life cannot be pictured.

(That the nature of the universe is not accessible to the untrained mind, nor the nature of the psyche to the uninitiated.)

Under the gaze of science, it is said, all the basic units of matter shed their substance.

It is declared that it is absolutely and forever impossible to determine the position and velocity of an electron at the same time. (That the observer changes what is observed.)

Thus it is clear that science will never know the position of all the particles in the universe and that science cannot forecast the history of the universe for all time.

The behavior of the single atom remains mysterious. No reason can be found for why one atom rather than another begins to disintegrate. No laws can be formulated for the behavior of the atom.

It is asked whether or not it is a quality of nature to be vague and lawless, or whether it is a limitation of our vision which makes nature seem elusive.

(The memories of women suffering from hysteria are said to be false. Those who said they were raped by their fathers, it is decided, were seduced by their mothers.)

It is asked if the universe would exist if it were not perceived.

It is said that "all the choir of heaven and furniture of earth . . . have not any substance without the mind."

Still, prediction is a goal of science, it is said.

And it is determined that since the single electron cannot be defined, electrons will be studied as groups.

That the probable behavior of a single electron can be derived from a picture of the behavior of the group, that the nature of the electron will be defined as part of a structure of electrons.

The behavior of populations is studied.

It is calculated in the year 1950 that of 12,170 women between the ages of twenty-five and thirty-four, 4,160 worked outside the home and 7,870 worked inside the home.

The domestic pattern is discovered. It is determined that organization around the function of the housewife is a principal pattern governing the female role.

Waves of probability are discovered. Probabilities of velocity are measured.

(If statistically one third of all electrons have a speed of 1000 to 1100 seconds, the probability of finding one electron at that speed is one third, it is said.)

(Yet it is admitted it is impossible to find one electron at any speed.)

Bits of matter, thus, are said to have "tendencies to exist" and atomic events are said to have "tendencies to occur."

The universe, it is now declared, is finite.

Space and time have limitations; space is shaped by mass, time by events. No mass can travel faster than the speed of light. The sun is burning itself out, the stars are dying embers, the heat of the cosmos turning cold, matter dissolving to radiation, energy dissipated into space.

There will be no light, no change. Time itself will end. Existence will diffuse like a vapor into the insatiable void.

It is said that small boys live in awe and fear of their fathers.

(The concept of providence is said to be an infantile re-creation of the father.)

That from the love the boy feels for his mother comes a desire to murder the father, but that in turn the boy lives in fear of the father, believing his father will castrate him.

(That in order to abate his anxieties, man took up an "attack upon nature . . . forcing it to obey human will," it is written.)

And it is said that girls are born castrated.

That she does not have a penis is said to be a "momentous discovery" in the destiny of a girl. This wound to herself is said to develop like a scar. And it said that she will pass from self-hatred to hatred of her mother and then hatred of all women.

(It is said that women invented plaiting and weaving to hide their genitals. That even nature caused the growth of pubic hair for this purpose.)

And it is decided that woman becomes debased in the eyes of small boys when they see she does not have a penis.

We open our mouths. We try to speak. We try to remember.

That the clitoris is a prototype for inferiority is held to be self-evident.

And it is said that small girls develop an envy of the penis and that women bear a natural hostility toward men, a jealousy.

1896   Dementia praecox is diagnosed.

1911   The cure for dementia praecox is said to be found in the restoration to consciousness of certain memories, and the illness is renamed schizophrenia.

In illnesses of the mind, it is said, symptoms are projected like foreign bodies into the normal state. The ego is split, and like the splitting of a crystal, it fragments along lines predetermined by its structure.

(A young woman at her father's deathbed dreams her arms are venomous snakes. She fears the snakes will kill her father. After his death, she forgets this dream. Later, she cannot move her arms.)

The atom is bombarded with the neutron and is split, releasing other neutrons, which in turn split more atoms, fire, light and sound. The chain reaction is invented.

1941   Plutonium is discovered.

1945   Hiroshima, Nagasaki, are destroyed by atomic explosion.

Antimatter is found.

A particle with a charge opposite to the electron is found. And it is said that when the positron meets the electron, both are annihilated in radiant energy.

And it is speculated that the supernova results from chance meetings of galaxies of matter and antimatter.

An instinct toward death is said to exist in the human psyche.

It is said that "besides the instinct preserving organic substance and binding it to even larger units," there is another instinct, "which would seek to dissolve these units," to bring them back to death.

That when harnessed, this instinct for destruction in men seeks power over nature.

That in woman her body predisposes that she turn this instinct for destruction inward.

("a new fantastic toilette, Russian half-boots of violet-blue velvet trimmed with ermine, a robe of the same material, held up by narrow strips and tassels of the same fur . . .)

That the female cell, the ovum, in the act of fecundation, being wounded, is primordially masochistic.

(. . . a matching, close-fitting, short patelot, also richly trimmed and lined with ermine; a high cap of ermine in the style of Catherine the Second . . .")

That the infant girl wishes to be eaten, devoured by her father, that later she wishes to be beaten or whipped by him, that young girls dream of rape, that the grown woman wishes to be pierced.

That women have a lust for pain.

(. . . with a small plume of heron feathers, held in place by a diamond pin, her red hair loose down her back . . .)

And it is also written that when a woman steps out of the sphere of passivity, when she becomes too active, she endangers the men around her.

("Thus she ascends on the driver's seat, and holds the reins herself," it is written. "How she lashes on the horses. The carriage flies along like mad.")

The meson is discovered, the lambda, the sigma, the eta, the muon, pion, cascade, kaon, are discovered.

Thirty kinds of elementary particles are discovered.

It is suggested that the elementary particles may not be fundamental. Man's notion of nature is again threatened. Her face is changing, it is said. And it is suggested that a structure invisible to measurement is beneath the particles.

But it is also argued that there are no elementary particles.

Every question about the essential nature of things, it is said, leads to another question.

Of the nature of earth, rock, river, cloud, light, wind, breath, flesh, of mules, of horses, of birds, of the body of woman, womb, breast, vulva, hair, it is acknowledged these are still unknown.

It is written that we are both spectator and part.

And time does not flow universally. The universe is amorphous, without fixed design, always subject to change. There is no absolute space. Time and space are one.

We are the rocks, we are soil, we are trees, rivers, we are wind, we carry the birds, the birds, we are cows, mules, we are horses, we are Solid elements, cause and effect, determinism and objectivity, it is said, are lost. *matter. We are flesh, we breathe, we are her body: we speak.*

LAND

HER CHANGING FACE

Territory

> I saw everything as no man had ever seen before.... I felt
> like an explorer in medicine who first views a new and important
> territory.
>
> MARION SIMS, M.D. (on the invention of the speculum)

> Consider Him who chose to be born of a virgin.... Freely he
> penetrates viscera known only to Himself and with greater joy en-
> ters paths where none has ever been. These limbs, He feels, are
> His own: unsoiled and unshared by any man....
>
> FORTUNATUS (bishop of Poitiers, 530–609), *Opera Poetica*

> ... a countrey that hath yet her mayden head, never sakt, turned,
> nor wrought.
>
> SIR WALTER RALEIGH, "Discovery of Guiana"

Sea.   Mountain.   River.   Plain.   Forest.   Gorge.
Field.   Meadow.   Rock.   Plateau.   Desert.   Mountain.
Valley.   Sea.   He is the first. Truly he has come farther than
any man before him. His eyes have beheld what has not been seen
before. What newness he is blessed with, what freshness! None of the
beauty of this land has been brought down, no part soiled. He is the
first to tread here. Only the mark of his shoes effaces the soil. Pine.
Otter. Canyon. Musk ox. She gives up her secrets. He is the first to
know, and he gives names to what he sees. He records the existence
of these things. He is thinking to preserve these moments for poster-
ity. He draws a map of his way across this land. And he charts the
shape of the place. Behind the mountain range. On the other side of
the valley. Down the riverstream. Across the gorge. He finds the un-

known irresistible. He believes what is hidden in this land calls to him. He feels undiscovered grasses tremble in wait for him, he imagines mysterious lakes glistening revelation, he knows there are meadows, ignorant of his being, which will open to him. He has a taste for knowledge. Missouri River. Council Bluffs. Sioux City. Despite all dangers, he penetrates farther. Cheyenne River. Knife River. White Earth River. He vanquishes darkness. He vanquishes despair. Bearpaw Mountains. Big Belt Mountains. Great Falls. He places his life in the balance. Clark Pass. Yet he is brave. Lewis Hellgate. Yet he is ardent. Snake River. And the wilderness embraces him. He is taken up by wildness. He becomes wild. Now the secrets of this place are his and each of his footsteps is a triumph. Windstorm. In facing down danger, he has become more than himself. Thunderstorm. He is conqueror. Lightning. He has pierced the veiling mountains, ridden the rivers, spanned the valley, measured the gorge: he has discovered. Now nothing of this place is unknown, and because of his knowledge, this land is forever changed. This was his dream.

The Struggle

> She should never have looked at me
> If she meant I should not love her!
>
> LORD BYRON, "Christina"

> . . . he will find enough to damp his ardor.
>
> FRANCIS PARKMAN, The Oregon Trail

He writes that the scenery is tame, graceful and pleasing. That there is an abundance of streams, level plains too wide for the eye to measure, green undulations like the motionless swells of the ocean. Yet whoever looks on the land, he writes, will find enough to damp his ardor. His wagons will stick in the mud, he writes, his horse will break loose, harness give way, axletree break. His bed will be of mud of the richest consistency, and he will find little to eat since this country strangely produces little game. He may travel for a fortnight, he writes, without seeing the hoofprint of a deer, or the sign of a prairie hen. Yet he will find wolves and they will howl at night and skulk around him by day. His horse will step in badger holes. Le-

gions of frogs will croak and bellow from every marsh and mud pud-
dle, and mosquitoes will rob him of sleep. Snakes, too, will glide
under his horse's feet or visit his tent at night. And when he is thirsty,
after a long day's ride over the prairie under the scorching sun, when
he finally comes to a pool of water and stops to drink, he will find
tadpoles in the bottom of his cup. And every afternoon, with a pro-
voking regularity, he can expect a thunderstorm which will drench
him to the skin.

The Abyss

> She claims him with her great blue eyes
> She binds him with her hair;
> Oh, break the spell with holy words,
> Unbind him with a prayer!
>
> JOHN GREENLEAF WHITTIER, "The Witch of Wenham"

> This wild abyss,
> The womb of nature and perhaps her grave.
>
> JOHN MILTON, *Paradise Lost*

> He wandered like a forgotten ghost that has passed into the land
> of the spirits.
>
> JOHN JAMES AUDUBON, "The Lost One"

Suddenly he finds he cannot see. He is surrounded by fog and the
grass is taller than he is. With every step, his ignorance deepens. He is
lost. He cannot see his way out. Huge gray trees spread giant boughs
over him. Rank grass extends on all sides. No living being crosses his
path. The land is like oblivion. His cabin is lost to him. He runs on,
hour after hour. But with each movement he loses more the sense of
where he is. Chill and heavy dews descend. Night falls. Now he is in
the midst of darkness and he is filled with terror. His body is filled
with fatigue. He is hungry. Now he hears animals about him, but he
cannot kill them. In the midst of abundance, he will starve. He has lost
all knowledge. He knows only his own smallness, his own need, and
that he must appear small to the animals, the trees, grasses, skies. He
is helpless. (He prays to almighty God.) He wanders like a ghost into
the land of the forgotten. With each step this place pierces through
him to reveal more clearly his desperation.

Guide

She knew her skill and she knew it well. She could speak more than
one language. She spoke their language, and she spoke her own,
which they could not speak. (The father, it was recorded, frequently
disposed of his infant daughters in marriage to grown men, for the use
of their sons.) She had learned all the customs of their people and of
her own people, which they did not know. (The compensation, it was
written, given in such cases consisted of horses or mules delivered to
the father.) She could ride horses in any terrain, navigate rivers, she
could do all that they could do, and she could do more. She bore a
child. She foraged for food. She fed them what she had dug from underground, which they had never before tasted. (Sacajawea, they
noted, had been disposed of before she was captured by the Minnetarees. Her husband, more than twice her age, had two other wives.
Though he did claim her as his wife, because she had had a child by
another man he did not want her.) She knew this land which they had
never seen before, for which they had no maps. She told them she had
lived in this land as a child, that she had been taken from this place,
from her girlhood. Where they were afraid they could not go on, she
was familiar. (As a child, she had been captured) She led them (by the
Minnetarees) through this territory (from these Indians, it is said) she
helped them (Charbonneau either purchased her) secure horses (or
won her by gambling) she went on with them (and afterward) leading
them out of the territory (he married her) to which she was born. She
was well liked by them. They adopted her son and he learned their
ways. (They sent a party to the sea) and if certain words blistered her

lungs (and reported seeing a whale) if some words burnt through her tongue (and they wrote) if some words (the Indian woman had begged) had eaten like fire in her belly (to see the "large fish") still she showed no such pain (and was, therefore, permitted to join the party to the beach) and she had survived.

Possession

> Indians told him stories of a fabulous island called Bimini where gold, delicious fruits, and all that man might desire could be found in abundance. Furthermore, the island had a fountain which had the virtue of restoring youth to any old man who drank from it or bathed in it.
>
> LOUIS B. WRIGHT and ELAINE FOWLER, *The Moving Frontier*

> When you look at them with their clothes on you imagine all sorts of things; you give them an individuality like, which they haven't got of course. There's just a crack there between the legs. . . . It's an illusion! . . . all that mystery about sex and you discover that it's nothing—just a blank . . . there's nothing there . . . nothing at all. . . .
>
> HENRY MILLER, *Tropic of Cancer*

Coming through finally to the end, having traversed the entire entrance to this territory, as if to an opening suddenly, he came to a sea, a wide ocean, another horizon, again a new possibility greeted him as silently as all the forests he had braved: He is disappointed. This land he has devoted himself to has turned out to be a delusion. She is a house of mirrors. Now the sea beckons, as did her plains, her mountains, her passes, valleys, deserts. And beyond this sea, now finally, in an awakened state, he knows will simply be another land, begging entrance, so that he might submerge himself in her darkness, to find what secrets? Only this silence again. To himself quietly he admits there is no fountain, no endless lining of gold, no secret marked for him. He will age like every other traveler before him, like men who are born and die, only having traveled the length of a woman's body. Any part of his body he has lost in this, he sees now, will not come back to him. He is cast over with weariness and yet the land, he sees, is not tired, she is constantly renewed, as if his passage meant nothing to her, and her indifference seems to him a relentless cruelty of nothingness in the face of his search. But he will have something. On this bluff, high above the sea, he leaves a flag. This land will bear his name. After him will come other men who will pronounce these syllables and acknowledge his ownership. And they will change the face of this land.

Primogeniture

> In law, rule of inheritance whereby land descends to oldest son.
> *Columbia Desk Encyclopedia*

We shall tell you who gained and who lost In this way *for there were those* the fathers *who held* knew that their names *and those who did not* would live on *those who were known* and that the great estates *and those* testifying to their glory and fame *who were unknown* would live on *those whose lives were vanished* and that the power which spread from those holdings of land *those whose labor* would continue, generation after generation *like the labor of the fields, of the soil,* to be great in the minds of the living *would pass like the passing of breath from the living.*

Use

> On the arable land the cultivators will be increasingly mechanized, the management and operation of the machines being the responsibility of one group of workers. Field sizes will have been reshaped and enlarged to make cultivation easier.... Weeds will be almost entirely controlled by means of herbicides.... Crop varieties bred to meet the needs of mechanized farming ... The crops will be protected against pests and diseases, from seed time to harvest, by insecticides and fungicides.
> SIR WILLIAM SLATER, "Farming as a Science-Based Industry," *The World in 1984,* vol. 1 (1964)

> The very use man makes of woman destroys her most pernicious power: weighed down by maternities, she loses her erotic attraction.
> SIMONE DE BEAUVOIR, *The Second Sex*

> Putting virgin soil under cultivation initiates a breakdown of what may be called the "body" of the soil.
> WILLIAM A. ALBRECHT, "Physical, Chemical, Biological Changes in Soil Community," *Man's Role in Changing the Face of the Earth*

He breaks the wilderness. He clears the land of trees, brush, weed. The land is brought under his control; he has turned waste into a garden. Into her soil he places his plow. He labors. He plants. He sows. By the sweat of his brow, he makes her yield. She opens her broad lap to him. She smiles on him. She prepares him a feast. She gives up her treasures to him. She makes him grow rich. She yields. She conceives. Her lap is fertile. Out of her dark interior, life arises. What she does to his seed is a mystery to him. He counts her yielding as a miracle. He sees her workings as effortless. Whatever she brings forth he calls his own. He has made her conceive. His land is a mother. She smiles on the joys of her children. She feeds him generously. Again and again, in his hunger, he returns to her. Again and again she gives to him. She is his mother. Her powers are a mystery to him. Silently she works miracles for him. Yet, just as silently, she withholds from him. Without reason, she refuses to yield. She is fickle. She dries up. She is bitter. She scorns him. He is determined he will master her. He will make her produce at will. He will devise ways to plant what he wants in her, to make her yield more to him.

He deciphers the secrets of the soil. (He knows why she brings forth.) He recites the story of the carbon cycle. (He masters the properties of chlorophyll.) He recites the story of the nitrogen cycle. (He brings nitrogen out of the air.) He determines the composition of the soil. (Over and over he can plant the same plot of land with the same crop.) He says that the soil is a lifeless place of storage, he says that the soil is what is tilled by farmers. He says that the land need no longer lie fallow. That what went on in her quietude is no longer a secret, that the ways of the land can be managed. That the farmer can ask whatever he wishes of the land. (He replaces the fungi, bacteria, earthworms, insects, decay.) He names all that is necessary, nitrogen, phosphorus, potassium, and these he says he can make. He increases the weight of kernels of barley with potash; he makes a more mealy potato with muriate of potash, he makes the color of cabbage bright green with nitrate, he makes onions which live longer with phosphates, he makes the cauliflower head early by withholding nitrogen. His powers continue to grow.

Phosphoric acid, nitrogen fertilizers, ammonium sulfate, white phosphate, potash, iron sulfate, nitrate of soda, superphosphate, calcium cynanamide, calcium oxide, calcium magnesium, zinc sulfate, phenobarbital, amphetamine, magnesium, estrogen, copper sulfate, meprobamate, thalidomide, benzethonium chloride, Valium, hexachlorophene, diethylstilbestrol.

What device she can use to continue she does. She says that the pain is unbearable. *Give me something,* she says. What he gives her she takes into herself without asking why. She says now that the edges of what she sees are blurred. The edges of what she sees, and what she wants, and what she is saying, are blurred. *Give me something,* she says. What he gives her she takes without asking. She says that the first pain is gone, or that she cannot remember it, or that she cannot remember why this began, or what she was like before, or if she will survive without what he gives her to take, but that she does not know, or cannot remember, why she continues.

He says she cannot continue without him. He says she must have what he gives her. He says also that he protects her from predators. That he gives her dichlorodiphenyltrichloroethane, dieldrin, chlorinated naphthalenes, chlordan, parathion, Malathion, selenium, pentachlorophenol, arsenic, sodium arsenite, amitrole. That he has rid her of pests, he says.

And he has devised ways to separate himself from her. He sends machines to do his labor. His working has become as effortless as hers. He accomplishes days of labor with a small motion of his hand. His efforts are more astonishing than hers. No longer praying, no longer imploring, he pronounces words from a distance and his orders are carried out. Even with his back turned to her she yields to him. And in his mind, he imagines that he can conceive without her. In his mind he develops the means to supplant her miracles with his own. In his mind, he no longer relies on her. What he possesses, he says, is his to use and to abandon.

Exploration

> The development of the middle west did exact its price of natural resources. . . . As husbandry gave way westward to wheat-growing, the land was looked on less as homestead and more as speculation, to be cropped heavily and continuously for grain, without benefit of rotation and manuring, and to be sold at an advantageous price, perhaps to reinvest in new and undepleted land.
>
> CARL SAUER, "The Agency of Man on the Earth"

> Mars speaks with red silence. Once we could not have answered. Only a few short years ago we knew that we sat on a world that would birth and death us, find and forget us. But now this host of

once lost children grown up to be saved adults, gives answer.
Mars, we *hear*. Mars, we *move*. Mars, we *arrive*.
RAY BRADBURY, "A Martian Chronicle—With Chicken Soup"

It is said that in his old age (Automatically, at their command the shovel extends) he fears he is losing his powers (and extracts a sample) that the aging of his body (of soil) makes him frantic (which is placed) and thus frantically (in an incubation chamber) he searches (aboard the spacecraft) for a young woman. (The soil is kept) Some say (perfectly dry) being close to youth (and is incubated) makes him younger (for five days at 50 degrees) or at least he feels younger (under an arc lamp that simulates Martian sunlight). Others say (A quartz window) that proving he can still (filtered out ultraviolet light) attract a young woman (that might have caused) restores him (spurious signals). And still others point out (On radioed command from earth) that in capturing (the test chamber was filled) a young, even a virginal woman (with Martian atmosphere) he has proven his prowess (Then the experimenters) once again. (sent up a radio command) But in all cases (that added a whiff of radioactive carbon) he must (dioxide and carbon monoxide) be free of his wife (to act as tracers in the experiment) at least temporarily (On earth, green plants) for her age (take in carbon dioxide) reminds him of his age (and if there were life on Mars) and of his limitations (vapor in the chamber would contain) his encroaching weakness (traces of carbon) and death.

TIMBER

WHAT WAS THERE FOR THEM

What They
Found

... Many a business depends for its success on some girl who is
smart enough to see to it that her boss gets his work done, who
sometimes even does his work for him, who keeps everybody satisfied and happy, and who has enough foresight to control new situations as they occur.

How do you go about finding such a jewel? ...

RICHARD and RUBIN, *How to Select and Direct the Office Staff*

Suddenly the settlers of the Oregon country found a fortune on
their doorsteps. The Green Desert took on a new luster, with
treasure hanging from every branch.

ELLIS LUCIA, *The Big Woods*

Saw logs are a form of circulating capital. . . .

JOSEPH ZAREMBA, *Economics of the American Lumber Industry*

He is like a man in a dream who has discovered a treasure. He has
come upon a forest untrod by human beings for hundreds of years. A
dream. Transformation. In a trance, he makes figures. The numbers
of the trees. Their size. Three to four million board feet for every forty
acres, he whispers to himself. Centuries of growth. Centuries of rainfall. The very moisture of the air is golden. This is the Comstock of the
timber world, he declares.

Fir, Cedar, Hemlock. Sequoia, ripe for the cutting. Gradually, what
this greenery can be becomes clear to them. They are astonished.
Breathless. Wherever they turn they see timber, timber, timber. They
call this green gold.

Machinery, boilers, engines, pump augers, axes, chain saws, hauled
in from the city. Sawmills, cookhouses, bunkhouses built. The woods

are alive. (Glasses tinkle beyond the swinging doors, squeals of girls, the rousing shouts from the saloons, empty oaken kegs in the alleys, the thick forest of tall masts in the harbor, this last and greatest timber bonanza.)

By autumn, trees falling, moving upstream. (Wrenched from the Western wilderness) Two thousand board feet a day, three million, six hundred and seventy-three thousand, seven hundred and ninety-seven board feet a year. Sixty-four thousand shingles, forty-two thousand, one hundred and three feet of piling, two hundred and twenty-three masts and spars. (They see $70,999.) And each year increasing.

How the Forest Should Look

> There is but one way in which the office manager can control scientifically; that is by standardization . . . The office manager should, therefore, continually direct his efforts to having each operation . . . always done in exact accordance with the manner he has prescribed.
>
> LEFFINGWELL and ROBINSON, *Textbook of Office Management*

> Proper regrowth and efficient forest management of our present and prospective forested areas will assure sufficient lumber for domestic requirements and a profitable export trade.
>
> NELSON C. BROWN, *Lumber*

> Foresters will have worked out more precisely the types of forest to establish on different soils to give the greatest sustained yield, and species of trees used will have been bred for this purpose.
>
> E. M. NICHOLSON, "Orchestrating the Use of Land," *The World in 1984*, vol. 1 (1964)

The trees in the forest should be tall and free from knot-causing limbs for most of their height. They should not taper too much between the butt and the top last saw log. They should be straight. (Among applicants, a person with high intelligence should be sought. She should be an expert typist. A stenographer. She should be diplomatic, neat and well dressed.)

Trees growing in the forest should be
useful trees.
For each tree ask if
it is worth the space it grows in.

Aspen, Scrub Pine, Chokeberry, Black Gum, Scrub Oak,
Dogwood, Hemlock, Beech are weed trees
which should be
eliminated. A thousand
cubic feet of one species can be
worth more than the same
quantity of another. (Standard
procedures for clerical work
should be initiated. Find out
the purpose of each kind of
work, ask, "Is this
work necessary?") Find out
which species are of
highest value
to the consumer, and
plant these.

For harvesting trees, it is desirable that a stand be
all of the same variety and age. Nothing should grow
on the forest floor, not seedling trees, not grass not
shrubbery. (In one case,

nineteen girls all
working on the same operation
were using ten
different methods.) Clearcutting
the virgin stand and replanting
the desired
species is
recommended.

In the well-managed forest poor and surplus trees
have been thinned to make room for good trees. In
such a forest there is no room for overripe trees,
past their best growing years, for diseased trees or
damaged trees, branchy or badly shaped trees.

(Is she accurate? Neat in her work and personal habits?
Is she loyal? Can she be trusted? Is she courteous?

Does she have a pleasing telephone personality?)
The forest
is more easily
managed if
it is large and the
trees should be planted close together
so they will grow straight and
tall to reach the light. (There
should be one central stenographic
pool to render
service for the entire
office instead of
small groups of uncontrolled
stenographers throughout
the office.)

        (Is she emotionally stable? Is she responsible? Ver-
        satile? Creative? Consistent? Confident? Does she
        have a good memory? Is she alert to the needs of
        others? Does she

try her best? Can she spell?
Does she learn from) The
forest should be close to
a sawmill. (When the
work is centralized each
stenographer will
produce more than
would otherwise be the) Trees
bred to grow more
rapidly, to be more
healthy, sounder,
taller, thicker, straighter and
of more
use to the
consumer should
gradually replace their
inferiors. (The study
of human aptitudes, the selection

of the human element best
fitted to perform any
task) in this
way the forest
will yield, and
yield again what is
desired.

Class

The study of human aptitudes, the selection of the human element
best fitted to perform any particular task, is therefore an essential
principle of the science of management, which from its very nature
is not and cannot be wholly confined to inanimate objects.

LEFFINGWELL and ROBINSON, *Textbook of Office Management*

Wood for use in the manufacture of shingles should have the following properties: (1) durability (2) freedom from splitting in
nailing (3) dimensional stability (4) light. . . .

PANSHIN, HARRAR, BAKER and PROCTOR, *Forest Products*

(Third-Class Clerk: Pure routine concentration, speed and accuracy. Works under supervision. May or may not be held responsible
for results.

Second-Class Clerk: No supervision of others, exhaustive knowledge of details.

First-Class Clerk: More responsibility.

Senior Clerk: Occasionally independent thinking and action, tech-
nical varied work, exceptional clerical ability and extensive knowledge
of business. Must be dependable, trustworthy and resourceful.)

For paper (Does she catch on
easily?) Spruce, Southern Yellow Pine,
Hemlock (Learns very rapidly, catches on
easily, learns without
difficulty). For toothpicks, White
Birch (needs repeated instructions,
dull). For baskets, Beech, Elm, hard
and soft Maple, Black and Yellow
Birch (How does she control
her emotions?) For railway ties,

White Oak, Douglas Fir, Tamarack, Southern
Pine, Gum, Beech, Maple (Too easily
moved to anger or
depression. Tends to be
overemotional) For mine
timbers, Douglas Fir (usually well-
balanced, well-balanced,
unusual balance) Red Oak, Maple, Beech
(of responsiveness and control, unresponsive)
Birch, Ash Chestnut (apathetic) For veneers
(Tends to be unresponsive)
Beech, Birch, Maple, Cotton-
wood.

The
Measure

Nationwide we estimate that we have 37.5 billion board feet of
uncut timber under contract . . .

A. W. GREELY, Associated Chief of the Forest Service
in a letter to Joseph McGrathy, Vice-President
of the National Association of Home Builders

   She picks up a piece of fabric with each hand from two piles to her
left and right. (11,000,000,000 fence posts) She brings the pieces together and superimposes the corners to correspond. (10,000,000,000
railroad ties) With her knee she raises the machine foot. (450,000,000
telephone poles) She positions the right-hand corner in the machine
⅛ inch beyond the edge of the foot. She lowers the foot. She stitches
along the fabric edge to the next corner, both her hands guiding the
fabric to maintain an accurate stitch line (2,400,000 board feet cut in
160 years) her feet controlling the machine; she continues similarly
with the rest of the garment.

   *We can recite the names to you of Loblolly Pine in the coastal plain
of the Southeast, and in the Monongahela Woods of West Virginia we
can tell you about the growing of Hemlock, Yellow Birch, Sugar
Maple, Magnolia, Basswood, what color the leaves turn if they turn,
and their odor and the bark smell too, and in the southern highlands
of the Blue Ridge Mountains we remember Scarlet and Black Oaks, we
remember Cherry, we remember Beech and Birch Beech, and Holly.*

(Calculate that in order to complete this task she must have a sense of touch, she must have a sense of vision, she must have a sense of movement.) *And in the Green Mountains of Vermont we can say we have seen White Pine and Oak and Spruce and Maple and Beech, and Lodgepole Pine in Bitterroot, Montana, and Douglas Fir in the Olympic National Forest, these names bringing back the quietness of the forest to us* (In order to do this work figure she must have judgment; figure she must have anticipation, figure she must have perception; figure she must have coordination. Figure she must have a sense of time.) *bringing back the names of forests to us, and how many we knew there to be.* (She must use her finger, wrist and hand dexterities.) *Shoshone Forest, Snoqualmie Forest, Molalla Valley, Starwein Ridge, Bald Hills Ridge, Prairie Creek, Selway River, how many, French Pete Creek, the Appalachia, there were, the Allegheny, the Sierra, the Rockies, untouched, Adirondacks, Cumberland, in their pride, Ozark, Cascade, San Andreas, Big Belt Mountains, the Rockies.*

She must use her mind. She must think to keep her fingers free of the machine. She must think to keep the seam sewn straight. She uses her vision. She must see if the pieces of cloth fit together. She must see the fabric slide through the machine. She uses her willpower. She must keep her mind on this work before her, she must stay here, she must not let her eyes wander, she must not let her mind wander, she must keep her thoughts on the work before her, she must keep working, she must not think of standing up and walking out the door, she must not think too often of the time, she must keep her eyes in focus, she must not think of where she would like to be, she must not dream, she must use her will, her power, here.

Production
(Current of the
Years)

It was no longer from the vision of material poverty that she turned with the greatest shrinking. She had a sense of deeper impoverishment, of an inner destitution compared to which outward conditions dwindled into insignificance. It was indeed miserable to be poor, to look forward to a shabby, anxious middle-age, leading by dreary degrees of economy and self-denial to gradual absorption in the dingy communal existence of the boarding house. But there was something more miserable still—it was the clutch of solitude at her heart, the sense of being swept away like a stray uprooted growth, down the heedless current of the years.

EDITH WHARTON, *The House of Mirth*

In the summer of 1854, the bark was stripped from its trunk . . . for the purpose of exhibition in the East. . . . At different distances upward, especially at the top, numerous dates and names of visitors have been cut. It is contemplated to cut a circular staircase around this tree. . . .

The Yosemite Valley

Seven men stand about the tree, which is now fallen and exposed. Two hold axes; one, his left foot forward, knees bent, leans back on the heel on his right foot, and rests his right hand on the handle of the ax, whose blade rests on a ledge of the tree. The man himself stands on that same ledge, a ledge that must have been created by the felling of that tree. One can see it juts out from the otherwise flat circle of a trunk, and that the final cuts and wedging must have been done on the other side, so that this side fell first, tearing with it as it fell a greater portion of the trunk, hence this ledge. On the same torn place stand three other men. To the far left at the edge, one of them has driven his ax into the tree, so that it stands handle up without his holding it. He supports himself with one hand on the trunk and another on a plank of wood which rests on the forest floor. As one studies the faces of these four men, one feels they are smiling and then one sees they are only partly smiling, except for one man on the ground in front of the tree, who rests his elbows on the ledge, just where a great, long saw for two men is placed, and buckles up the exposed trunk. He is the only man with a real grin. An almost boyish smile, his teeth showing. And in contrast to the other men, with something unnamed reserving them, he seems almost foolish, maybe even a little slow. At the right edge, standing on the ground also, but to the side, and partially obscured by a seedling tree, or a fallen branch, leaning in a proprietary way, with his left hand on the outer bark, his right on his hip and his head angled outward toward the camera, is the man who must have been the job boss. He has a wry, commanding look too, one eyebrow up scrutinizing, and he wears a different sort of hat than the other men. His is a bowler, covered with a dust that shows white in the sepia tint, and must have been sawdust. On the top of the log, arms folded, is the oldest man. He has a mustache which shows white or gray and he is of a slighter build than the other men. His jaw is set and unsmiling, but his eyes are obscured by his hat brim, and one could not say what he was thinking. Nor any of the men, for that matter, except the fact that they have felled it (in all except the man who stands aside and even some in him) one reads a certain vulnerability into their postures, a shyness even, a fear. On the log itself, in the exposed trunk, is carved the figure "17½" and afterward the abbreviation for feet. From its size this tree can be identified as a redwood, and the surrounding trees too have the foliage, bark and size characteristic of that species. One redwood, a portion of whose bark and trunk can be seen in the left corner, grows at such an angle toward the felled tree, one wonders if branches of the two trees had at one time perhaps touched. In the lower-left-hand corner of the photograph, one reads the legend: "18 ft. diameter, Redwood tree cut, Noyo River, January 10, 1933, Union Lumber Co. Fort Bragg, Cal."

WIND

"Listen, I have stood being shut up as long as I can   I cannot go on any longer. . . . But they would not let me go   'In a little while you will be better; in a little while you will be all right; in a little while you can go home' I can't stand this concrete floor any longer. They told me last Spring I could go home. And every hour I was ready. . . ."

LARA JEFFERSON, *These Are My Sisters: A Journal from the Inside of Insanity*

California 1984—To those of us who remember the hurricanes of the 1960's, with their grimly girlish names and their incredible viciousness, a certain excitement has gone out of life. It turned out that hurricanes could be prevented rather easily.

DR. ROGER REVELLE, "A Long View from the Beach," *The World in 1984*, vol. 1 (1964)

In all cases, these terrible storms began over oceans where water had absorbed more energy from the sun than is normal. (Sh-sh-sh! Don't say anything about it to the nurses—but a patient is running away!) Evaporation was very high. Warm, humid air rose with speed from the surface of the sea. As it rose, steam became water, and the heat of this becoming caused the air to rise still higher, which caused more steam to change to water, which caused more rising. (See! There she goes. Sh! Let her get started—don't say a word about it. Go back over there and act like you don't know anything!) Colder air rushed in where the warm had risen, but this air too became warm, and rose, and became water, and rose. (Maybe she can make it. Oh, I hope she does! Won't they be mad when they find out about it? Don't you dare say a word. Won't they be mad. Oh, won't they be mad!) Gradually a vortex was formed, and the speed of the air increased enormously, spinning about itself, until the disturbance spread tens of thousands of square miles, and a new hurricane had begun its career of murder and destruction.

It is suggested that the formation of hurricanes might be stopped if the excess heating and evaporation of the oceans could be stopped. (When she got to the trash burner, instead of turning back to the door where the nurse had waited, she dashed off around the corner of the building.) It was thought this might be accomplished by spreading a thin layer of reflecting material on the face of the ocean. (By the time she reached the road she had far outdistanced her pursuers, but a car was coming to a stop in her path and two men stepped out to meet her.) This would send the light back before it could illuminate and warm the water. (She saw their intention, and without slacking pace, swooped up two rocks from the roadside. But they caught her. She has not often been out of a straitjacket since.) It was then postulated that a substance might be found that would not be dissolved by water, that would weigh less than the water, that could be produced in large masses with little effort, and that then, in this way, dangerous areas of the sea could be masked from the light which might brew disaster in them.

COWS

THE WAY WE YIELD

She is a great cow. She stands in the midst of her own soft flesh, her thighs great wide arches, round columns, her hips wide enough for calving, sturdy, rounded, swaying, stupefied mass, a cradle, a waving field of nipples, her udder brushing the grass, a great cow, who thinks nothing, who waits to be milked, year after year, who delivers up calves, who stands ready for the bull, who is faithful, always there, yielding at the same hour, day after day, that warm substance, the milk white of her eye, staring, trusting, sluggish, bucolic, inert, bovine mind dozing and dreaming, who lays open her flesh, like a drone, for the use of the world.

Appearance

> The shoulders are molded within the steeply oval outline which confines the upper part of the body, so that their smooth, sharply tapering curve offers no resistance to the fluid progress of the rhythmic contour around the form. The arms continue the shoulder line almost without modification. . . . The hands suggest the pattern of a slender urn, from which fingers break into small elongated serpentines.
>
> "On the Madonna of the Long Neck," S. FREEDBERG,
> *Parmigianino: His Works in Painting*

> All animals should be taught to pose.
>
> YAPP, *Dairy Cattle*

She must have a feminine appearance and an absence of tendency to lay on fat. She should be in good flesh but not beefy. Her chest broad and deep, shoulders within, vertebrae and hips prominent and firm, muzzle large, mouth broad, nostrils large and open, head erect, neck slender, her eye alert and placid, her hips wide apart and level, her back straight, her rump long and wide and level, her skin mellow, her hair . . .

Her Breeding

> Glad us maiden, mother mild
> Through thine ear thou were with child
> Gabriel he said it thee.
>
> Anonymous, 13th-century lyric

> Breeding will, during the next twenty years, become more and more scientific. Already we are seeing the results of the work of geneticists in the poultry industry, and the breeding of dairy cattle is rapidly following on similar lines. . . .
>
> SIR WILLIAM SLATER, "Farm as a Science-Based Industry,"
The World in 1984, Vol. 1

She is bred for the fat in her milk. The sire is chosen through a measure of the fat in his daughter's milk. That calf whose daughter's milk may be unworthy is eliminated as a sire. (He is approached in a standing position. Two slits are made in the bottom of his scrotum; the testicles are drawn out; the cord for each testical is broken or severed. The end of the cord is touched with a hot iron. Or the cord is cut with an instrument which crushes the end of the cord as it is cut.)

One bull with superior genes may sire thousands of calves without servicing a single cow. The sperm of a sire may be introduced into the vaginal canal of a cow one thousand miles away. Even the ovum can be transported. One may extract a fertile egg and place it in the belly of a rabbit. This rabbit may be carried great distances or even flown across oceans. (Afterward, the egg is extracted from the belly of the rabbit and introduced into the womb of another cow, who will bear the calf.)

Udder

Beata cujus ubera
Summo repleta munere
Terris alebant unicam
Terrae polique gloriam . . .

(Thou whose blessed breasts, filled with a gift from on high, fed
for all lands the unique glory of heaven and earth)

BEDE, "Adesto, Christie, Vocibus"

It is not difficult to appreciate that a cow's udder is highly important to a great industry and even to the welfare of the peoples of
the world.

YAPP, *Dairy Cattle*

The udder should be held snugly to the body and be of good tex-
ture. It should not be too large in size lest it be subject to injury. Large
meaty udders that hang low and swing back and forth as the animal
walks are an inconvenience. They are more difficult to milk than the
well-formed udder.

Milking

He gives her the kiss she had longed for . . . and so great is the
power of that kiss that at once she conceives and her bosom swells
with milk. . . .

BERNARD OF CLAIRVAUX, *In Cantica Canticarum*

There is more than one kind of milking machine. In one using suc-
tion, the teat cups are rigid and have no liners. The upper rim of the
teat cups is fitted with a rubber gasket which forms an airtight contact
with the base of the teat. (Several sets of teat cups of different sizes
are needed to fit different sets of teats.) Then a vacuum is applied
which draws the milk from the teat while a pulsation opens and closes
the line.

Another machine works with the aid of atmospheric pressure and
uses a teat cup with both a rigid outer wall and an inner wall of elastic
rubber, with an airtight chamber between these two.

(If the cow experiences difficulty in letting down her milk she may
be injected with oxytocin, the hormone science has discovered to be
responsible for this process.)

Preparing the cow for milking will take .42 minutes. It will take .20 minutes to rise and attach the milking units, .20 minutes to place the teat cups on the cow, 1.27 minutes to machine strip the cow, .06 minutes to move the milking cart from cow to cow, and .18 minutes to replace the head on the pail. Both the movement of the cart and the manipulation of the pail can be eliminated if all stalls are equipped with units attached to one central machine with pipes running from each stall to the milk room.

Habits

(The cow may begin to show bad habits. She may suck her own teats or those of other cows. Secure a metal anti-sucking device and fasten it in the cow's nostrils, or put a halter on her, and on the halter strap a nose strap covered by another strap through which sharp nails point outward. She may kick: secure a set of hobbles and fasten these on her legs.)

Birthing

> Lawdy, Lawdy, them was tribbollashuns! Wunner dese here womans was my Antie en she say dat she skacely call to min he e'r whoppin' her, 'case she was er breeder woman en' brought in chillun ev'y twelve mont's jes lak a cow bringin' in a calf. . . .
> MARTHA JACKSON, b. 1850, in *Alabama Narratives*

> Mary has wept! Mary has wept! . . . Weeping is fecund. There never has been a sterile tear. As the rain that falls from on high irrigates the countryside and prepares it to receive, in all fertility, the crops and seed and fruit that will in time come to ripeness, so it will happen in the realizing of the spirit.
> ARCHBISHOP OF SYRACUSE, *Il Pianto di Maria a Siracusa*

Every twelve months the cow should be calved. (When the young girl is bleeding at her time of the month, she hides her condition, she is careful that no blood shows on her clothing.) Her peak period for the production of milk (When the woman has a child growing in her womb she may hide this or she may hide herself) occurs between the third and eighth week after calving. (She may speak of a child, but she does not speak of her womb or vulva.) After this period, the production of milk declines daily. (During her labor, she lies in a room alone.)

A cow should be permitted (At certain times the pressure of her blood is measured) to remain dry (or the beat of the heart of her child is listened to or the width) for four to eight weeks (of her cervix is calibrated) after calving. (She is denied any relief of her pain. Or she is drugged until she seems to sleep. She is told that in a wakened state she may be dangerous to herself or to her child.) The productive life of a dairy cow is from 3.6 to 7.5 years. *(The pain of our labor is imaginary, it is our nature to be hysterical, we are told, the pain of our labor is natural, it is in our nature to suffer, we hear. The pain of our labor is pleasure, this is how we become women, it is said.)* And the average productive life of a cow lasts five years. (During the birth, her feet are put in metal stirrups.) After this, the cow is no longer worth her keep.

The Calf

> I never saw my mother, to know her as such, more than four or five times in my life; and each of these times was very short in duration, and at night. She was hired by a Mr. Stewart who lived about 12 miles from my home. She made her journeys to see me in the night, traveling the whole distance on foot, after the performance of her day's work. She was a field hand, and a whipping is the penalty of not being in the field at sunrise. . . . I do not recollect of ever seeing my mother by the light of day.
>
> FREDERICK DOUGLASS, *An American Slave*

When the calf is born (her hands are strapped to the table) she is allowed to remain with her mother for twenty-four or in some cases thirty-six hours. (She may not touch the infant during birth.) The calf drinks the colostrum, the first milk, which science has determined will aid her growth. But after this first milk (The doctor who delivers the child does not look on her; he covers her vulva with a sheet and feels under the sheet for the head of the infant) she is separated from her mother and placed in isolation from any grown cow. (Or he shines a bright light between her thighs but does not allow her to see his hands as they turn inside her.) On rare occasions a calf may be allowed to run with her mother in the fields. But normally separation is necessary so that the calf will learn to drink from a pail. Teaching this is a difficult task: all food must be withheld from the calf for twenty-four hours. Then place your fingers in her mouth and she will suckle, and then this hand with the calf's mouth around it must be placed in the bucket of milk (And when the child is born) and then the calf will suck in some milk. (it shall be given the name) She may raise (of the father) her head from the bucket and refuse to drink. Again, fingers must be placed in her mouth *We lie alone* again her head must be placed in the bucket. *The pains come on. They come closer and closer together. Some of us cry for our mothers. Some of us scream angrily at God. We are strapped down. We are injected with substances. Some of us are frightened. Some of us die. We grow sick. We lose consciousness; pain carries us away.*

The Cows Speak

> At the sight of their mothers the calves skip so wildly that their pens can no longer hold them; they break loose, lowing all the while and gamboling.
>
> HOMER

We are the cows. With our large brown eyes and our soft fur there was once something called beauty we were part of. It is this we remember when we bellow. When we stand still and gaze at you. Our noses were wet, we know that, we know we once nuzzled you as you pulled with your hands on us, as the milk rushed warm against our bellies, rushed through us, sighing, sighing within us as it flowed, or as the tongues of our calves licked our teats and our skin shivered, and the calf's mouth closed over us, and we remembered the shaking body as it slid from our thighs, and as we licked it, amazing and new, over its skin, licked it clean, as now it licks us, nuzzles us, its brown eye staring into our eye, skin and fur, one against the other, the one and the same, one shiver, and one sigh, one warm rush of sweetness in the mouth, and the soft bodies, growing nightly, soft against ours, to run with us, we remember that once we stood together in the fields, we remember what we were then, what it was then to be part, to be part of our beauty.

We Are Mothers

> . . . A woman who weeps always becomes, in the very act, a mother, and if Mary weeps beside the cross of Jesus—I can tell you that her weeping was fertile and made her a mother.
>
> ARCHBISHOP OF SYRACUSE, *Il Pianto di Maria a Siracusa*

When we awaken, there is a child given to us. We are mothers. We feel a pain where the vulva has been cut. We are mothers. We feel that the skin of the child is soft. The face to us in sleep is beautiful. The small body lying against our body vulnerable. The cries move us. Secretly we remove the child's clothing, the blanket, the diaper. We fondle the body. We love this body, because we are part of the body. We are mothers.

We are heavy with bodies. If men bore children, we imagine, they would burst from their heads, not their asses, and be fully grown, and dressed, and godlike, with no need to eat, no substance pouring from their substance. But we are mothers. (She is a great cow. She stands in the midst of her own soft flesh, with hips wide enough for calving; who lays open her flesh, like a drone, for the use of the world.) *And we labor. We labor like . . .*

MULES

. . . So de white man throw down de load and tell de nigger man tuh pick it up. He hand it to his womanfolks. De nigger woman is de mule uh de world so fur as Ah can see. . . .

ZORA NEALE HURSTON, *Their Eyes Were Watching God*

We are the mules. Offspring of the he-ass and the mare. We cannot procreate our own kind together; nature did not create us: we were bred for domestic labor. Though we work hard, our very name signifies obstinacy and stupidity. Yet that is the very nature of our work, obstinate and stupid. We have the strength of staying power. Though our labor is necessary and though we were bred for that purpose, no one envies us; no one yearns to do the work we do as finely as we do it. We are despicable. If we go on, cleaning the toilets, washing the floors, dusting the furniture, lugging the groceries, cutting the beans, folding the laundry, if we go on, bearing the children, washing their faces, their asses, their noses, carrying their feces away, feeding them from our own bodies, if we go on, our hair pulled up in bandannas, our hands smelling of garlic, our noses filled with dust, our backs bent close to the earth, our ears hearing only inarticulate cries, our eyes hard with obstinate labor, our mouths shut for all but necessity, our brains only calculators for simple quantities, three cups of flour, ten yards of flannel, fourteen pounds simmered in butter, vinegar and rags, water and rags, pins in the soap, vegetables on Tuesday, cotton in hot water, wool in cold, if we go on, changing the sheets, administering dosages, we are despicable, and if we stop in our tracks, speech not having been bred in us, we articulate nothing, our nature is mysterious, mulish, but that is what we are bred for, we are a useful beast, you who feed us and house us in exchange for our labor say, but difficult to handle, still, men count mules among their riches and among their godlike accomplishments, to have ordered nature, to have made an animal.

And we know we are not logical. The mule balks for no apparent reason. For no rhyme or reason. *We remember weeping suddenly for no good reason.* Spiteful and kicking, angry out of nowhere, like a hurricane, with almost no warning, and incomprehensible, brutish

And despite all the solutions we apply and all the scrubbing of cloth and wood and porcelain, still there are always stains; and no matter how often we wash, washing the smell of excrement from our hands so we may prepare food, washing the smell of food from our hands, still the odor stays. And because she is bestial, not fit for thought, she is clumsy with the dullness of labor.

But the mule does have a certain grace. She is sure-footed. She can turn, with the plow harnessed to her, her weight pulling the blade through the soil, on the steep side of a mountain, not sliding or stumbling at the incline. She can follow men up through the steepest mountain pass; carrying food and water. (So that the mule-driver is as necessary to an army as is the gunner.) And is this grace bred into her?

Bred or not, it is the grace of labor. It at least is a strength and has that spare beauty of function, of things that are what they are, the definition, the line, the movement, essential.

And if we find this grace through our labor, with our fingers finding the loose thread in the garment, our ears late at night hearing the cries no one else hears, catching the milk in the pot as it begins to boil, the body bent over rocking, rocking, the pieces of cloth sewn together in patterns, the taste of thyme with rosemary and the different odor of oregano, or the grace, the grace of crisis, the fever, the steady application of cold cloths, the grace of economy, the soup of leftovers, the reuse of the bed covering in a skirt, or the seeing of the barely seeable, the unnamed, the slight difference in the expression of the eyes, the mood, the slow opening, the listening, the small possibility, barely audible, nodding, almost inarticulate, yet allowing articulation, words, healing, the eyes acknowledge, this grace of the unspoken, spoken in movement, the hand reaches, the blanket is wrapped around, the arms hold this mulish daily grace, without which we do not choose to continue, and if we find this, we have something of our own.

This is our secret grace, unnamed, invisible, surviving.

THE SHOW HORSE

The Bit

> Be ye not like to horses and mules which have no understanding:
> whose mouths must be held up with bit and bridle, lest they fall
> upon thee.
>
> *The Book of Common Prayer*

The right thumb of the rider holds the center of the bridle in front
of the horse's face and above her head so that the bit is in front of the
horse's mouth. The right hand is placed under the horse's jaw. If
the horse does not open her mouth when the bit touches her teeth, if
she clenches her teeth, the rider presses his left forefinger on the
toothless bars of the lower jaw, which will make the horse open her
mouth and accept the bit. The thicker the bit, the milder its effect on
the mouth of the horse. The bit should neither pull up the corners of
the mouth nor touch the teeth. The noseband must be tight but not so
tight that the horse cannot breathe. And she must be able to accept
tidbits from the rider's hand. The throat latch, however, should be fas-
tened loosely.

Nature

> [The horse] is by Nature a very lazy animal whose idea of heaven
> is an enormous field of lush grass in which he can graze undis-
> turbed until his belly is full, and after a pleasant doze can start fill-
> ing himself up all over again.
>
> CAPTAIN ELWYN HARTLEY EDWARDS, *From Paddock to Saddle*

A perfect hostess in a household with servants gives the impression that she has nothing whatever to do with household arrangements, which apparently run themselves. In a servantless

household, she has the cleaning, marketing and as much cooking as possible done in advance, so that an absolute minimum of her time is spent on these chores while her guests are with her.

EMILY POST, Etiquette

It is the horse's extreme sensitivity to pain, especially in the mouth but also all over her body, which allows the rider to control her with the pressure of his own weight, the movements of his legs, and with the aid of the bit, the bridle and the rein, the riding whip, the long whip and the spur.

It is the timorous nature of the animal coupled with this sensitivity that allows her to be trained. The horse is not aggressive; her only defense is to flee. Therefore the horse reacts to pain by running away from the pain. If the rider stands at the horse's head and taps her flank with a long whip, the horse will move away from the discomfort.

In addition, the horse has a prodigious memory, is a social animal, has a desire to please and a need for security, and all these qualities are used in her training. Her faults are nervousness, laziness and an excitability that is at times unpredictable.

Education

Differences emerge too in the instinctual disposition which gives a glimpse of the later nature of women. A little girl is as a rule less aggressively defiant and self-sufficient, she seems to have a greater need for being shown affection and on that account to be more dependent and pliant.

SIGMUND FREUD, "Femininity"

To train horses, it is essential that we have a very clear understanding of the way in which their small minds work and appreciate how limited they are in this department.

CAPTAIN ELWYN HARTLEY EDWARDS, From Paddock to Saddle

Oh how lovely is her ignorance!

JEAN JACQUES ROUSSEAU, Émile

The horse is not designed for carrying weight; she has a structure similar to a rectangular box with a leg at each corner, and the rider places his weight on the weakest part, the unsupported center. Her legs and feet are not designed for trotting on hard roads or galloping. And jumping is entirely unnatural to the horse. But through an arduous process of training, the body ill-designed for this task can become a carrier of weights and learn to adjust her own balance for that purpose.

Therefore the body of the horse must be reshaped. A horse in the correct form has a rounded top line accompanied by a lowered head and neck and hind legs engaged beneath the body; to achieve this form the teacher uses exercise, strapping, and encourages higher head carriage. Thus formed, the horse carries weight and can develop paces, balance and movements at the bidding of first the teacher and then the rider.

The horse has a natural curvature of the spine, perhaps as a result of the fetal position of the unborn foal. This curvature prevents the animal from moving on a straight line so that the hind feet follow exactly the track of the forefeet. Therefore the horse is trained in exercises to correct this natural crookedness by increasing the flexibility in the lumbar vertebrae. This straightening improves the mechanical efficiency of the horse.

Grooming

She is brushed all over her body with a dandy brush in the direction that the fur grows. She is brushed with the body brush in round, scrubbing movements. She is polished with a linen cloth until she shines.

Her eyes, her lips, her nostrils, under her tail, are washed. Bits of sand, dust, manure, pebbles, mud, grass, weeds, are taken from her hoofs with a pick. Oil is rubbed into her foot.

She is clipped. (So that she does not have the naked look of a fresh cut, this is done before the show.) The scissors move against the fur, leaving only her mane, her tail and a saddle mark.

(The groom places a saddle on her back and clips around it so that when the saddle is removed, a saddle of fur remains on her back.)

And now that she is clipped her rider must protect her. The grease that was natural to her, that protected her from the cold and the wet, has been removed. She is vulnerable to the weather. He must provide for her a warm woolen blanket to put under her and a lined rug to put over her.

She may have her fetlocks clipped for showing in summer.

On certain occasions, good form requires that her mane and her tail be braided. Her hair is sewn or tied with ribbons.

Dressage

Girls ought to be active and diligent; nor is that all; they should also be early subjected to restraint. This misfortune, if it really be one, is inseparable from their sex; nor do they ever throw it off but to suffer more cruel evils. They must be subject, all their lives, to the most constant and severe restraint, which is that of decorum: it is, therefore, necessary to accustom them early to such confinement, that it may not afterwards cost them too dear; and to the suppression of their caprices, that they may the more readily submit to the will of others.

JEAN JACQUES ROUSSEAU, *Émile*

She must not swing her arms as though they were dangling ropes, she must not switch her self this way and that; she must not shout and she must not, while wearing her bridal veil, smoke a cigarette.

EMILY POST, *Etiquette*

The teacher should insist that the horse stand still and on all four legs during the process of mounting and until asked to move on by the rider. Fidgeting on the spot or moving on without command must not be tolerated.

ALOIS PODHAJSKY, *The Riding Teacher*

The movements that the show horse executes have no use in themselves but exist as part of the show of dressage, manifesting how obedient she is, how well she keeps her balance, how complete is the mastery of her rider.

To "Go Large" she rides straight along the walls of the riding school, taking the corners precisely on an arc of a circle of three steps' diameter.

The "Circle" is performed in either half sector of the school by inscribing a circle of sixteen to eighteen meters.

A "Volte" is the smallest circle the horse may perform; it is six steps in diameter and may be done in the corners, along the walls or on the center line. The volte is performed only once.

The "Half Volte and Change" consists of a half circle and a straight line on which the horse is led at an angle of 45 degrees back to the wall, where her position is changed.

"Serpentines all along the wall" may be ridden as single or double loops. For the single loop, the horse, after passing the second corner of the short side, is taken on a single track approximately five meters from the wall, thus describing a flat arc, and halfway through the school she is taken back in the same manner. For the double loop the curve of the single is repeated, but the horse does not move from the wall more than three meters. Both arcs must be of the same size.

The "Half Pass" is performed on parallel tracks, usually on a diagonal of the school. The horse's head is bent slightly at the poll in the direction she is going. The rest of her spine is held straight. If her shoulders move laterally more than her haunches, she will move on circular tracks, and this is classic direct rotation. If her haunches move more than her shoulders and on circular tracks, she does a classic inverse rotation.

A common fault in the half pass occurs when the horse's quarters are pushed ahead of the shoulders. Another occurs when the horse falls onto the leading shoulder in loss of balance owing to her not being straight.

Difficulties in training a horse to perform are these: nervousness or laziness, qualities which it has been decided are part of the horse's nature. Calmness and patience are recommended for the former. For the latter, the long whip.

Physical problems may be a long back or weak hindquarters, making it either difficult or painful for the horse to carry a rider or train for long hours. These may be eliminated partially by gymnastic training. Another difficulty is the oversensitive mouth of most high-spirited horses: this necessitates a light use of the bit.

If the horse lets her tongue hang out, this is counted as a serious fault. This may be prevented by a manipulation of the bit.

Whenever the horse performs well, the rider offers her a lump of sugar.

The collaboration of horse and rider is essential to performance. When it is possible, a nervous horse should be led by a calm rider and a phlegmatic horse by a nervous rider.

As One

> The ego's relation to the id might be compared with that of a rider to his horse.
>
> SIGMUND FREUD, "The Dissection of the Psychical Personality"

> The onlooker should have the impression that two creatures are fused together, one thinking, the other executing the thoughts.
>
> ALOIS PODHAJSKY, *The Riding Teacher*

The rider loves his horse. He dreams of her at night. He sees her sometimes in a fury of wildness, her excitable frenzies pouring over his body in waves; his head tossing becomes her head, a silky black mane on the pillows, large nostrils flaring, the long neck flailing back and forth, throwing the sheets to the floor, hoofs kicking at the walls, and one eye, wild-staring, unknowing, hurtling now, seven hundred pounds, crashing through the wall, galloping blood-bright at the teeth where the bit has been torn away, a white frothy sweat, running through the dark night, all night: he is not the rider but the horse, riding, riding, riding. But in the morning she is calm. She is his mare. He speaks softly to her. She is supple. She responds quickly to his least movement. They have developed a silent language. If he presses with his left thigh, a subtle movement, imperceptible to the onlooker, she moves immediately to the right, her feet graceful, her head high, executing with exquisite grace his barely whispered will. It is as if she reads his mind and peacefully lets his thoughts enter and guide her body. They are beautiful together, seemingly effortless, artful, her back seems part of his ass, her legs are his legs, they ride as one.

The Stable

> . . . the stable and the return to it after work is the greatest reward we can give our horse.
>
> CAPTAIN ELWYN HARTLEY EDWARDS, *From Paddock to Saddle*

When does the horse first know that the rider has left her side? Even when his weight is no longer on her back, his hand may be connected to her mouth, by the rein, by the bit. And even when his hand is off the rein, his eyes may be upon her. When can she be certain he is gone? Does she listen to his footsteps as they recede? Then does she remember? Does she remember that she has a tongue, that she can push it between her teeth and over her lips? Does she feel a sense of dread as she lets it out? Does she feel a sense of shame, apart from the rider, when she rolls on her back? Is this a private ecstasy? Is she in fear of being discovered? Does she dread and not give this dread a name? Does she love the dark privacy of her stall? The smell of hay newly laid, the food that is brought every day at the same precise hours, always fresh, always familiar. Never changed. Does she love even the sound of the chain on her halter as it is run through the manger ring? And when she is led out, finally, to the riding school or the track, even at her moment of triumph, even after she has waited for this, as the flowers are put over her silky neck, does she dream of the stable? Does she dream of returning?

Love

> Love gets its name (*amor*) from the word for hook (*amus*) which means to capture or to be captured.
> ANDREAS CAPELLANUS, *The Art of Courtly Love*

Though she loves her stable because of the comfort, because she can always count on it to be there, because it is her private world and it is where she rests and is fed, she waits there. It is in the stable that she waits for her rider. It is only when her rider appears that she leaves her stable, that she moves. She loves to please her rider. It is her rider who rubs her flanks, who carries bits of food in the white flesh of his palm, who speaks to her softly, kindly. It is her rider who has trained all her movements, her rider who tells her what she must do from one moment to the next. Her rider who possesses a secret knowledge of a series of memorable movements whose purpose she cannot decipher, a knowledge above her capacity to understand, her rider who knows how to produce food and pleasure, for she is so entirely stupid and helpless that she cannot even feed herself without his aid, let alone know what or where to go, to do. The horse has no wish for freedom. She waits the occasional visits of her master, who day after day seems more powerful, more wise, taking on a majesty the horse would never dream of for herself. When he is in her presence, her thoughts are riveted on him. She likes no one else to ride her. Is this not love the horse is feeling? But she is mute. The rider has named her and so he must also name her feelings. He decides that she loves him.

HER BODY

I wish they all had but one body, so that we could burn them all at
once, in one fire!

HENRI BOGUET, *Discours des Sorciers*

Her body is a vessel of death. Her beauty is a lure. Her charm a
trap. She is irresistible. Her voice is deceit. Her word a plot. Her gesture a snare. She plans her seduction. She cannot help herself. Her
mind is a theater of seduction. She is incapable of other thought. Her
body was made for seduction. For her all other thought is a mask, a
guise for her single purpose. Her skill is ultimate. She will stop at
nothing. Underneath grace, she is grasping; beneath her singing is a
siren. Her mouth sucks. The air around her becomes a whirlpool. She
is treacherous. Closeness with her is drowning, intimacy suffocation.
She blinds. The innocent cannot see her real shape. Behind her sup-
pliant flesh is a maw, a devouring hole, an abyss. Death. Destruction.
Darkness without light. Nothingness. She will eat the flesh she appears to love. Her hunger is never satisfied. To yield to her one demand is to yield to endless demanding. In her is a depth so profound,
she darkens all light. The voyager never finds his way out. She is an infinite ocean. Inside her body is hell. Burning. When she is angry all
life stands still in terror. At the gate of her womb is a wound which
bleeds freely. It is a wound that will never heal. She is mutilated. She
is damaged. She will never forgive existence for this. Her every act is
an act of mutilation, of distortion. She is a plague. A disease. The
blood from her wound will sour milk. It will spoil fruit or the fermen-
tation in wine; it will break the strings of a violin; it will poison food;
cause disease, death in battle, impotence and shrinking. The color of
her blood is the color of calamity, of fire, of evil. The smell is offensive,

the smell is a warning. She loves blood. She asks for slaughter. She asks for sacrifice. Her sinister wish is for castration. For more wounding, for endless mutilation. Her vulva has teeth. Her stare can petrify. Her womb is a grave. She cannot help herself. She devours even herself. Her passion is endless, without reason, without boundary, existing only for itself, careless, arrogant, lavish, indulgent, mindless, inexorable, cruel, selfish, she will not stop of her own will; her body will not stop being; if she were set free, to do as she willed, her body would never stop, all being would be destroyed except her being, which at last her hunger would not spare, she would consume herself; in her body is the seed of nothingness.

We discover one day, with our hands on the pot of boiling water, seeing it in our mind's eye wash endlessly out over the familiar face speaking to us, we are angry. The pot moves. The pot appears to move across space. We are stunned. The pot holds danger. Burning. Pain. Our hands have become malevolent. Evil. Destroying. When we see this our hands go limp. They are paralyzed. The pot stops in midair. The boiling water, which we had dreamed of throwing over him, pours over us. At first we feel nothing, only the wetness. The red skin. The blisters. We are in pain. The pain is excruciating. We cannot escape it. We cannot escape. It hounds us. It tells us we should not exist. It is everywhere, our own voices screaming, we hear our own voices, there is nowhere we can hide, the pain is inescapable, telling us, over and over, of our murderous impulses, our appetite for death.

We begin to feel the heat of our own bodies. Our thighs close together. The lips of our vulvas swell. We feel the outlines of our breasts, their weight, the nipples inside of our blouses. There is wetness in the dark space inside us. We can smell ourselves. We begin to think of hands. Of skin. Of tongue. Of hair. We want to rock. We want to shut our eyes. We want to press the insides of our bodies together, our lips together, to suck, we feel the blood flowing in our vulvas, we become voracious, we stop thinking, our thoughts fly into shapes, into colors, our mouths open, we hear ourselves, we hear our sounds, our breathing, we shut our eyes, we hear our breathing, these sounds overwhelm us, we can think of nothing else, passion has taken us over, our bodies have possessed us. There is no place we can hide. They follow us everywhere with their beating, with their wetness; they are unmerciful; they lead every thought to themselves; they enter dreams; they take us into darkness, and in darkness they seize us totally. We yield. We forget our names. We lose ourselves forever.

One day we look down and see we have become gigantic. Our nipples are long and brown, our breasts have become huge, our bellies are swollen so large we cannot see our vulvas. Each day we grow larger. We fear this growing has no respect for the insides of our bodies. We begin to feel we might burst. We become afraid. We fear we are possessed with violence.

She finds blood streaked between her legs and in the toilet. She finds blood on her dress. Blood all over her clothing. She cries. What she washes away comes back. She wraps up paper towels and puts them between her legs. She tries to wash the blood from her dress. There are stains, long pink shapes. She dresses again. She ties her sweater around her waist so that you will not see the pink shapes. She washes her hands, takes the red from under her nails. She cleans the toilet, the floor. When she walks, she feels towels between her legs. She worries that the edge of them will show through her dress, that *you* will know she is wearing them. She walks home as quickly as she can. She will let no one walk with her. She finds her mother. She whispers to her mother what has happened. Her mother's face is flushed. She takes the girl to the back of the house. They lock themselves in the bathroom. She removes her clothing. The men are not allowed in the back of the house while they do their work. Her mother soaks the girl's clothing. She gives her napkins to put between her legs. The girl bathes. She washes all over. Finally, the women emerge. There is no sign of blood, only on the napkin, which is shielded, which is private, which is hidden, which will be wrapped in paper and in a bag be discarded. They do not say what they were doing, mother and daughter. Before your embarrassed faces, they keep their secret.

Skin

There was the leg-screw or Spanish boot, much used in Germany and Scotland, which squeezed the calf and broke the shin-bone in pieces . . . and the "lift" which hoisted the arms fiercely behind the back; and there was the "ram" or "witch-chair," a seat of spikes, heated from below. . . .

H. R. TREVOR-ROPER, *The European Witch-Craze*

Before I applied the pressure bandages to prevent swelling, I took a final look at my work. The woman before me was no longer forty-five but a lovely person with the taut firm beauty of youth.

DR. ROBERT ALYN FRANKLYN, *Beauty Surgeon*

. . . no one ever speaks of "a beautiful old woman" . . .

SIMONE DE BEAUVOIR, *The Coming of Age*

Our faces begin to die. We are full of defect. Our brows, for instance, are lined. (For transverse wrinkles of the forehead, the skin above the frontal hair line is excised and the lines are eliminated by lifting the skin of the forehead in a resection.) *Our flesh is aging. Our chins sag.* (For ptosis of the chin, a resection of the tissue is performed which tightens the skin in a transverse direction, to elevate the point of the chin.) *We call the furrows over the bridge of our noses "worry lines." We try not to worry; we try not to move the muscles of our faces.* (For glabellar wrinkles, silicone is injected into the dermis and beneath it in small amounts.) *We are wizened. Our lips are pursed.* (For lip wrinkles, surgical abrasion is indicated.) *Our cheeks and our temples sag.* (An incision is made from the juncture of the ear lobes to the cheek.) *Our jaws droop; our necks have folds.* (An incision in the cheek to the supratragul notch.) *We find wrinkles cover our faces.* (A solution is made of 3cc of 88 percent USP phenol, 2cc distilled water, 5 to 8 drops of Croton oil and 12 to 18 drops of Septisol. A cotton-tipped applicator is dipped into the solution. Excess fluid is blotted away with a sterile sponge. The solution is painted onto the surface of the skin to be peeled. The skin is stroked lightly until there is a frosty appearance to the surface. The skin is blotted dry. A tape mask of waterproof tape is applied. The face is kept motionless for twenty-four or forty-eight hours. The face may burn or swell. A dry crust is allowed to form after the tape is removed. The crust is soaked away with a warm saline compress. Antibiotic lubricant is applied.) *Our hands reach to our faces. We lay the insides of our fingers on our cheeks. Our palms cradle our chins. Skin against skin. We feel the blood rush in our temples. We blink. Our eyelashes brush against the lines in our hands. We breathe through the spaces between our fingers. This is strangeness. Our hands are familiar. We know these hands. But we do not know these faces. This skin. Its smoothness; its tightness. We shut our eyes. We try to turn away from ourselves. None of this fear of ourselves shows back to us in the face we see reflected before us.*

Hair

> . . . perhaps nothing was so effective as the *tormentum insomniae,* the torture of artificial sleeplessness . . . even those . . . stout enough to resist the *estrapade* would yield to . . . this slower but more certain . . . torture, and confess themselves to be witches.
>
> H. R. TREVOR-ROPER, *The European Witch-Craze*

> When I think of women, it is their hair which first comes to my mind. The very idea of womanhood is a storm of hair—black hair, red hair, brown hair, golden hair,—and always with a greedy little mouth somewhere behind the mirage of beauty.
>
> FRIEDRICH NIETZSCHE, *My Sister and I*

Fine light hairs covering our backbones. Soft hair over our forearms. Our upper lips. The body takes on the adult contour of hips and breasts. *Hair tickling our legs. Lying against our cheeks.* The accessory reproductive organs reach maturity. *Hair rounding over vulvas. Hair curling from under our arms. Our noses.* The uterus descends into the pelvis. *Hair surprises us. Betrays us. Our secrets.* A solution is applied to the skin, excising each strand. The solution is applied again. The solution is applied again. The solution is *We are covered with black coarse hair.* The follicle is decomposed at the root with an electric current. *Hair grows wild all over our bodies.*

Breast

> . . . one might also be grilled on the *caschielawis,* and have one's finger nails pulled off with the *turkas* or pincers; or needles might be driven up to their heads in the quick.
>
> H. R. TREVOR-ROPER, *The European Witch-Craze*

> The female breast has been called "the badge of femininity." In order for the breast to be aesthetically pleasing, it should be a relatively firm, full breast which stands out from the chest wall and states with certainty, "I am feminine."
>
> JOHN RANSOM LEWIS, JR., M.D., *Atlas of Aesthetic Plastic Surgery*

> . . . I was feeling pretty well pleased with myself. I had just taken the after pictures of a bust operation you would have to see to believe.
>
> DR. ROBERT ALYN FRANKLYN, *Beauty Surgeon*

The surgeons view the female breasts from above, from below. The surgeons say the breasts must look their best if the female is standing, sitting or lying supine. They remind themselves that it is in the supine position that the breast is most likely to be seen naked. They say that as well as having a pleasing contour, size and symmetry, no scars should be visible. They see that when the female lies supine her breasts fall laterally. Thus they conclude that incisions lateral to the breast are less likely to be seen than incisions medial to the breast. In order to reduce the size of the breast, they say, lateral incisions are not so obvious as scars. (The physician looks for a material with which to increase the size of the breast. He is determined. He is obsessed. He will not accept failure. When other doctors say it cannot be done, he becomes more determined. He finds a new material in the cockpit of an airplane. He tests it for hours. He makes it from raw material, but he cannot make it to the right dimension. He tries another material. The body rejects this material. The body eats this material. He finds other materials, those that are too hard; those that do not hold their shape. He works at night. In stolen hours, sacrificing sleep. He prays. At last he finds the material made to the right dimension. He tests it endlessly. It is impervious, he finds, to time, to temperature, to moisture, to body fluids, to bacteria. It is easily shaped by scissors. Easily sewn into place, easily molded. One morning he molds the plastic in the shape of a breast. In twenty minutes he makes a one-and-one-half-inch incision under the breast, slips in the plastic and sews the incision. His patient is transformed, he writes later, in thirty minutes.) To enlarge the breasts, the surgeons say, incisions may be made at the side of the breasts near the fold, around the areola, in the shadow of the underbreast, or on the chest under the breast. But the least visible incision, they say, will be in the shadow of the underbreast.

Clitoris

In the water torture, the *question de l'eau,* water was poured down the throat of the accused, along with a soft cloth to cause choking. The cloth was pulled out quickly so that the entrails would be torn.

ROSSELL HOPE ROBBINS, *The Encyclopedia of Witchcraft and Demonology*

The only bodily organ which is really regarded as inferior is the atrophied penis, a girl's clitoris.

SIGMUND FREUD, "The Dissection of the Psychical Personality"

We are not told of the existence of the clitoris. The existence of the clitoris is denied to us. We feel but we have no name for what is feeling in us. We say nothing of this feeling. The denial of this feeling is not called a lie. The denial of the clitoris is not called a lie. The denial of the clitoris is never spoken. No one speaks of the clitoris as existing or as not existing. The labia are folded back. The hood is located. At the beginning of the vulva is found. *We are told that we do not have this feeling. We are told that this feeling in us is excessive. We are told that excessive feeling is a sign of illness.* A mass. Deep pins are passed underneath the mass, and elastic ligatures are tied around the mass and under the pins. *We deny having this feeling. We are terrified that we might have this feeling. We bury even the memories of this feeling. We give it no name. We keep it secret from ourselves.* The mass is excised. Tissue posterior to it is sectioned. Deep sutures are tied as the pins are removed. *We do not know we keep secrets. We forget how much we deny. We say we despise learning. We say we despise knowledge. We recognize that we are dumb. We are not good at inventing names. We could not tell you what it would be:* to touch truth, to cut away lies.

Vulva

No limits hindered the ingenuity of the witch judge; one of these creatures, Judge Schulties, at Erwitte, cut open a woman's feet and poured hot oil into the wounds.

ROSSELL HOPE ROBBINS, *The Encyclopedia of Witchcraft and Demonology*

Lucy spent a whole hour crouched on her knees and elbows for tied [*sic*] only by opium and hope against the searing, racking operative pain.

SEALE HARRIS, *Women's Surgeon*

> He gathered up all of the vesico-vaginal fistulae he could, embodied in black female slaves (the first three named Anarcha, Lucy, and Betsey), and housed them "in a little building in his yard." For four years he operated and failed, thirty times on Anarcha alone. . . .
>
> G. J. BARKER-BENFIELD, *Horrors of the Half-Known Life*

From childbirth our vulvas are torn open. We feel what is inside us exposed. That our bodies give off odors. That we are horrifying. The edges of the opening are scarified. They are closed together. *We touch ourselves. We place our hands over our vulvas. We search.* To put the clitoris out of reach, the lips of the vagina are sewn together. *We cannot swear that we are virgins.* A hymen is sewn into place. *Our vulvas are too sensitive to touch.* Nitric acid is applied to destroy the mucous membrane of the vestibule. The labia minor is removed. *Our vulvas close against entry. We are frigid. Our husbands cannot enter us. We are sterile.* Ether is administered. The body is rendered unconscious. The vagina is relaxed. *Our vulvas will not open. We allow no entry.* The hymen is excised. The vaginal sphincter muscle is sectioned. The pubic nerve is cut. The vagina is incised. Dilators are placed in the canal. *We are hysterical. We cry without reason. We are slight. We are sickly.* The physician applies leeches to the vulva. *We are hysterical.* It is said that we are too concerned with the clitoris. That the vulva must be trained to receive, to seek penetration, that in this seeking girls become women.

Womb

> There were the *gresillons*, which crushed the tips of fingers and toes in a vise; the echelle or "ladder," a kind of rack which violently stretched the body; . . . the tortillon, which squeezed its tender parts at the same time. . . .
>
> H. R. TREVOR-ROPER, *The European Witch-Craze*

> It is almost a pity that a woman has a womb.
>
> 19th-century physician

We grow thin. We are peevish. We are irritable. We have fits of crying. We cannot sleep at night. We cannot defecate. We cannot digest our food. We vomit. Our heads ache. Our backs ache. We exhibit madness. We are melancholy. We touch ourselves. We cannot help touching ourselves. We grow morbid. We believe we will be struck dead. For problems of the womb, marriage is prescribed. Childbirth is prescribed. (The first incision is made straight, not curved, from one indentation to the next, regardless of previous scars on the abdomen, in the skin.) For problems of the womb, complete rest is prescribed. The absence of all stimulation. The cessation of all movement. Absolute passivity. (The next incision is made in the subcutaneous tissue down through the fasciae in the midline to one and one half inches only.) Injections are made into the uterus of linseed tea, water, milk. (Fascia is cut open by going under the subcutaneous tissue. The scissors are placed in the space between two rectus muscles and opened in the line of incision. This gives a space into which the forefinger of each hand is now placed.) The uterus is cauterized with silver nitrate, or with the hydrate of potassium, or by means of a white-hot instrument. (The peritoneum is held by two straight forceps. It is incised and stretched sideways so that it is completely open to the size of the skin and fascial openings.) It is decided that the cervix should be amputated. *We have not learned the name for clitoris. We do not know what to call our vulvas. We have never seen our own vulvas. We know nothing about our wombs. These are mysterious to us. Clearer to us are our hands. Clearer to us are our feet. We do not invoke these dark places within us. These do not belong to us. These belong to men, we learn, only the men touch them, only the men seize them, name them, only the men have seen them. These are not part of us.* It is decided that the neck of the womb ought to be removed to allow for the egress of menses and the ingress of sperm. (The uterus is now lifted out of the pelvis. Tissue between the uterus and tube and the ovary is cut with scissors. The bladder is pushed down off the cervix and vagina. The bladder peritoneum is cut and separated off. The peritoneum on the posterior surface of the uterus is cut. The uterus is pulled further out of the incision. The uterine vessels are clamped. The tissue toward the lower end of the cervix is cut. The vagina is entered. The uterus is held out of the incision. The vagina is entered laterally. The cervix is grasped. The vagina is cut anteriorly and posteriorly. The uterus is pulled to the left. The remaining tissue is cut. The uterus and cervix are removed.)

BOOK
TWO

SEPARATION

The Separations

in His Vision

and Under His Rule

I felt a Cleaving in my Mind—
As if my Brain had split—
I tried to match it—Seam by Seam—
But could not make them fit.

The thought behind, I strove to join
Unto the thought before—
But Sequence ravelled out of Sound
Like Balls—upon the Floor.

EMILY DICKINSON, 1896

WHERE HE BEGINS

Separation

> I begin to sing of rich-haired Demeter, awful goddess—of her
> and her trim-ankled daughter whom Aidoneus rapt away, given to
> him by all-seeing Zeus, the loud-thunderer.
>
> *Homeric Hymn to Demeter*

Her womb from her body.   Separation.   Her clitoris from her
vulva.   Cleaving.   Desire from her body.   *We were told that
bodies rising to heaven lose their vulvas, their ovaries, wombs, that
her body in resurrection becomes a male body.*

The Divine Image from woman, severing, immortality from the garden, exile, the golden calf split, birth, sorrow, suffering. *We were told
that the blood of a woman after childbirth conveys uncleanness. That
if a woman's uterus is detached and falls to the ground, that she is unclean.* Her body from the sacred. Spirit from flesh. *We were told that
if a woman has an issue and that issue in her flesh be blood, she shall
be impure for seven days.* The impure from the pure. The defiled
from the holy. *And whoever touches her, we heard, was also impure.*
Spirit from matter. *And we were told that if our garments are stained
we are unclean back to the time we can remember seeing our garments
unstained, that we must rub seven substances over these stains, and
immerse our soiled garments.*

Separation. The clean from the unclean. The decaying, the putrid,
the polluted, the fetid, the eroded, waste, defecation, from the unchanging. The changing from the sacred. *We heard it spoken that if a
grave is plowed up in a field so that the bones of the dead are lost in
the soil of the field, this soil conveys uncleanness. That if a member is*

severed from a corpse, this too conveys uncleanness, even an olive pit's bulk of flesh. That if marrow is left in a bone there is uncleanness. And of the place where we gathered to weep near the graveyard, we heard that planting and sowing were forbidden since our grieving may have tempted unclean flesh to the soil. And we learned that the dead body must be separated from the city.

Death from the city. Wilderness from the city. Wildness from the city. The Cemetery. The Garden. The Zoological Garden. *We were told that a wolf circled the walls of the city. That he ate little children. That he ate women. That he lured us away from the city with his tricks. That he was a seducer and he feasted on the flesh of the foolish, and the blood of the errant and sinful stained the snow under his jaws.*

The errant from the city. The ghetto. The ghetto of Jews. The ghetto of Moors. The quarter of prostitutes. The ghetto of blacks. The neighborhood of lesbians. The prison. The witch house. The underworld. The underground. The sewer. Space Divided. The inch. The foot. The mile. The boundary. The border. The nation. The promised land. The chosen ones. The prophets, the elect, the vanguard, the sanctified, the canonized, and the canonizers. *We were told that when he tried to rape her, she said, "No, it is against God's wishes." That although she was stabbed fourteen times, she did not raise her hands to stop him, but only to prevent her defilement. That she forgave him afterward. That her mother forgave him. We were told that because of these acts she was blessed, that we were to look on her as a saint.*

Anger from her body. Intellect from her body. Separation. Interrogation. Purification. The test by fire. Space Divided: Heaven from hell. Time Divided: Mortality from immortality. Cataclysm. The last judgment. Judgment from emotion, from sensation. Sensation from idea. The sensation of color from the ray of light. Optics. Music from the sound wave. Acoustics. The laws of nature from nature. The lasting from the transient. *The story came down to us that he feared she might conceive a son and that this son might depose him.* The immutable from the mutable. *Res extensa. Res cogitans.* Splitting. Reduction. Sensual fact peeled away from number. Number. Measurement. The measured from the immeasurable. Quantity from the cave of illusions. The mind from the body. *Thus we heard that he coaxed her to him and then he opened his mouth and swallowed her whole, that he was then seized with a raging headache, that his skull seemed to burst, that from his skull was born a daughter in his image, wielding a sword and shouting.*

Her will from her body. The knower from the known. The speaker from the mute. Self from self. From the nocturnal. From the nightmare. Discovery from dream. Her will from her body. *We were told in a story that he pursued her. That she fled from him. She fled into the water. She became a fish. He became a beaver. She leaped ashore. She became an otter, a pig, a fox, a mare, a lion. He became a lynx, a bear, a wolf, an elk, a tiger. She became a goose. He became a swan. That he forced her to his will and she bore his daughter.*

Her name from her daughter. The named from the unnamed. The spoken from the spoken. The daughter from the mother. *Somewhere we heard the story that she who made the earth yield, the seed grow, had her daughter taken from her. We heard that one day when her daughter was playing in the fields the earth separated and that from this gaping crevice sprang her abductor. That she dreaded him. That not knowing he had blessed this event, she cried out for help from her father. That not knowing one nearby could hear from her cave, she cried out rape. That wishing for her mother she cried out again and again and her voice rang against mountains and across seas until it reached her mother's ears.* Cleaving. The part from the whole. The reduction of the element from the compound. Nitrogen from liquid air by boiling. Oxygen from air by boiling. Hydrogen from water by electric current, by steam passed over hot carbon. *We knew from this story that her mother was seized with pain when she heard her daughter's cry. It occurs to us that she must have felt herself rent apart. That she flew like a wild bird, we were told, over land and sea, asking what had happened to her daughter. That no one would tell her the truth.* Carbon dioxide separated from limestone by heat. Iodine oxidized from sea water, bromide oxidized from sea water, chlorine from the electrolysis of salt, fluorine from the electrolysis of salt. *We remembered that finally she met one who had heard her daughter's cry. That together they searched for her, that together they carried torches, that they learned the story together of her daughter's rape, that the sunlight told them she was lost to her mother. That her mother became bitter, we knew, that she was unforgiving, that she left herself, that she lived in the body of an old woman, in the body of a housekeeper, and played the part of a nurse. (That she cared for the son of a king, while she shaped the body of this boy over her fires into immortality.) That finally she revealed herself in rage. But that though she demanded to be recognized for who she was, no recognition would appease her. That she remembered her daughter, the soft hair down her spine. Her daughter's voice. Her terror. And that she could do nothing to save her. She ate nothing. She drank nothing. She refused existence. She was mute. She withheld herself. She was numb. And the earth would not yield, and the seed would not sprout. The land was devastated and the sea shrank into itself in an agony of loss and the sky was black with dread.* Silver from lead. Copper. Gold. Silicon from sand, quartz, rock, crystal, potassium from sylvite, carnalite, langbeinite from ancient sea beds, platinum from iridium, osmium, palladium from alluvial deposits, manganese from oxide, silicates and carbonates from the floor of the oceans, plutonium from uranium, uranium from pitchblende, uraninite, carnotite, phosphate rock.

Loss. Grief. Parting. The gentle from the terrible. Suffering from knowledge. Separation. Tearing away. Breaking. The skin of the sea otter *we were told* from the sea otter *that the world would be tested by fire,* the tusk of the elephant *that souls would be weighed* from the elephant *and judged according to a balance sheet* the pelt *of each life* of the fox from the fox *that there is a book* the feather of the egret *in which everything has been inscribed* from the egret, the weed *that the risen will wear this book around their necks as a passport* from the flower, the metal from the mountain, uranium from the metal, plutonium from uranium, the electron from the atom, the atom splitting, energy from matter, the womb, spirit, from her body, from matter, cataclysm, splitting, the chromosome split, spirit burned from flesh, desire devastated from the earth.

The Image

SPANISH DANCER (oil, cardboard) *We testify* WOMAN AND CHILD (ink, chalk, paper) *that we were called woman.* WOMAN IN WHITE MANTILLA (oil, canvas) *We were called woman* STANDING NUDE WITH RAISED ARMS (gouache) *and we were called nature* HEAD OF A WOMAN (sepia wash) *and we were the objects* HEAD (oil, canvas) THE DRESSING TABLE (oil, canvas) BOTTLE OF RUM (oil, canvas) *of his art.*

LANDSCAPE (oil, canvas) STILL LIFE (oil, canvas) THE MODEL (oil, canvas) WOMAN IN AN ARMCHAIR (gouache, watercolor) TABLE IN FRONT OF AN OPEN WINDOW (gouache, watercolor) WOMAN WITH FAN (oil, canvas) TWO NUDES (gouache, pencil) STILL LIFE (oil) *We were the objects* SEATED DANCER   WOMAN AT THE BEACH   MOTHER AND CHILD   HEAD OF A WOMAN   MATERNITY   SEATED NUDE   THREE NUDES *of his art* Mata Hari (her navel is like a round goblet) Salome (always filled) Delilah (her belly like a heap of wheat) Eve (surrounded by lilies) Lolita (her breasts like two young roes) *and these were the names* Helen of Troy (her eyes) Guinevere (like fish pools) *we were given* Clytemnestra (the joints of her thighs) the Sirens (like jewels).

The Sirens *We say* (She was a Phantom) *these were the names* (of delight) *we were given.* Annabel Lee (a lovely apparition sent) *We say these were the stories* La Belle Dame Sans Merci *of our lives.* (To be a moment's ornament) *We were called* Miss Prue and Pamela and Dora, old bag, old bawd, Potiphar's wife and Hera, the nagging wife of Zeus (my wife with the hourglass waist) *we were called* Lilith and the Daughters of Zion, Jezebel and Madame Flaubert and the nagging wife of Socrates (with the wait of an otter in tiger's jaws) and bitch and crone and cunt and the Lady of the Lake (with eyelashes like strokes of childish writing) and the nagging wife of Abraham Lincoln *and we were called* Justine, *we were called* Lady Brett Ashley, *we were called* The False Duessa, harlot, heifer, mare and the nagging wife (my wife with the matchstick wrists) of Rip Van Winkle (whose neck is pearl barley) *we were called* quail, slattern and Lady Macbeth (whose throat is a golden dale) *we were called* shrew, *we were called* sow, *we were called* vixen (with the springtime buttocks, and sex of seaweed and stale sweets, with mirror sex, with eyes of wood always under the ax).

We say we were called woman WOMAN SLEEPING *we were called* good as gold WOMAN IN AN ARMCHAIR *we were called* Sonia Semyonova, Little Dorrit WOMAN'S HEAD AND SELF-PORTRAIT *and we were called* Patient Griselda WOMAN IN A GARDEN   HEAD OF A BULL AND JUG (oil, canvas) CAT EATING A BIRD (oil, canvas) WOMAN SEATED IN ARMCHAIR (oil, canvas) WOMAN AND BIRD CAGE BY WINDOW WOMAN IN ARMCHAIR HEAD OF A WOMAN WITH EARRINGS WOMEN

OF ALGIERS PORTRAIT OF DORA MAAR PORTRAIT OF JACQUELINE
PORTRAIT OF MME. H.P. WOMAN IN A TURKISH COSTUME IN ARM-
CHAIR NUDE UNDER A PINE TREE WOMEN AND CHILDREN THE
SABINES NUDE SEATED NUDES STANDING NUDE RECLINING WOMAN
NUDE WOMAN WITH BIRD BUST OF A WOMAN WOMAN STILL LIFE
WOMEN STILL LIFE WOMAN WOMAN WOMAN WOMAN WOMAN
WOMAN WOMAN WOMAN WOMAN WOMAN WOMAN WOMAN WOMAN
WOMAN WOMAN WOMAN WOMAN WOMAN WOMAN WOMAN WOMAN
WOMAN WOMAN WOMAN WOMAN
WOMAN WOMAN WOMAN
WOMAN WOMAN
WOMAN

WOMAN
Woman of   Woman belonging to
Woman given to   Woman sent for (But
the women, it was written, and the little ones,
and the cattle and all that is in the city, even all the
spoil thereof shalt thou take unto thyself; and thou shalt eat
the spoil of thine enemies.) Woman taken, WOMAN (It is written that
the whole mind and body of woman changes by virtue of the male
power of fecundation *in coitu.*) subjugated, woman drawn hither and
thither (And it is written that the meaning of woman is to be meaningless.) woman known (And it is pronounced that as a man knows a
flower or a tree, and possesses these objects with his mind, that in the
moment of carnal knowledge both husband and wife are changed forever; he can never return to ignorance, she never returns to virginity.)
wife, wife of, wife belonging to (And the body of the wife, it is set
down, is part of the body of the husband. And it is recorded that of
that body, she is the flesh, and he is the head.)

Marriage

Dearly beloved, you have come here to be united into this holy estate *We are the empty vessel* it behooveth you, then, to declare, in the
presence of God and these witnesses *we are the body the flesh* the
sincere intent you both have. *We are one with him* Who giveth this
woman to be married to this man? *and he is the one.* Wilt thou have

this man to be thy wedded husband *We bear his name* to live with him after God's ordinance in the holy state of matrimony? *His knowledge is our knowledge, what he asks of us we give.* Matter impressed. *We are the background, the body, we receive.* Matter impressed with heat. The enlarging of the molecule. The polymerization of material. The desirable flexibility. The formation of plastic. *We have heard the story of the foolish virgins who were not always waiting for the bridegrooms. We wait.* The making of plasticity. The material molded to desire. The synthesis of polyamide. The coupling of hexamethylene diamine with adipic acid. Nylon. *We have heard the story of Zeus's mother, of how she forbade marriage to Zeus, of how she feared the violence of his lust.* The material shaped. *Of how Zeus raped his mother.* Phenol mixed with formaldehyde. *We comply.* Bakelite. The material shaped at will. Ethylene reacting with chlorine. Polyvinyl chloride. Polystyrene. Plexiglass. Polythene. Polythylene. *We know that after Zeus married Hera he angered her with infidelity. And we heard that after she rebelled against him he hung her from the sky, putting golden bracelets around her wrists and anvils about her ankles.* The material easily shaped. *We obey.* Artificial rubber. Artificial wood. Artificial leather. Easily used. Teflon. Silicone. Corfam. Malleable. Cellophane. Polyurethane foam. Mutable. Glass fiber resins. Bent to use. DDT 24-D. Ammonic detergent. *We have heard the story of Daphne. That she did not want to marry. That when Apollo pursued her, she fled. That when he seized her, she would not yield and she called out for help to her father, and that her father changed her to a laurel tree. And we heard that after this Apollo told her,* "Your leaf shall know no decay. You shall always be as you are now, and I shall wear you for my crown." Benzene. Hexachloride. *We yield.* Dichlorobenzene solvents. Polypropylene plastics. Design. The formation of the earth in strata. The convenient stratification of the elements. The utility of the complexities of the earth. The convenience of resources. The availability of treasure. *We were told that we exist for his needs, that we are a necessity.* Mineral salt. Coal. Metallic ores. *That it is in our nature to be needed.* The production of soil for agriculture. The general dispersal of metals useful to man. The disposition of certain animals for domestication. The provision of food and raiment by plants and animals. The size of animals in relation to man. The convenience of the size of goats for milking. The convenience of the size of ripened corn. The value of labor. The labor theory of value. Her labor married to his value. *We were told that Zeus swallowed Metis whole* Her labor *that from his belly* disappearing *she gave him advice.* Her labor not counted in his production. *We are the empty vessel, the background, the body.* His name given to her labor. The wife of the laborer called working class. The wife of the shopkeeper called petit bourgeois. The wife of the factory owner called bourgeois. *We were told that since it is in our nature to be needed* wilt thou love him, comfort him, honor him, obey him *that his need is our need* and keep him in sickness and in health *and that his happiness is our happiness* and forsaking all others, keep thee only to him *in all things.* so long as you both shall live? *And if we should suffer at his hands* In the presence of God and these witnesses, I take thee *we must have wished for this suffering* to be my wedded husband *that his sins are our sins* and plight thee my troth *that without him, we are not* till death do us part.

HIS POWER

HE TAMES WHAT IS WILD

The Hunt

> Is it by its indefiniteness it shadows forth the heartless voids and immensities of the universe, and thus stabs us from behind with the thought of annihilation when beholding the milky way?
>
> HERMAN MELVILLE, *Moby Dick*

> And at last she could bear the burden of herself no more. She was to be had for the taking. To be had for the taking.
>
> D. H. LAWRENCE, *Lady Chatterley's Lover*

She has captured his heart. She has overcome him. He cannot tear his eyes away. He is burning with passion. He cannot live without her. He pursues her. She makes him pursue her. The faster she runs, the stronger his desire. He will overtake her. He will make her his own. He will have her. (The boy chases the doe and her yearling for nearly two hours. She keeps running despite her wounds. He pursues her through pastures, over fences, groves of trees, crossing the road, up hills, volleys of rifle shots sounding, until perhaps twenty bullets are embedded in her body.) She has no mercy. She has dressed to excite his desire. She has no scruples. She has painted herself for him. She makes supple movements to entice him. She is without a soul. Beneath her painted face is flesh, are bones. She reveals only part of herself to him. She is wild. She flees whenever he approaches. She is teasing him. (Finally, she is defeated and falls and he sees that half of her head has been blown off, that one leg is gone, her abdomen split from her tail to her head, and her organs hang outside her body. Then four men encircle the fawn and harvest her too.) He is an easy target, he says. He says he is pierced. Love has shot him through, he says. He is a familiar mark. Riddled. Stripped to the bone. He is conquered, he says. (The boys, fond of hunting hare, search in particular for pregnant females.) He is fighting for his life. He faces annihilation in her, he says. He is losing himself to her, he says. Now, he must conquer her wildness, he says, he must tame her before she drives him wild, he says. (Once catching their prey, they step on her back, breaking it, and they call this "dancing on the hare.") Thus he goes on his knees to her. Thus he wins her over, he tells her he wants her. He makes her his own. He encloses her. He encircles her. He puts her under lock and key. He protects her. (Approaching the great mammals, the hunters make little sounds which they know will make the elephants form a defensive circle.) And once she is his, he prizes his delight. He feasts his eyes on her. He adorns her luxuriantly. He gives her ivory. He gives her perfume. (The older matriarchs stand to the outside of the circle to protect the calves and younger mothers.) He covers her with the skins of mink, beaver, muskrat, seal, raccoon, otter, ermine, fox, the feathers of ostriches, osprey, egret, ibis. (The hunters then encircle that circle and fire first into the bodies of the matriarchs. When these older elephants fall, the younger panic, yet unwilling to leave the bodies of their dead mothers, they make easy targets.) And thus he makes her soft. He makes her calm. He makes her grateful to him. He has tamed her, he says. She is content to be his, he says. (In the winter, if a single wolf has leaped over the walls of the city and terrorized the streets, the hunters go out in a band to rid the forest of the whole pack.) Her voice is now soothing to him. Her eyes no longer blaze, but look on him serenely. When he calls to her, she gives herself to him. Her ferocity lies under him. (The body of the great whale is strapped with explosives.) Now nothing of the old beast remains in her. (Eastern Bison, extinct 1825; Spectacled Cormorant, extinct 1852; Cape Lion, extinct 1865; Bonin Night Heron, extinct 1889; Barbary Lion, extinct 1922; Great Auk, extinct 1944.) And he can trust her wholly with himself. So he is blazing when he enters her, and she is consumed. (Florida Key Deer, vanishing; Wild Indian Buffalo, vanishing; Great Sable Antelope, vanishing.) Because she is his, she offers no resistance. She is a place of rest for him. A place of his making. And when his flesh begins to yield and his skin melts into her, he become soft, and he is without fear; he does not lose himself; though something in him gives way, he is not lost in her, because she is his now: he has captured her.

The Zoological
Garden

Wild, wild things will turn on you
You have got to set them free.

CRIS WILLIAMSON, "Wild Things"

In the cage is the lion. She paces with her memories. Her body is a record of her past. As she moves back and forth, one may see it all: the lean frame, the muscular legs, the paw enclosing long sharp claws, the astonishing speed of her response. She was born in this garden. She has never in her life stretched those legs. Never darted farther than twenty yards at a time. Only once did she use her claws. Only once did she feel them sink into flesh. And it was her keeper's flesh. Her keeper whom she loves, who feeds her, who would never dream of harming her, who protects her. Who in his mercy forgave her mad attack, saying this was in her nature, to be cruel at a whim, to try to kill what she loves. He had come into her cage as he usually did early in the morning to change her water, always at the same time of day, in the same manner, speaking softly to her, careful to make no sudden movement, keeping his distance, when suddenly she sank down, deep down into herself, the way wild animals do before they spring, and then she had risen on all her strong legs, and swiped him in one long, powerful, graceful movement across the arm. How lucky for her he survived the blow. The keeper and his friends shot her with a gun to make her sleep. Through her half-open lids she knew they made movements around her. They fed her with tubes. They observed her. They wrote comments in notebooks. And finally they rendered a judgment. She was normal. She was a normal wild beast, whose power is dangerous, whose anger can kill, they had said. Be more careful of her, they advised. Allow her less excitement. Perhaps let her exercise more. She understood none of this. She understood only the look of fear in her keeper's eyes. And now she paces. Paces as if she were angry, as if she were on the edge of frenzy. The spectators imagine she is going through the movements of the hunt, or that she is readying her body for survival. But she knows no life outside the garden. She has no notion of anger over what she could have been, or might be. No idea of rebellion.

It is only her body that knows of these things, moving her, daily, hourly, back and forth, back and forth, before the bars of her cage.

The Garden

> And the man said, The woman whom thou gavest to be with me, she gave me of the tree, and I did eat. . . . Therefore the Lord God sent him forth from the garden of Eden, to till the ground from whence he was taken. So he drove out the man; and he placed at the east of the garden of Eden Cherubims, and a flaming sword which turned every way, to keep the way of the tree of life.
>
> GENESIS 3:12, 23, 24

She was in the garden, sequestered behind bushes, as night came, just as the other children were called in, and so she stayed quiet, she said, as a mouse, so that she could be out there alone. And when the cries of the others had gone indoors, in this new silence she began to hear the movements of birds. So she stayed still and watched them. Then she felt, she said, the earth beneath her feet coming closer to her. And she began to play with the berries and the plants and finally to whisper to the birds.

And the birds, she said afterward, whispered to her. And thus when, hearing her mother's frightened voice, she appeared finally from the dark tangle of trees and shrubs, her face was so radiant that her mother, amazed to see this new joy in her daughter, did not tell her then what she knew she would soon have to say. That those bushes her daughter hid behind can also hide strangers, that for her shadows speak danger, that in such places little girls must be afraid.

HIS VIGILANCE

HOW HE MUST KEEP WATCH

Space Divided

> Bring out number, weight and measure in a year of dearth.
> WILLIAM BLAKE, *The Proverbs of Hell*

> Miletus initiated the practice if the mathematical "plat," based
> not on a topographical reality but on numerical configurations.
> SIBYL MOHOLY-NAGY, *Matrix of Man*

The mile.   The acre.   The inch and the foot.   The gallon and the ton.   The upper and lower, left and right, side, front, back, under, ante, post. The large and the small. Number and name. Perimeter. Classification. Separation. Shape.

Space Divided.

The Mile.   As in thirty miles north of Oklahoma City (is a plant for the manufacture of plutonium) or six miles west of St. Louis (is the St. Louis Public Zoo) or one mile and a half north of Soledad (lies the Central Facility for Soledad State Prison) or two hundred miles southwest of Berlin (in the district of Bamberg, there once existed a house for the trying of witches) or six miles west of the city of Corona (is the California Institution for Women) or two miles south of Napa (is Napa State Hospital for the mentally ill).

Space.   The Acre. For example, 500,000 acres (of the Ozarks have been sprayed with herbicide) or 936 acres (comprise the central facility at Soledad) or 199 acres (are in the California Institute for Women) or 81 acres (are part of the St. Louis Zoo).

Space.   The Inch and the Foot. Divided. As in eight foot long (pencil-thin metal rods are used to store the plutonium) or thirteen feet by seven feet by nine feet (is judged the proper size for a cell used for continual separation and solitary confinement) or fourteen to eighteen inches (should be the thickness of the walls dividing cells) or eighteen inches (of stone should separate the cell from the corridor) or five thousand square feet (is the size of a pool accommodating several seals and one sea elephant) or fourteen thousand square feet (are allotted for the primate house) or thirty feet (are needed to widen the public ramp for the lion show).

Divided.   The Gallon. The Ton. As in a million and one half gallons (of 2,4-dichlorophenoxyacetic acid and 2, 4, 5-tetrachlorophenoxyacetic acid are stored on Johnston Island) or forty thousand tons (of 2, 4, 5-tetrachlorophenoxyacetic acid were dropped over the Vietnamese countryside) or tons (of toolproof steel were used in the construction of Sing Sing Prison).

Divided.   Upper and Lower. At the Side. Under. Left and Right. Ante. Space. As in upper and lower (chapels were in the two-story building) or at the side (was an outbuilding which was the torture chamber) or under (the building ran a stream used for test by immersion) or to the right (of the entrance hall was the warder's room) or to the left and right (of the corridor leading to the chapel opened eight separate cells) or to the right (are cell blocks and shops for hardened criminals who will not leave their quarters) or on the left (is the hospital for the abnormal) or antechambers (for the judges adjoined the chapel) or on the upper story (are cages for lions) or on the lower (are rest rooms for the public) or to the left (of the hospital was the death house).

Space Divided, as in Large and Small.   The largest of three (arenas is the chimpanzee show) or the small (mammal house) or a small (room on the upper story called the confession chamber).

Divided.   Name. Number. As in the name Hexenhaus (House of the Witches) or the number eighteen (cells and a room for a warder) or twenty-six (witches could be held in the house at any one time).

Divided by Perimeters and Classifications, such as a twelve-foot-high chain-link fence (secured at the bottom to a concrete curb and topped by three strands of barbed wire, with ten armed guard towers, lined in two parallel rows of five) or such as four classes of inmates (800 average, 150 a disciplinary group, 150 defective or abnormal, 400 an honor group) or such as the three classes of animals (Reptiles, Birds, Mammals) or the three classes of structures needing remodeling (by priority: First Priority, aviary, lion house, seal basin, west parking lot, east refreshment pavilion, et cetera; Second Priority, reptile house, small mammal house, et cetera; Third Priority, primate house, lion show, and so forth).

Space Divided by Separations, as in separate corridors (are provided for the guards and the prisoners) or each floor is separated from the other floor, or there are eight separate cell blocks, or the dining room has two separate entrances (so that the classes of inmates may be kept separate) or there are several separate cottages (a cottage for colored girls, a cottage for the younger girls, a cottage for older women, a cottage for women on the honor role, a cottage for women being disciplined, a cottage for the incorrigible), or as in separation is enforced (in the Auburn system by a rule of silence, and because the inmates must keep their eyes downward and walk in lock step).

And finally, the Divisions of Space are seen as Shapes, such as an elliptical arc (forms the outside wall of the upper and lower chapel in the Hexenhaus) or a square (the shape of the lion house) or a circle (the shape for a prison in which there may be constant surveillance from the center) or such as the rectangular shape of a cell.

Or the shape of a measuring rod.

Time Divided

The very words from which she will get into the way of forming sentences should not be taken at haphazard but be definitely chosen and arranged on purpose. For example, let her have the names of the prophets and the apostles, and the whole list of patriarchs from Adam downward. . . .

ST. JEROME, *Letter on a Girl's Education*, 403 A.D.

Time.   The hour.   The minute.   The second.   His clock. His universe ticking, he says, like a clock. (The number of man-hours it takes him to do a job.) His life span. The life span of a normal man.

Time and the generations.   As in the generations of Esau. (And these *are* the generations of Esau the father of the Edomites in Mount Seir: These *are* the names of Esau's sons; Eliphaz the son of Adah the wife of Esau, Reuel the son of Bashemath the wife of Esau. And the sons of Eliphaz were Teman, Omar, Zepho, and Gatam and Kemaz. And Timna was concubine to Eliphaz Esau's son; and she bare to Eliphaz, Amalek: these *were* the sons of Adah Esau's wife. And these *are* the sons of Reuel; Nahath and Zerah, Shammah, and Mizzah. . . .)

His Time.   The years. As in the years of his reign. As in the reign of Ramses II. As in the Jefferson years. As in the Stalinist period. Time and his discoveries. As when Columbus discovered America. As when Cabot discovered America. As when Americus Vespucius discovered America. (As when Balboa discovered the South Sea, Cortez discovered Vera Cruz, De Soto discovered the Mississippi River, Hudson discovered the Hudson River, as when Watson discovered DNA.)

Time.   Time Divided. As in the Period. As in the Epoch. As in the Dark Ages. His Middle Ages. His Renaissance. As in the Ages of Man. As in the Iron Age. As in the Age of Industrialization. As in the Atomic Age. (And when he discovered iron, and when he discovered electricity, and when he split the atom, and when he invented plutonium, 2,4,5-tetrachlorophenoxyacetic acid and 2,4-dichlorophenoxyacetic acid.) Time divided and measured. As by the active life of plutonium (as in 250,000 years), as by traces of insecticide found in tissues five years later, as by contamination of the water supply for more than five years.

Time divided and measured.   Time marked by events. As in history. As in the history of his events. As in the Battle of Thermopylae. As in the First Punic War. As in the Peloponnesian Wars. The Sack of Rome. The Norman Conquest. The Conquests of Charlemagne. As in the Crusades. As in the Hundred Years' War. The War of the Roses. The Thirty Years' War. The Seven Years' War. The American Revolution. The French Revolution. As in the Congress of Vienna. And the fall of the Maginot Line. Time.

Time.   Time divided by his thoughts. As in the Age of Reason. As in the Age of Ideals. As in the Classical Age and the Mannerist Period. Time divided. Divided by his words. As in the Homeric Age, or the Age of Chaucer, or the Age of Shakespeare. Time. Time divided by what he believes, as in the Age of Belief. As in his Reformation. And the Death of God. As in the Decadent Age and the Age of Anxiety.

Time and his history. And the history of his creations. As in the history of the zoological garden. (The paradeisos, the menagerie, the period of the classical zoo, the modern zoological garden.) As in the history of incarceration. (The house for the interrogation of witches, the jail, the stocks, the prison, the reformed prison, the mad-house, the mental hospital, the detention camp, the concentration camp, the New Life Hamlet.)

Time and his creations. As in the Mechanical Age and the Age of Technology.

Time. Time divided by events. By his history. As in his birth. As in the ceremony of circumcision. The ceremony of becoming a man. The ceremony of graduation. And the ceremony of his ordination. The ceremony of his retirement. Time marked by events. Such as the time of His Birth. Such as the date of His Death, and the day of His Ascension.

Silence

> I am reminded that a great compliment of my childhood was: "She's such a quiet girl."
>
> MICHELLE CLIFF, *Notes on Speechlessness*

In that photograph of the child and her mother there is a wide space between them and wide space all around them, and all that space seems to be filled with silence. The child looks as if she might have cried but is not crying. Her eyes look down intently to the ground. Her hands grip the wire of a barbed-wire fence. Maybe she has just tried to say what she felt. Maybe the language did not come to her, she could not find the words. Maybe what she felt got turned in her mouth into other words. She has that look of desperation on her face, that she had tried to speak and given up.

In the mother's body is a different kind of helplessness. She stands with one hand on her hip, another shading her eyes from the sun, looking toward her daughter. Whatever her daughter tried to say was not something she could understand. And her posture might be righteous, or even angry, if there were not a clear longing in it. As if the child's attempt at speech had touched an old buried place in her, and so she lingers, half turned to her daughter, half turned away, knowing she will never grasp that feeling and thus already having given up, yet not able to turn from it.

And they stand there forever that way, locked in silence.

HIS KNOWLEDGE

HE DETERMINES WHAT IS REAL

What He Sees (The Art of It)

> Watched all night by the dead body of a friend of Mrs. P——
> . . . Peace to his soul! I made a good sketch of his head, as a
> present for his poor wife. On such occasions time flies very slow
> indeed, so much so that it looked as if it stood still, like the hawk
> that poises over its prey.
>
> JOHN JAMES AUDUBON, *Journal*, August 11, 1821

For weeks upon weeks he observed the habits of this bird. He could
create in his mind the posture of the animal as it perched on the highest limb of a magnolia tree. He could predict every movement of the
bird; he knew his habits. Now as the bird circled his nest, the artist
knew he would light there and remain. He had planned this event. He
had disturbed the nest of this eagle since he knew then that the bird
would stay there, surveying the extent of the damage, and protecting
what was his. So the painter did not hurry as he went to find his gun,
and he took his time loading it. Then he sequestered himself in weeds
about the tree and aimed slowly and carefully. At the sound of the gun
the eagle flapped his wings, but could not bear himself into the air and
finally fell to the earth. The artist, holding the dying bird in his hands,
expressed his wonderment at the expression of the eagle's eye, which
at one and the same time blazed as if illuminated with fire, and glazed
over with death. As the sun descended the eagle died.

Now he was excited. He had a fire built and spent the next hours
preparing the bird, stuffing him, mounting him. He had acquired this
skill through years of labor and experiment. He used wires to pierce
and hold together the body of the bird in the posture he desired and

the result of his efforts created an effect whose grace and naturalness were later said to have rivaled life.

The next morning he ascended to the top of the magnolia tree, and in great danger and with enormous labor he succeeded in sawing off the limb on which the eagle had once rested. This then he attached the eagle to, perching in all his grandeur, an emblem, it was said, of freedom and glory.

Finally he would capture the eagle on paper by placing the body against a background ruled with division lines in squares to correspond to similar divisions on his own paper. And if necessary, in addition, he would measure parts of the bird with a compass. He was meticulous and painted with great accuracy even every barb on every feather, so great was his love for his subject. And in this way, he preserved the birds of America.

The Anatomy Lesson

> It is obvious that we cannot instruct women as we do men in the science of medicine; we cannot carry them into the dissecting room. . . .
>
> WALTER CHANNING, *Remarks on the Employment of Females as Practitioners in Midwifery, by a Physician*

The medical student is overcome with feeling. She vomits when she ought to be lifting the corpse's arm, breaking it against the stiffening of death. She associates her own body with the coldness of this one, trembles before it. No measure is taken to relieve her fear. No one asks her to describe it or sing it out. No ceremony exists to reveal it. She is told instead she must learn to move about the human body without feeling. (She must leave feeling behind.) No one wonders if there might have been a use for that feeling—it is discarded before it is examined. She shall never know about death. The anatomy lesson becomes lifeless.

And now this probing of the body gives us no help against our fear of death. Yet isn't that why we wanted to see the body, despite our loathing, despite our fear, because of the fear, our feeling?

Acoustics (What He Hears)

> They said that the animals were clocks; that the cries they emit-
> ted when struck were only the noise of a little spring which had
> been touched, but that the whole body was without feeling.
>
> LA FONTAINE, cited by Loren Eiseley, *The Firmament of Time*

> Wisdom, Circuit Judge: David Wiley, the appellant, and Eugene
> Cunningham, a co-defendant, were arrested on March 17, 1971,
> in connection with an alleged sexual assault . . . on twelve year old
> Maxine Lewis . . . they were charged with carnal knowl-
> edge . . . and taking indecent liberties with a minor child. . . . The
> jury found Wiley guilty. . . . The principal issue on appeal is
> whether there was sufficient corroborative evidence to take the
> case to the jury. We find there was not sufficient corroborative ev-
> idence.
>
> *United States v. Wiley,* 492 F. 2d 547 (D.C. Cir. 1973)

It is said that what is heard is a delusion of the senses. That sound consists of waves. That the wave is a momentary shape produced by energy traveling through molecules of air, or wood, or steel. Whether this wave is heard by the human ear as sound, it is said, depends on the frequency of the vibration of the sound. It is said that there are vibrations too rapid for the human ear and vibrations too slow, that vibrations of sound increase in warmer or thicker media, that the structure of the inner ear increases or decreases the frequency of sound waves, that sound waves of one frequency mask the presence of those of another frequency so that the ear hears only one sound when there are two, that many sounds together are heard as undifferentiated noise, that there is no absolute relationship between what produces sound and what is heard, that what is heard is a delusion of the senses and cannot be said to be real.

(It is established in the law that the testimony of an alleged victim of rape must be corroborated. It is said that corroboration is required because the complainants in such cases too frequently have an urge to fantasize or a motive to fabricate. Therefore the credibility of the alleged defiled, it is said, must be approached with skepticism, especially when the complainant is a young girl.)

It is therefore said that sounds do not exist without ears and a mind to hear them, that all sound exists only in the mind. (And the evidence that shortly after the alleged event a witness said that he saw the alleged victim on the street, crying, in a disheveled condition, upset and without a coat though the day was cold, and that she told him she had been attacked and pointed to her alleged attackers a short distance away, is held not to be corroborative, nor is the evidence of another witness that she appeared to him crying and saying that she had been raped held as corroborative since this is evidence that some event took place but not necessarily evidence that sexual intercourse took place.) And since sound is a product of the mind, it is further argued, it is absurd to believe that sound can exist in an unthinking substance, in the violin, or the wood of the violin.

And since all evidence for the existence of matter is sensual evidence of a like deceptive kind, existing only in the mind, it is concluded that matter exists only in the mind. (It is therefore the judgment of this hearing that the defendant was innocent of rape and that no such crime took place.)

His voice. She hears his voice speaking. He tells her she is always defending herself. For no reason, his voice implies. She tells him that while he was away, she was sick and the baby cried. He tells her that she has told him this to make him feel guilty. He raises his voice. His arms flail out as he speaks. His voice sounds violent to her. Her body flinches. She holds back the words she was going to speak. She feels a weight descend inside her. Her mouth is dry. She puts no name to this. She does not tell herself she is afraid. She does not pronounce the word "violence." His arms stop again and again short of her cheeks, of her breasts. She convinces herself that she is imagining danger. That she has no reason to defend herself, she says. That perhaps she is even now, in her fear, conjuring this up in him. That perhaps she is seeking a reason to hate him. She is ashamed for hating him. She tries again to speak with him. She says that she is tired. He falls into silence. I am tired, she says again. He turns his head away. She wonders if she has used the right words. She wonders if the tiredness in her body is real. Did you hear me? she asks. "Did you hear," she finds herself screaming. He walks out of the room. A violence fills her. Her voice lacks air. Words spit from her mouth. BASTARDSONOFABITCHIHATEYOU, she rasps. Her voice becomes ugly to her. Her words come back on her. She disowns this voice. There is no hearing, no response. She is surrounded now by silence. The voice that started in her dies within her.

The soldiers testify. They report she was killed in action. (They say the instruction was given to them in order to avoid problems: pay the women money or kill them after you are finished.) The general testified that these were rumors, stories told in jest. (They said they kept her five days before they killed her.) The journal reported the cases were all uninvestigated. The inquiry excluded mention of. . . . (Her hands were bound behind her back. Her mother ran after the soldiers with her scarf. One of them tied it around her daughter's mouth.) They testified that they had never learned her name.

Since the existence of matter is unverifiable *Each of us can say we have heard footsteps behind us* and since sensual data are deceptive *each of us tried not to show fear* it is questioned if there is any reason *since in acting the part of the victim* to examine what is called reality *we may become the victim* or if there is any way *each of us has hidden what we are* that anything can be known *each of us has denied desire* since no existence can be verified *since it has been said to us that it is our own lust* to be known and therefore *which is lived out in the body of the rapist* how can the act of knowing be known *and our terror which inspires attack* and therefore neither mind nor body *and our own guilt* can be said to exist *which attacks us through his hands* and therefore all existence *even to the point of our own death* is denied.

Reason

They said that in order to discover truth, they must find ways to separate feeling from thought *Because we were less* That measurements and criteria must be established free from emotional bias *Because they said our brains were smaller* That these measurements can be computed *Because we were built closer to the ground* according to universal laws *Because according to their tests we think more slowly, because according to their criteria our bodies are more like the bodies of animals, because according to their calculations we can lift less weight, work longer hours, suffer more pain, because they have measured these differences* and thus these calculations, they said, constitute objectivity *because we are more emotional than they are* and based they said only on what *because our behavior is observed to be like the behavior of children* is observably true *because we lack the capacity to be reasonable* and emotions they said must be distrusted *because we are filled with rage* that where emotions color thought *because we cry out* thought is no longer objective *because we are shaking* and therefore no longer describes what is real *shaking in our rage, because we are shaking in our rage and we are no longer reasonable.*

The Argument (One Thing from Another)

> Gentlemen, we are opposed to the legislation but we are not opposed to natural beauty.
>
> ROBERT E. LEE HALL, President, National Coal Association
> Testimony,
> Senate Interior and Insular Committee

> In Paris, during the ninety years ending in 1876, not a successful Caesarian section had been performed.
>
> ALAN GUTTMACHER, *Into This Universe*

> *Enfin, se l'on ne peut sauver que la mère ou l'enfant, en se servant de l'opération césarienne, sans espérance bien fondée pour l'autre, lequel des deux est-on obligé de préférer?*
>
> Messieurs les Docteurs en Théologie
> de la Faculté de Paris, 1733°

In defense of this operation, to cut away the mountaintop (one hundred and five tons in the bucket of the steam shovel) to reveal the seam of the coal (the cliff exposed, like an unfinished road, like a washboard, topsoil carried away, slate and pyrite exposed) they cited a vital contribution to the nation.

In defense of this operation, to cut into her womb (an incision made diagonally under her navel, across her abdomen or vertically under her navel to her pubis, or vertically to the right and below her navel) they cited his eternal soul. In defense of this decision (hemorrhage from the uterus into the abdominal cavity, severe pain, severe shock, infection of the wounds) they mentioned charity over justice.

In defense of this act (pyrite oxidizing, sulfuric acid in the water, fish poisoned, ponds red with acid, plants, trees disappearing) they put forward a greater good.

°Finally, if one can save only the mother or the infant, in doing the Caesarian operation, without hope of saving the other, which of the two should be chosen?—Doctors of Theology of the Faculty of Paris, 1733

Yes, they argued, considering only justice, the life of the unborn should be sacrificed to save the life of the mother. Yes, they exclaimed, they are not opposed to natural beauty. But does not charity ask that the mother prefer the life of her unborn infant over her own life? they asked. But "beauty," they argued, is only a relative term, and beauty, they said, has been said to exist only in the eye of the beholder.

Yes, they said, we do have the right to struggle against whatever endangers the life God has given us. And they said, yes, in areas set aside just for the purpose of natural beauty one might object to these mines. But, they argued, this infant is innocent and therefore who can say that this innocent endangers the life of his mother? But, they said, the same operation might be tolerated in other areas because it provides a material essential to the nation. Yet, they argued, it is true that the innocence of the infant does not deprive the mother of her rights. But is not this infant, they warned, in danger of going without baptism, and does not charity demand she choose his eternal soul over her temporal life? Is not her temporal life clearly inferior? they argued.

And considering the economy of this place, they argued, the jobs and the income these mines will bring, they said, might one not look on these mines as "things of beauty and joy forever"?

But should the mother *We were urged to weigh* they argued risk her life *the mother's life* when she is not herself in a state of grace? *against the life of her unborn.* Does she not risk her own eternal soul? *We were urged to weigh our lives against the lives of our children. Our survival against the beauty of this place.* But no, they said (And they argued that the coal company was not responsible for the floods in those places where rubble had fallen into the streams since the rainfall was an act of God) it is not necessary for the mother's life to be free of all guilt, they argued, she need only experience contrition, she need only have lived a life based on the Christian sacraments, if she wishes to sacrifice her life for her unborn child. (And which is of more beauty, they asked, this place or the welfare of the nation?) And to give one's life for one's brother is considered an act of ardent charity, they said, therefore these metaphysical decisions always being difficult *And we did not choose the beauty of this place* they finally concluded *we did not choose each other* that the life of the unborn infant should be preferred over the life of the mother. *We never chose ourselves.*

HIS CONTROL

Childish Fear

> I have small hands and feet like a woman. Could I have been meant to be a woman?
>
> FRIEDRICH NIETZSCHE, *My Sister and I*

> A man desiring a youth was obliged to abide by legal procedure. . . . When of age, a boy could be courted and often many admirers would vie for his favor in open competition with gifts, flattery and even cash. Once a suitor was approved, the lucky man was permitted to possess the boy by rape.
>
> FLORENCE RUSH, "Greek Love: The Sexual Abuse of Male Children"

> See how
> all men
> were women once
> when they were small.
>
> MARTHA KING, *Women and Children First*

This darkness. He cannot sleep in this darkness. They tell him there is nothing to fear and he tries to believe Them. He tries his best to believe Them but still he is frightened. This darkness deepens into the darkest corners of his room at night. They say all the terrible creatures he has described to Them are part of his dreams. But this frightens him more. He does not know how to say this to Them, but it frightens him more that these creatures live in his dreams, because now they are closer to him. They are inside him. He is utterly helpless against them. They say such creatures do not live in houses or in cities or anywhere he has ever been. But They do not know how alone this makes him, for now he knows he is the only one who has ever seen them. The creatures crowd into his room whenever the darkness allows them to come. So he continues every night to plead to Them for light. And every night They protest that he is dreaming, that no one has ever heard of what he describes, until finally, giving in to his panic, which does continue despite Their efforts and his, giving in to these tears and clingings of his, They leave the light on in the room. Sometimes They even sit with him. They are there; They soothe him to sleep with these words; They protect him. And then as he starts to drift off, overcome by tiredness, the softness of his bed surrounding him, he is overwhelmed with gratitude, and so clutches one of Their hands even in his sleep. He knows he could not exist without Them. The thought of Their death terrifies him. Without Them he would not be fed. Without Them he could never live in this house. He could not even cross the street. Without Them he would never learn the names for things. (They gave him his own name.) They explain the mysterious to him. Their knowledge is endless, and Their voices grand. Yet They cannot satisfy his need to know. They tell him there are things he cannot understand. They keep secrets from him. They tell him what is best even when he cannot understand why. They tell him what must be. Even though he cries They are unyielding. And even though he pleads with Them They say no. Even though he pleads until he feels his smallness before Them becoming infinitely smaller, They show no sign of yielding. He searches Their faces for a sign. He is always watching Them, Their bodies, Their eyes, to see what They will do, if he has displeased or pleased Them. If They praise him, he is pleased with himself. He imitates what They do. He makes his voice grand. He makes himself tall. He dresses in Their clothes. He imitates Their walk, Their gestures. A smile crosses one of Their faces. He believes he is pleasing Them; he believes he has become one of Them; They begin to laugh. He uses his grand voice. They cease listening to him. He swaggers in Their presence. They turn as if They did not see him. They tell him he must go to bed. And then he is making noise. And then he is saying bad words. And then he is pounding his fists and kicking his legs and his face is covered with snot and They are carrying him up the stairs. And he sits alone in the darkness, until They come back to comfort him. The anger run out of his body now, he lets Them hold him, lets Them rock him to sleep, he feeling good now, feeling soft in Their arms, except that he holds on to Them with one hand tight, one hand awake even in sleep because of his fear, this fear of the dark.

Speed

> The *Futurist Morality* will defend man from the decay caused by slowness, by memory, by analysis, by repose and habit. Human energy centupled by speed will master time and space. . . . The intoxication of great speeds in cars is nothing but the joy of feeling oneself fused with the divinity.
>
> F. T. MARINETTI, "The New Religion Morality of Speed"

> No material body can move faster than the speed of light.
>
> ALBERT EINSTEIN and LEOPOLD INFELD,
> *The Evolution of Physics*

The race-car driver is fearless. He speeds past death. In his speed is endless virility. As a lover he amazes flesh. Women fall. He is like lightning in his gestures. His will pervades all matter. He sees no boundaries. He tolerates no entanglements. Nothing must slow him down. Slowness is his enemy. If he engenders children, he does not remember them. Memory is his enemy. He does not stay in one place. He never spends time. Time is his executor. In his quest for greater and greater speed, he casts away whatever gives him weight. Weight is his enemy. He seeks weightlessness. He casts away excess. He does not tolerate the superfluous. He wants only the essential. His life is reduced to the essential. At the speed of light, which he longs for, he would shed even his body. But still he would have weight, still gravity would determine his path, still he would curve toward the earth. He glides as quickly as he can over surfaces. He does not want to touch the earth. Friction is his enemy. The smell of friction is the smell of burning is the smell of death. He cannot afford to think of death. Death is the commander of his enemies. He sheds his knowledge of death; he cannot afford to fear. The air is filled with anxiety. Space is filled with longing. He must traverse space instantly. (He must not give in to longing.) He must take the air by surprise. (He must not give in to terror.) As his speed increases, so does his power. He takes everything. Everything yields to him. He never waits. His hands move with infinite speed. What he steals vanishes. He keeps no records. He has no time. No memory. He moves. Motion is all he knows. He does not know what he moves through. The world is a blur to him. *We are a blur to him.* To the world he says that clear outlines and separate existences are illusion. Only I exist, he says. The sides of your bodies, he states, wash into nothingness. Every irrelevant detail disappears from his sight. The line of his movement alone is clear. He worships the straight line. He abhors change of direction. Change of direction is his enemy. Curves are his enemy. He wants to be more than light, more than an electromagnetic wave, which has weight, which curves. He wants to be pure number, proceeding without the passage of time infinitely forward. This is his dream. Nothing will distract him. He will dream only of the future. He will escape gravity. He will escape his enemies. In his solitary world of speed nothing enters to disturb this dream. He is like a sleeper rapidly vanishing. *We cannot imagine his destiny. His destiny terrifies us.*

Burial

> Fuel assemblies were shipped by truck . . . and were uncrated on arrival and stored under water for an average of five months to let shorter-lived radioactive wastes decay. Fuel elements were then taken out, chopped into pieces, and the spent fuel was dissolved in nitric acid. The hulls of the fuel elements and all other hardware were rinsed off and sent to the burial ground.
> GEORGE G. BERG, "Hot Wastes from Nuclear Power"

> That had been long settled: "Fling them into the canal, and all traces hidden in the water, then the thing would be at an end." So he had decided in the night of his delirium. . . .
> FYODOR DOSTOYEVSKY, *Crime and Punishment*

He separates energy from matter. (This evening, however, on coming out into the street, he became acutely aware of his fears. "I want to attempt a thing like that and am frightened by these trifles," he thought. . . .) What is left over he calls waste. ("One death and a hundred lives in exchange—it's simple arithmetic. Besides, what value has the life of that sickly, stupid, ill-natured old woman in the balance of existence . . . ?") He discovers that this waste is dangerous to him. ("Of course she does not deserve to live," remarked the officer, "but there it is, it's nature.") He determines to rid himself of this waste. ("Oh, well, brother, but we have to correct and direct nature. . . .") He sends this material to where (He laid the ax on the ground near the dead body.) he cannot see it (He remembered afterward that he had been collected and careful, trying all the time not to get smeared with blood. . . .) to where he cannot touch it (He rushed at her with the ax; her mouth twitched piteously, as one sees babies' mouths when they begin to be frightened) or smell it, to where there is no evidence of it. (Fear gained more and more mastery over him, especially after this second, quite unexpected murder.) He sends it into rivers and creeks. ("Fling them into the canal, and all traces hidden in the water. . . ." But to get rid of it turned out to be a very difficult task.) He releases this waste into the ground. (At last the thought struck him it might be better to go to the Neva.) He lets it flow into open-bottomed trenches. ("Here would be the place to throw it," he thought. . . . "Here I could throw it all in a heap and get away.") He sends it in concrete-lined drums into the sea. (He bent down over the stone, seized the top of it firmly in both hands, and using all his strength, turned it over.) He says he will let it melt into the Antarctic ice cap. (Under the stone was a small hollow in the ground, and he immediately emptied his pockets into it. Then he seized the stone again and with one twist turned it back . . .) He says he will drop it between the continental plates, at the bottom of the ocean (. . . he scraped the earth about it and pressed it at the edges with his foot.) and hope it will work its way to the core of the earth. (Nothing could be noticed.) He says the atmosphere will absorb this material. (He hid his face in his hands again and bowed his head. Suddenly he turned pale) He says the rivers will wash it away. (got up from his chair, looked at Sonia . . .) That the oceans will take in this substance (A sort of insatiable compassion . . . was reflected in every feature of her face . . .) the earth will bury this matter (His sensations that moment were terribly like the moment when he had stood over the old woman with the ax in his hand and felt that "he must not lose another minute.") that the core of the earth will receive this threat ("I know and will tell . . . you, only you. I have chosen you out . . . I chose you long ago to hear this . . .") and take this danger from him ("Lizaveta! Sonia! Poor gentle things, with gentle eyes . . . Dear women! Why don't they weep? Why don't they moan? They give up everything.")

HIS CERTAINTY

Quantity

> Mathematics is thought moving in the sphere of complete abstraction from any particular instance of what it is talking about.
>
> TOBIAS DANZIG, *Number, The Language of Science*

> Granted, granted that there is no flaw in all that reasoning, that all I have concluded this last month is as clear as day, true as arithmetic. . . .
>
> RASKOLNIKOV in Dostoyevsky, *Crime and Punishment*

He says that through numbers   1   2   3   4   5   6   7   we find the ultimate reality of things   8   9   10   11   He says   12   13   14   that quantities are the most rigorous test of things   12   13   He says God created numbers and our minds to understand numbers   14   15   16   He says the final proof   16   17   is always a sum   18   19   20   (Counting. She is counting. The number of seconds in a minute, the number of minutes in an hour, the number of hours) He measures the distance from his land to his neighbor's land. He measures his wealth. He numbers his wives. He numbers his children   21   22   23   24   25   26   He weighs what will be traded (1 Faning Mill $17.25, 1 red-faced cow $13.25, 1 year-ling calf $4.25) He calculates the worth of what he has (1 plow $1.60, 1 Wench and child $156.00, 8 fancy chairs $9.25) He assesses the value of what is his. (He measures the gallons of milk she produces. He measures the board feet they yield. He measures the hours she works, the value of her labor.)

He tells us how big he is. He measures his height. He demonstrates his strength. He measures what he can lift, what he can conquer. He calculates his feelings. He numbers his armies. *He measures our virtue. He counts the reasons why we fell.* (570 through poverty, he says, 647 through loss of their parents or their homes, 29 orphaned with elder brothers and sisters to care for.) *He counts the reasons why we fell from grace.* (23 widowed women with small children, 123 servant girls seduced and discharged by their masters.) *He tells us how strong he is.* He counts the sperm in his seminal fluid. He numbers his genes. . . . (She numbers the seconds. She numbers the hours. She numbers the days.)   27   28   29   30   31

Counting. They count. They count one billion suffering from hunger.   32   33   34   35   They count twelve thousand dying of starvation.   36   37   38   39   He counts the number of children being born.   40   41   42   He measures the growth of food.   43   44   45   He calculates the sum.   46   47   48   He says that through quantities we find ultimate reality. (She is counting the number of days in a week. The number of months in a year.)

He tells us how rich he is. He is counting his possessions and all he might possess. He measures his intelligence. He measures the coal in the ground. He calculates his life expectancy. He estimates the oil in the sea. He adds up the value of his life. He measures productive acres. He calculates the value of his existence.   49   50   51   52   53

He tells us how long he will live. He measures his neighbor's land. He numbers their children, the bellies of their cows, the spans of their horses, the numbers of their bridges, their cities, their hospitals, their armies. He counts their dead. He counts his dead. He calculates. He calculates the sum. *He gives us the final proof.*

54   55   56   57   58   59   60   (She has numbered each second of each hour of each day of each year. She has been counting.)   61   62   63   64   65   66   67   68   69   70   71   72   73   74   75   76   77   78   79   80   81

He counts   82   83   necessity. He counts what he imagines to be necessary. He says six combat divisions are necessary; he counts thirteen training divisions as necessary, four brigades, two maneuver area commands.   84   85   86   87   88   89   He   says   1,700 ballistic missiles are needed and seven hundred bombers.   90   91   92   93   94   He   counts   bombs,   he   counts   70,000 bombs.   95   96   He says when people. He counts the number of people. He says when people have nothing they starve. He counts four hundred million on the edge of starvation. He says when starving people are fed. He counts ten million children risking death from starvation. When starving people are fed, he says, they reproduce. He counts. 97 98 99 100 101 (She has numbered her children. She has counted the days of their lives. On this day, she can say, this one learned to pronounce her name. In this month, she can say, this one learned to walk. She has counted the moments.) 102 103 104 105 106 He has counted. 107 He has counted the effects. 108 109 One roentgen, he says 110 111 shortens a life by 3.5 days. 112 113 114 One hundred roentgens will shorten a life. 115 116 by one year 117 and one thousand roentgens by ten years. 118 119 120 121 122123124125126127 Counting. They have counted the targets. Of 224 targets they count, 71 were cities. They count the bombs. 128 129 130 They count 263 bombs and 1,446 megatons. 131 132 133 They count the dead to be 42 million. They imagine 42 million to be dead. They count the injured to be 17 million. They imagine 17 million injured.

134 135 136 137 *He tells us how powerful he is.* 138 139 And they count what they imagine will survive. They count 23 percent of electrical machinery. They estimate 28 percent of fabricated metal products. They say 29 percent of rubber products. Thirty percent of apparel. Thirty-four percent of machinery. Forty percent of chemicals. Fifty-one percent of furniture. 138 139 140 141142143144145146

(Counting. She has counted on this life continuing. She has counted on continuing. Each day she has counted, each day she has done what she must, done what she must to go on.)

147148149 57 percent of food, 60 percent of construction, 89 percent of mining, 94.6 percent of agriculture. Counting. He is counting how much. He is counting how much tragedy is acceptable. He imagines ten roentgens of radiation. 150 151 152 He imagines the birth of one million defective children. Counting. He counts 153 154 155 156 157

Counting. We count each second. No moment do we forget. We live through every hour. We are counting the number he has killed, the number he has bound into servitude, the number he has maimed, stolen from, left to starve. We measure his virtue. We count the value of our lives. We are counting the least act of the smallest one, her

slightest gesture, and we count the ultimate reality of her breath
barely visible now in the just cold air, 1, 2, 3, we say, as it shows itself
in small clouds, 4, 5 and 6, and disappears from moment 7, 8, 9 to
moment.

Probability

> The theory of chance consists in reducing all the events of the
> same kind to a certain number of cases equally possible . . . and in
> determining the number of cases favorable to the event whose
> possibility is sought.
>
> PIERRE SIMON DE LAPLACE, "Concerning Probability"

> . . . within a mere ten to fifteen years a woman will be able to buy
> a tiny frozen embryo, take it to the doctor, have it implanted in
> her uterus, carry it for nine months, and then give birth to it as
> though it had been conceived in her own body. The embryo
> would, in effect, be sold with a guarantee that the resultant baby
> would be free of genetic defect. The purchaser would also be told
> in advance the color of the baby's eyes and hair, its sex, its proba-
> ble size at maturity, and its probable I.Q.
>
> DR. E. S. E. HAFEZ

Where he begins. How he begins. Where he begins to doubt.
Where he begins to doubt how he began. If this should happen. If he
does this. Where he begins to think himself a prisoner (Supposing that
a thin coin is thrown into the air with opposite faces, heads and tails.
To figure the probability of throwing heads at least one time in two
throws, it is shown that four equally possible cases may arise, heads at
first and at second, heads at first and tails at second, tails at first and
heads at second, and tails at both throws.) of fate. How circumstance
determines him. If he does this. Each step. If he moves this way. Each
possibility. Where he arrives. All the dangers. He has no assurance.
Where he begins, he has no assurance, he does not know what will
happen.

(And thus the first three cases being favorable to the event, the
probability is equal to three quarters and it is a bet of three to one that
heads will be thrown at least once in three throws.)

And he considers that he may not have begun. That this may not
have been his starting place. That he may never have seen this place.
That he may have been born differently. That he may have been born
blind. That he may have been born someone else and not himself.
That he may not have been born.

(And discovering the numerical correspondence between the number of groups of hereditary qualities and the number of pairs of chromosomes and determining that there are twenty-three chromosomes, there are then over a million possible kinds of germ cells, and two such sets will give a possible number of combinations which is vastly greater.)

He sees her swelling. She is growing bigger. What is beginning in her he does not know. What will come out of her he does not know. (The doctor guides a four-inch needle through the abdominal wall, into the peritoneal cavity, through the uterine wall, and lastly, into the amniotic sac.) But what is inside her grows without his willing it. (This must be done without nicking a blood vessel, or any of the blood-filled sinuses laced around the uterus, without penetrating the fetus, or any portion of the umbilical cord, not trusting to luck, not blindly, but knowing exactly how the fetus lies and the location of the placenta.)

He says she is a mystery to him, that he does not know what is inside her, that he cannot penetrate her. (The amniotic fluid obtained in this way reveals if the fetus suffers a genetic defect, and if it is male or female.) He knows there is no mystery in him. What he does is always perfectly clear. And if he can learn what will happen next, he says, then what he will do will also be clear. (To carry out conception in vitro, oocytes, surgically freed from the ovary, are placed in a glass tube, in a carefully balanced fertilization medium into which spermatozoa are introduced. After fertilization, oocytes are then washed and transferred to a culture medium.) The movements of his life, he says, are determined by the predictable lines of logic. Each move he makes is an improvement, he declares. All his efforts lead to betterment. His body was made to struggle for this, he says. His mind was meant to find the way. He was determined at the beginning, he says, to determine what will happen. He fulfills necessity, he says. The history of his life (In order to alter genetic structure) may have been predicted (the plasmid DNA was snipped open with a restriction enzyme) from events in the past which in turn were determined (and into the broken ends of the ring, synthetic rings of DNA were attached) by the events in the past, so that what exists could not be otherwise, he points out, and what will be (with DNA complementary to plasmid DNA acting as glue) is inevitable.

Gravity

Sooner or later the uniformly moving body will collide with the wall of the elevator destroying the uniform motion. Sooner or later, the whole elevator will collide with the earth destroying the observers and their experiments.

ALBERT EINSTEIN and LEOPOLD INFELD,
The Evolution of Physics

. . . it is always possible to be "oriented" in a world that has a sacred history, a world in which every prominent feature is associated with a mythical event.

MIRCEA ELIADE, "A Mythical Geography"

The scientists are in a box. There are no windows. Nothing tells them which is right side up. The walls are empty. The ceiling and the floor are the same. They are standing in a perfect cube. Every surface is a square. This they measure and prove with their rulers. The scientists prove by experiment what is the nature of this world. One drops his handkerchief into space. It does not fall to the ground. It rests where the scientist's hand left it. Over time the handkerchief still does not move. This experiment is repeated with another scientist's eyeglasses. The scientist's eyeglasses do not move from where he has placed them in space. This experiment is repeated with different objects. First they push the eyeglasses, lending them motion, then the handkerchief, a pen, a piece of paper, and then their ruler. Each object moves continuously across space until it collides with the opposite wall. The scientists are delighted. They discover they are living in a perfect inertial system. Every body continues in a state of rest or motion. They will continue resting infinitely. They are delighted with this perfection. But gradually one scientist allows a question to enter his mind. It occurs to him that they do not know if they are at rest in an inertial system or if they are moving at a continuous rate of acceleration. Perhaps in a vacuum. Perhaps, and now the scientist feels a sense of disquiet, perhaps they are in a field of gravity, and *are* therefore accelerating continuously. He realizes that they do not know for certain where they are, nor where they are going, if they are going. He decides to break through the cube. Suddenly air rushes in. (They were suffocating, he realizes.) Through the hole he has made he sees the face of the earth coming closer and closer.

"Do you suppose that what we thought was true is not true?" he says with alarm. "We are falling," he admits, "down." Headfirst, the scientists dive from their cube. "I know where we are now," the doubting scientist shouts. "We are in a field of gravity." "And we are no longer falling at the same rate," another observes, "because of the resistance of the air." "Air!" another scientist sighs. "We are certainly not at rest now," the scientists assent. "We *are* moving," they agree.

"We know where we are now relative to the earth," they pronounce.

"And we know where we are going," another adds quickly.

"To the earth," they whisper.

"Where we were born," one says.

"And we know what will happen next," all of the scientists choir back. "We will all of us die."

HIS CATACLYSM

THE UNIVERSE SHUDDERS

Prophets

> I am become Death, the shatterer of worlds.
>
> SRI KRISHNA, the Exalted One, as spoken in the
> *Bhagavad-Gita* and remembered by J. Robert Oppenheimer
> at the moment of the first atomic blast

(NOAH)

We were told that Noah was chosen to hear the word of God. We were told that God said to Noah, "I will destroy man whom I have created from the face of the earth." That there was a flood. That it was unmerciful, and every living thing perished. (That it rained forty days and forty nights and every bit of the earth was covered with water, even the highest peaks of the highest mountains.)

(ISAIAH)

We were told that Isaiah had seen God and that God was angry. (That the anger of God will darken the earth, Isaiah said. That the people will be like fuel for his fire.

That God said He would be like a man of war, that He would cry, roar and prevail against His enemies.

That the daughters of evil would be uncovered. Their shame seen. Woe to rebellious children, He said. There would be no deliverance from this flame.)

(THE DOCTORS)

We were told that they knew what was inside the atom, and that they could destroy a city with it. That unfathomable energy was locked inside matter, heat, light, fire. That the sky would light up. That the heat would melt flesh. And the roar would be deafening.

Plutonium

We hear there is a substance and it is called plutonium. We hear that "they" are somewhere (do you remember the name of the state?) manufacturing it. We don't know how it is made. We think the substance uranium is used. We know it is radioactive. We have seen the photographs of babies and children deformed from radiation. The substance plutonium becomes interesting to us when we read that certain parts of the building where it is manufactured have leaks. We don't know really what this means, if it is like the leak in our roofs, or the water pipe in the backyard, or if it is a simple word for a process beyond our comprehension. But we know the word "leak" indicates error and we know that there is no room for error in the handling of this substance. That it has been called the most deadly substance known. That the smallest particle (can one see a particle, smell it?) can cause cancer if breathed in, if ingested. All that we know in the business of living eludes us in this instant. None of our language helps us. Not knowing how to drive, to cook on a gas stove, to soap the diaper pins so that they pass more easily through the diaper, to wash cotton in cold water so that it doesn't shrink, to repair the water pipes, or dress a wound. No skill helps us. Nor does quickness of mind, nor physical strength. We are like an animal smaller and more vulnerable than any nature has ever created. We have no defense. We try not to remember whatever we may know of plutonium.

Pollution

"I wish I could hold you," she continued bitterly, "till we were both dead! I shouldn't care what you suffered. I care nothing for your sufferings. Why shouldn't you suffer. I do! Will you forget me . . . ?"

EMILY BRONTË, *Wuthering Heights*

I did not have to remember these things, they have remembered themselves all these years.

Black Elk in John G. Neihardt, *Black Elk Speaks*

There is no turning away. There is no escape. Every attempt to destroy this matter brings it back again. For every head cut off a new one grows. Every particle ignited, the least bit of dust blown away, what rises in the air expanding, bursting into flame, incandescent, seeming to vanish, be gone forever, returns, returns, always comes back to him, unmercifully. What he has sent into the rivers comes back, blackens the shore, enters the land, feeds his crops, enters his mouth, festers in him. What he has burned gathers in the air, hangs in space, yellows his vision, stings his eyes; he breathes it. What he has worked out of the ground and transformed darkens the skies, gives out an odor he cannot forget, wherever he turns. What he has denied from his own body accumulates, grows, floats back to him, overwhelms him, gives him no way out. He has gone to the very root, he says, of existence. He has deciphered the secrets. As to the persistence of matter, he insists he can alter the structure of molecules. At his hands, the molecules change, and changed and changing they enter his skin, hide in what he eats, secrete themselves in his tissue, alter the molecular structure of his body. He goes inside the heart of life, he says. He takes apart even the form of matter itself, he strips energy from mass, he splits what is whole, he takes this force for his own, he says. But what he has split does not stop coming apart. Fractures live in the air, invisible fractures come into his body, split his chromosomes, unravel the secrets of life in him.

This secret life in us. The seen and the unseen. The speaking and the unspoken. The one who is what she ought to be and the one who is not. This other. The one from whom we are split away. Who follows us. Whose words lie under our tongues. Who speaks to us in our dreams.

Barely seen, soundlessly surrounding him, with hardly a breath of evidence, all he has burned, all he has mined from the ground, all he cast into the waters, all he has torn apart, comes back to him. He is haunted. Carbon monoxide, sulfur dioxide, beryllium, arsenic, peroxyacetylnitrate, formaldehyde, do not desert him. Dioxin, DDT, will not let him forget. Lead, mercury, live in his dreams. Strontium sticks in his bones. The equation for oxygen stays in his mind but he cannot breathe what he used to call air. The equation for water stays in his mind, but there is nothing he can drink that will not poison him. What the cells of his own blood should be he has recorded in his books, yet these cells begin to fight among themselves, some cells multiplying, and he is weakened by his own blood. *Who speaks to us in our dreams. Sings in our blood and will not be still there.* Every attempt he makes to order this world decreases his space. The dimensions of his life are filled with ghosts *Making us grieve for no apparent reason. Making us rage for no visible reason.* Filled with shadows, with tiny reminiscences. Nothing he has ever set his hand upon has forgotten that weight. *This fury in us that will not die, who has captured our bodies, who claims to have been with us for years. Who is making us see what we have not seen before.* He is haunted: all his victims speak in his body. He cannot escape pollution, there is no way for him to be free of these ghosts.

HIS SECRETS

WHAT IS SLEEPING WITHIN

Dream Life

> ... Niels Bohr, upon receiving the Nobel prize, revealed to the world that his dreams had depicted the structure of the atom. And August Kekule, the chemist, was likewise honored for the great advances made possible through his dream of the structure of the benzene ring.
>
> E. STANTON MAXEY, "Biopsychophysics—
> The Proper Study of Man"

> *Nel mezzo del cammin di nostra vita*
> *Mi ritrovai per una selva oscura*
> *Chè la diritta via era smarrita.*°
>
> DANTE ALIGHIERI, *Inferno*

He had left the true way when he was deep in sleep, and he cannot say how he came there. He looks back to see the dangers he has just passed, and is terrified. When he goes forward, he meets ferocious beasts on his path, three of them, and the last, he is certain, is very hungry. She pursues him. He runs from her into the presence of a man he slowly recognizes as one he had before taken as a mentor. This man has been known for his great power over words, and the sleeper takes this power as his own. When he makes a plea for help, this man tells him that the creature who pursues him has an insatiable appetite, that each bite she takes makes her want more, that he must choose a different road. This man offers to guide the sleeper to an eternal place, but he warns that there they will hear sounds of despair from spirits who live in pain, who endure a second death.

°In the middle of the journey of our life I came to myself within a dark wood whose straight way was lost.

[Marie Curie, 1867–1934]

I want to be left in peace.

MARIE CURIE, last words

In this mass of substances she searches for the elementary, for what cannot be reduced. Sifting through the residue of pitchblende, she removes pinecones and rocks. Over days and weeks, over years, she grinds this material, she dissolves it, she filters it, precipitates it, collects it again, dissolves it again, precipitates again, crystallizes and recrystallizes. Thousands of gallons become teaspoonfuls.

Finally, she can call this material pure. Yet it does not stay still. It gives off heat. Its emanations fill the air. It glows. Its rays pass through paper, glass, rubber, cloth, skin. A piece of metal placed near the radium but not touching it becomes radioactive. The pure radium burns itself away.

Now this substance has entered her hands. Her skin is burned. There are open sores. The lenses of her eyes become opaque. She cannot see. She has pains in her arms. She is exhausted. She collapses. She burns with fever.

Yet she will not allow these symptoms to be spoken of, and despite the complaints of her body, returns again and again to work this material.

But what the scientist touches she becomes. At her death, she declares, "I can't express myself properly." She says, "My head's turning." She tries to turn a spoon in a glass as though it were a rod in a beaker. She asks, "Has it been made with radium or mesothorium?" Its temperature becomes her temperature. She shakes with its coldness. "Thirty-eight degrees! I don't know if it's right. I'm trembling so." Its properties become her own; her body, the experiment. "I'd like to set myself straight, my head's turning." At the end, she speaks for herself. "What are you going to do to me," she says, "I don't want it," and demands, "I want to be left in peace."

[Sigmund Freud, 1856–1939]

What then [is] it? Those it is which [are] upon their altars, the image is of the eye of Ra and the image of the eve of Horus. O Ra-Tmu, the lord of the Great House, Prince, life, strength, health, of gods all, deliver thou from god that whose face is [in the form of] a dog, [and] his eyebrows like [those of] men, he liveth upon the enemy, watching bight that of lake of fire, devouring bodies and swallowing hearts, and voiding filth, not being seen himself. Who then is it? "Eater of millions" [is] his name. . . .

"The Papyrus of Ani," *The Egyptian Book of the Dead*

We displayed an unmistakable tendency to "shelve" death, to eliminate it from life.

SIGMUND FREUD, "Thoughts on War and Death"

The doctor's study is filled with figurines. They sit everywhere, stand everywhere, small gods staring out from glass cases, heads of goddesses assembled on tables, an army of deities at the front of his desk, facing the chair where he sat to write. (To his colleague he remarks that he must never abandon the sexual theory, that it must become a dogma, "an unshakable bulwark . . . against the black tide of mud of occultism.") On top of one glass cabinet sits a Greek vessel in the shape of a sphinx, and inside, Sakmet, the goddess with the head of a lioness. (He writes that religion to the common man is a palliative remedy, designed to explain the riddle of the world and assure him that a solicitous providence, in the form of a greatly exalted father, looks over him.) On the table to the right of his desk, with two other figurines, is the Egyptian figure of Imhotep, god of learning and medicine, holding a papyrus scroll in his lap. (In a lecture he says that he has taken the liberty to point out that that deep belief in psychic freedom and choice which men have "is quite unscientific and that it must give ground before the claims of a determinism which governs mental life.") Among countless others on his desk, Osiris, Isis, Amen-Ra, Isis nursing Horus, a Chinese tomb figurine, Aphrodite, Horus as a child. (He writes that "the patient must regard his doctor as a father," that "the father-transference is the only battlefield on which we conquer and take the libido prisoner.") A Janus head of Silenus and Minerva. On a table before his bookcase, the head of Bodhisattva, head of Buddha, bust of Seraphis (He records that in the early life of man, the sons lived in fear of death or castration from their father. That the brothers thus driven out of the family banded together and murdered the father, making a feast of his body) part of an Egyptian mummy cover. (And that in the childhood of each man lives a fantasy of murdering his own father.) In the cabinet between the entrance and the window, Egyptian funerary figures, six ushabti figures, named the "answerers" because they always respond to the call of their master. (During a discussion with a colleague about the decision of Amenophis IV to erase his father's name from the steles, Freud falls to a faint.) On a shelf, to the right of a vase filled with flowers, an Egyptian cobra, Uraeus, emblem of the Pharaoh's power, taken from a mummy's crown. (He writes that he will "suffer the just punishment that none of the undiscovered provinces of mental life which I was the first mortal to enter will bear my name or follow the laws I have formulated.") Centered above two bookcases, two Egyptian funerary steles, one with an inscription to the dead Hordiefnakht as he appears before the gods who will judge his fitness for the afterlife. (He fixes his death as occurring in 1918; suggests he will die in his forties of a rupture of the heart; on parting from his friends says, "Good-bye, you may never see me again," develops a fear of trains and writes that journeys on trains are common symbols of the fear of death.) In a bookcase, the Egyptian warrior goddess Neith, originally a female body with a penis. (Freud answers the puzzle of the androgyny of Neith by describing the castration fears of the young boy.) In front of his books, portraits of three women, Marie Bonaparte, Lou Andreas-Salomé and Yvette Guilbert. (He writes that femininity is a riddle he cannot solve.) In a cabinet two Near Eastern mother goddesses, on a table Horus, the falcon-headed god (As a child he dreams his mother, with an expression of sleep on her face, is carried into the room by three people with bird beaks and laid upon the bed.) between the Egyptian steles a bas-relief of the death of Patroclus. (He writes of a dream in which he seeks food from women in a kitchen, and then recalls as a child asking his mother if the words "From earth you come and to earth you shall return" were true, and he continues that his mother answered by rubbing the palms of her hands together and thus showing him the earth-colored skin of her hands.)

In his consulting room the engraving *La Leçon Clinique du Dr. Charcot,* depicting a hysterical female patient as she is shown to the members of the staff of Salpêtrière hospital.

[EMPEDOCLES, C. 495–C. 435 B.C.]

Fools! For they do not take the long view. . . .

EMPEDOCLES

He says that emanations are given off by all things that are created, and that these emanations enter into the pores of other created things. That sensation occurs when the emanation fits the pore. He says there are elements, homogeneous and unchangeable and indestructible, and those elements mix together to create all things. He says therefore that what we know as birth and death is a delusion. That we think of birth as a coming into being and death as annihilation, but that nothing can be created out of nothing, and that which is cannot perish utterly. There is no birth or death, he says, but rather there is change, and the mingling of things changed, and these are perceived by us as birth or death. All creation, he says, all dissolution, is but change.

[RENÉ DESCARTES, 1596–1650]

Am I not that being who now doubts nearly everything . . . ?
RENÉ DESCARTES, *Meditation on the First Philosophy*
in Which the Existence of God and the Distinction
Between Mind and Body Are Demonstrated

10 November, 1619, when I was full of enthusiasm, I discovered
the fundamental principles of a wonderful knowledge.
RENÉ DESCARTES, *Journals*

On this night of the tenth of November, he has three dreams. In the first, while walking in the street he is filled with terror and feels a great weakness on his right side, thus must bend over to his left side to get to his destination. He is embarrassed by this posture, yet he cannot straighten himself out. A wind whirls him around on his left foot, like a tornado. He tries to reach the church of the college he has seen ahead of him so that he might say a prayer. But at that moment he realizes he has passed an acquaintance without saying hello, yet the wind blowing in the direction of the church prevents him from turning back. But now he sees another man standing in the courtyard of the college. This man is friendly and calls him by name. He realizes with astonishment that those standing about are having no trouble standing up straight, but Descartes is still bent over and staggering.

He awakens and turns from his left side to his right, then prays for God to protect him from this dream. After two hours he falls asleep, dreams of a violent noise, and awakens again, seeing fiery sparks about the room. Thinking about the philosophical explanations for their existence, he focuses on various objects about the room, and this gives him a sense of peace which enables him to fall asleep again.

Now he dreams of finding a book on the table. Not knowing who put it there, he opens it and finds with delight it is a dictionary. Then under his other hand he finds an anthology of poetry titled *Corpus Poetarum.*° He opens the book and reads: "*Quod vitae sectabor iter?*"† But at this moment he notices a man, who hands him a poem beginning "*Est et non*"‡ and praises this poem. Saying this poem is by Ansonius, he leafs through the pages of the book to show the man Ansonius's "Idylls." But though he knows the order of the book, he is having trouble locating these poems. The man asks where he got this book, and Descartes answers he does not know, and that he also had another book, which has now disappeared. But at this moment the dictionary reappears, no longer as complete as it was before. Now he finds Ansonius's poems, but not "*Est et non.*" He shows the man what he says is a more beautiful poem, "*Quod vitae sectabor iter?*" Then he realizes when he finds some copper engravings in the book, which he says are very beautiful, that this is a different edition from the one he knew. The man disappears. Now he is aware he is dreaming, and still asleep, he interprets his dream. The dictionary is the interconnectedness of all science; *Corpus Poetarum* the closeness of philosophy with wisdom. Divine enthusiasm and imagination, he says, make the seed of wisdom in each spirit grow more profusely. "*Quod vitae sectabor iter*" is moral theology, or the counsel of a wise person.

When he awakens he decides that the spirit of truth had visited him to reveal to him the treasure of knowledge. And this dream, he said, led him to his "*méthode,*" and to seek ultimate truth in mathematical knowledge.

° "The Body of All Poets"—the collected works of all poets.
† "What path of life shall I follow?"
‡ "He is and he is not."

[ISAAC NEWTON, 1642–1727]

. . . so happy in his conjectures, as to so seem to know more than
he could possibly have had any means of proving.

DE MORGAN, "Newton," 1846

He said he made his discoveries by always thinking into them, that
he would keep the subject constantly before him and wait for the first
dawnings to open little by little into full light. His assistant recorded
that his efforts were prodigious at the spring and the fall of the leaf,
the fires scarcely going out day or night, sitting up all night until his
chemical experiments were complete. His assistant suspects, because
of Newton's pains and diligence at these times, that he reached for
something beyond human art and industry. In Newton's library are
found the titles *The Mirror of Alchemy, Musaeum Hermeticum, The
Philosopher's Stone, De Transmutatione Metalorum, De Occulta
Philosophia* and *Alchymia.* At his death a box of his papers is found
which during his life were never published. On examination, these papers are put away, not to be read or printed. Among these notes he
had written: "Because the way by which mercury may be so impreg-
nated has been thought fit to be concealed by others that have known
it, and therefore may possibly be an inlet to something more noble,
not to be communicated without immense danger to the world . . ."
Appended to his *Optics* is the query: "Have not small particles of Bodies certain Powers, Virtues or Forces, by which they act at a distance,
not only upon the Rays of Light for reflecting, refracting and inflect-
ing them, but also upon one another, for producing a great part of the
Phaenomena of nature . . ." and he speculates that these small particles might have attractive forces of an electrical nature; and he wonders if it might be that mass may be able to exchange with light. It is
said after his death that he most often had the truth before the proof.
Of himself he wrote that despite how he may appear to the world, he
felt himself to be like a boy playing on the seashore, diverting himself
by finding a prettier shell or smoother pebble than ordinary, "while
the great ocean of truth lay all undiscovered before me."

[CHARLES DARWIN, 1809–1882]

If Darwin's ill health was not, as some seem to think, a pretext to isolate himself with his work, neither was it, as Darwin had right to fear, an insuperable obstacle to his work. One reason why it did not prove fatal to his ambitions was the devotion and sympathy of his wife.

GERTRUDE HIMMELFARB, *Darwin and the Darwinian Revolution*

Beginning early in the day, after taking breakfast alone, and a walk, he worked in his study from eight until nine-thirty in the morning. Then he went into the drawing room with his family; he looked over the mail, and sometimes listened as a novel was read aloud, he resting on the sofa. ("All that we can do," he wrote, "is to keep steadily in mind that each organic being is striving to increase in a geometrical ratio . . .) He returned to his study at ten-thirty and emerged again at noon. (. . . that each at some period of its life, during some season of the year, during each generation, or at intervals, has to struggle for life or suffer great destruction. . . .") Then he took another walk, past the greenhouse, perhaps looking at an experimental plant, and then onto a gravel walk encircling an acre and a half of land, taking a specified number of turns, perhaps watching his children play, observing a bird, a flower. Or before he took too many spills, taking a canter on an old and gentle horse. ("What a struggle must have gone on during long centuries," he wrote, "between several kinds of trees each annually scattering its seeds by the thousands, what war between insect and insect—between insects, snails and other animals with bird and beasts of prey—) After this, lunch was served to him. And then he read the newspapers and wrote letters. If they were lengthy he dictated them from rough drafts. At three o'clock, he went to rest in his bedroom, smoked a cigarette, lay on a sofa, and listened again to a novel read aloud to him by his wife. (—all striving to increase, all feeding on each other, or on the trees, their seed and seedlings, or on the other plants which first clothed the ground and thus checked the growth of trees!") This reading often put him to sleep so that he complained he had missed whole parts of books. His wife feared the cessation of her voice would wake him. (Of the *Formica refescens,* he wrote, "So utterly helpless are the masters, that when Huber shut up thirty of them without a slave . . . they did nothing; they could not even feed themselves and many perished of hunger.")

At four he took another walk, and worked for one more hour. Then after another period of listening to a novel, he ate his dinner, played two games of backgammon with his wife, read some of a scientific book, and when tired finally, lay back again to listen while his wife read to him or played the piano. When he retired at ten or ten-thirty, he often lay awake for hours afterward in pain. On bad days, he could not work at all. (Of the process of selection he wrote: ". . . the struggle will almost invariably be most severe between individuals of the same species, for they frequent the same districts, require the same food and are exposed to the same dangers.")

In a letter to Lyell he claimed that he was bitterly mortified to conclude that "the race is for the strong," but that he would be able to do little more than admire the strides others would make in science. (". . . the swiftest and the slimmest wolves," he wrote, "would have the best chance of surviving and so be preserved or selected.") Because of his own ill health, and that of his grandfather and his brother, and mother-in-law and aunt (And he wrote: ". . . so profound is our ignorance and so high our presumption, that we marvel when we hear of the extinction of an organic being, and we do not see the cause, we invoke cataclysms . . .") and because of the sick headaches which his wife suffered ("natural selection acts only by preservation and accumulation of small inherited modifications, each profitable to the preserved being . . ." he wrote) he feared for the health of his children, of whom one died shortly after birth, one died in his childhood, and others suffered chronic illness.

In 1844, of his discovery of evolution, he recorded: "At last gleams of light have come and I am almost convinced (quite contrary to the opinion I started with) that the species (it is like confessing a murder) are not immutable."

[JOHANNES KEPLER, 1571–1630]

She was carried out of her house in an oak linen chest, and taken to the prison in Leonberg. She was then seventy-three years of age. (He writes that God himself "was too kind to remain idle and began to play the game of signatures, signing his likeness into the world.") There were forty-nine accusations against her, and numerous supplementary charges. She was said to have failed to weep when the Holy Scriptures were read to her. (He resolves the harmonies into regular polygons.) Katherine Kepler replied that she had shed so many tears in her life, she had none left. (The irregular polygons, and all figures that cannot be constructed by compass and ruler, he says, are unclean because they defy the intellect. *Inscibilis. Ineffabilis. Non-entia.* Unspeakable. Nonexistences. And this is the reason, he writes, "why God did not employ the septagon and the other figures of this species to embellish the world.") Her son Johannes Kepler answered the Act of Accusation by an Act of Contestation, which was refuted by an Act of Acceptation to which was submitted an Act of Exception and Defense which was answered by an Act of Deduction and Confutation. Finally, in her defense her son submitted an Act of Conclusion, one hundred and twenty-eight pages long. (He then discovers regular polygons inscribed in the movements of heavenly bodies. And of these he writes: "The heavenly motions are nothing but a continuous song for several voices . . . a music which . . . sets landmarks in the immeasurable flow of time.")

After that, her case, by order of the duke, was sent to her son's university, where the faculty found that Katherine should be questioned under torture, but suggested that proceedings stop at the *territio*—questioning under threat of torture. (As part of the harmony of the world, Kepler reveals that the ratio which exists between the periodic times of any two planets is precisely one and one half of the power of their mean distances.) She was led to the place of torture; the executioner was presented to her; all his instruments shown her and their effect on the body described. Great pain and dolor awaited her if she did not confess, she was told. The terror of the place had wrought confessions from many before her, but she said that even if they tore her veins from her body one by one, she had nothing to confess. (On discovering that the heavenly bodies move in ellipses rather than perfect circles, Kepler apologizes for having to bring a small cartload of dung into the universe in order to rid it of a far vaster quantity of dung.) She fell on her knees then and asked God to give a sign if she was a witch or a monster, and then said she was willing to die, that God would reveal the truth after her death. (He writes: "Yes, I give myself up to holy ravings. I mockingly defy all mortals with this open confession; I have robbed the golden vessel of the Egyptians to make out of them a tabernacle for my God. . . .") In this way, and due to the efforts of her son, and the respect he commanded in the world, Katherine Kepler was released.

[LINNAEUS, 1707–1778]

> The first step of science is to know one thing from another. This knowledge consists in their specific distinctions; but in order that it may be fixed and permanent distinct names must be given to different things and those names must be recorded and remembered.
>
> CAROLUS LINNAEUS

By naming and by knowing the names of things he proposed to see into the secret cabinet of God. Travelers from Madeira, Virginia, from all over the world, risked dangers in vast forests, on high cliffs, in the deepest chasms to send him packets of seeds. He catalogued American falcons, parrots, pheasants, guinea fowl, American capercaillie, Indian hens, swans, duck, geese, gulls, snipe, American crossbills, sparrows and turtledoves. He classified creation according to sexual organs; he gave each creature two names, a general and a specific name.

He wrote that riches vanish and stately mansions fall into decay, that even the most prolific families die out sooner or later and that the mightiest of states are overthrown, but that all of nature must be obliterated before the genera of plants and "he be forgotten who held the torch aloft in botany." But as he grew older, he suffered a stroke, and after this he began to lose more and more of his memory.

Gradually he no longer knew *Systema Naturae,* and after all this, in his last years, he forgot even his own name.

Nightmares

We dreamed we were the daughters of evil. But you are mistaken, we cried, there has been some mistake. And we cried to be accepted for our true identity. We produced documents. The testimony of our parents. But the documents were changed. And our parents said things were different from what we had thought. Did you lie to us? we questioned. But they would not speak to us. No one would speak to us. We were in rooms by ourselves. We were under the sheets. No one had accused us. We dreamed we were the daughters of evil, because we knew we were. We had been hiding this secret all our lives.

We dreamed we were speaking in tongues. That all we had ever felt, our whole lives, became clear to us. That language was beautiful. Lyrical. That we were singing. That we wept to recognize ourselves in these voices. But when we awakened, we dreamed, we could only remember babble, and all language was foreign.

We dreamed we traveled at the speed of light. And our flesh vanished to nothing. We were in the void. But before we reached this void we saw a glimpse. There was the world we always knew possible. In our fleshless bodies we felt our hearts drop infinitely. To see what we had given up. In our terror. In our desire to speed as fast as possible. To be away from the terrifying roar, the blinding light, the cataclysm, we had sped into the world of impossibility.

But there, behind us, green and still living, was this possibility—a day's walk back into a future we could have touched: Such tenderness, such joy.

TERROR

> Terror is the realization of the law of movement; its chief aim is to make possible the force of nature or history to race freely through mankind, unhindered by any spontaneous human action. . . . The rulers themselves do not claim to be just or wise, but only to execute historical or natural laws. . . .
>
> HANNAH ARENDT, *The Origins of Totalitarianism*

> You if you were sensible
> When I tell you the stars flash signals, each one
>   dreadful,
> You would not turn and answer me
> "The night is wonderful."
>
> D. H. LAWRENCE, "Under the Oak"

He speaks of the natural order of things and the regular movements of heavenly bodies. As for her efforts to make anything different, he directs her gaze to the skies. There is no caring in natural law, he says, things are as they are. As to any meaning in these movements, he says, he cannot say, but listen, he says, to the measurements. He is rarely very much over six feet tall, he says, and there are 5,280 feet in one mile, and the average distance from the earth to the sun, he says, is 93 million miles. Think about immensity, he tells her. The planet Saturn is 886 million miles from the sun. No star is less than 26 trillion miles away from the earth. Think of the smallness of this life, he says, and the vanity of supposing significance.

He reminds her she could not exist in that void. He says the average temperature of the human body lies at 119.5 Centigrade. Do you know how hot the sun is? he asks. The temperature of the sun, he raises his voice now, is 5,500 degrees Centigrade at its exterior, and, he leans forward and shouts, 40,000,000 degrees in its interior.

He tells her how perishable she is and how little there is to perish. A speck weighing usually only from forty to one hundred kilos. But the earth weighs 6,600,000,000,000,000,000,000,000 metric tons, he says, and the mass of the sun, he tells her triumphantly, is 332,000 times that of the earth, and the stars and the gases, the stars and the gases in this galaxy alone, he crows, are as heavy as 100 billion suns.

But at the speed of light, he lets her know, mass no longer exists; she is incapable of that kind of speed, he says, she would perish at that speed. And time in the sky, he tells her, is measured in light-years. From the earth to the moon, he says, is five and one half light-seconds. From the earth to the sun, eight light-minutes. The diameter of the whole solar system, he says, is not quite one half of a light-day. This is closeness, he says, this is intimacy. Distance, he says, is farther away, unimaginably, unspeakably vast. The nearest star, he tells her, is over four light-years away. Sirius, he says, is eight light-years away. To cross this galaxy would take 100,000 light-years. Even if she could travel at the speed of light, he says, she could never survive that journey. Her life would end thousands of years before she could reach her destination. She would die surrounded by the void. And this galaxy, he states now, is just part of an open cluster of galaxies three million light-years in diameter.

(Out of the corner of his eye, he sees a gesture. The image rubs against the inside of his head. Wakens him at night. Keeps his mind off what he is doing, his eyes out of focus. Of whom does this gesture remind him? Of what? So quick. And coming as it did from a woman. What did she have in mind from doing it? But this he thought he knew. Uncannily he thought he knew. And this he hated her for, the outrage of seeming to be like him, of imitating him, of mocking his dignity, of forcing in him some recognition, so that he might see himself *in* her. She did not know what she was doing, to imitate his carriage, to lift her head in that manner, calmly. There is something that repels him in that gesture. He has made other men laugh, many times, over that movement, telling how she drew herself up like a man, how silly she looked, dressed as she was, smaller than he, how out of place in that defiance. What was there to defy anyway? Just the natural order of things. But it was here, alone, out of the sound of their laughter, that the hatred came upon him. She was trying to steal something that belonged to him and of which she knew nothing. Her ignorance showed all over her as she tried to claim that her words were spoken with as much weight as his. And in this moment she made a mockery of his judgment. By imitating his certainty, she made him uncertain.

We recognize two sets of gestures. We know the stories of those gestures. How the one set of gestures was our own which we took care to conceal except among ourselves and they were like the gestures of any beings, carrying a simple air of earnestness that accompanies the performance of necessary tasks, and how the other gestures were performed for those others who looked to us for that slowness of wit which means dullness of feeling and an absence of pride. For if there were wit, or feeling, or a dignity, would not they have to know what we knew because in the privacy we had among ourselves we laughed, that speaking to each other, we could strip the dignity off them like bark, like the skin of an apple, that the truth of their movements, in our private moments, was laid bare, and then, yes, the skies and the stars were unmerciful witnesses.

And then ideas entered his head on certain nights in the shapes of dreams. On these wild nights, he saw himself in her body and then he moaned at the injustice of finding his humanity concealed and trapped in this way until he would wake up screaming in terror. And into these first moments of waking crept this doubt that seemed to edge into him and stick, creating an unnatural space between his soul and his flesh, this doubt of the justice of things after all. Suppose that gesture of hers meant her soul was like his. And then another thought came upon him, so terrible he could scarcely hold on to it. Suppose there is no difference between them except the power he wields over her. And suppose that in an instant of feeling himself like her, he let this power go, then would he not become her, in his own body even. And some part of him seemed to know what it would be to be her in his body, and how he came to know this he does not choose to remember. And he went no further that way in his thoughts because space closed in on him and slowly he had to push it back to give himself room to breathe. He had to push space as far as it could go, to the outer limits of the universe. And in that universe, vaster than he or she could imagine, that gesture of hers meant nothing. She may say the stars look like jewels on a velvet cloth. But he knew to distrust appearances. She had too much eagerness to attach meaning to things. He reminded himself that all this life is determined, that what meaning there is in the movements of matter is indecipherable, that he himself is made up only of particles in space. And beyond this, he tells himself, only the stars burn, burn in a dreadful void.)

What man sees taking place across the skies, he tells her, happened 3,000,000 years ago. What is happening at this instant, across space, he says, she will never know in her lifetime. He recites the figures to her. The Andromeda galaxy, he says, is over 2,000,000 light-years away. The Magellanic Clouds, 30,000 light-years in diameter, are 160,000 light-years away. There may be, he suggests, nearly 1,000,000,000 galaxies in this universe. And he tells her how all this began indifferently to her. He suggests there was an explosion. He says to her these explosions are still going on and have gone on, before she was born, after her death. He mentions in fact the Crab Nebula, 3,500 light-years away, which has been exploding for 900 years and increases in diameter by 120 million miles every day. Galaxies are moving away from this earth and one another, our galaxy is moving out, he says, everybody is moving, he says, some at the rate of 76,000 miles each second. And faint galaxies, he says, his voice filled with terror, at the edge of the universe, whose existences have been traced by radiotelescope, seem to be moving away 93,141 miles each second. And it is still unknown, he speaks these words slowly, if there are farther stars, moving faster away, still unknown if there are explosions or black holes toward which we move and what the fate of this earth will be, he says, is still unknown.

BOOK THREE

PASSAGE

Her Journey

Through the Labyrinth

to the Cave Where

She Has Her Vision

THE LABYRINTH

The Room of the
Dressing

> In woman dressed and adorned, nature is present but under re-
> straint, by human will remolded nearer to man's desire.
> SIMONE DE BEAUVOIR, *The Second Sex*

The spiraling descent. The legend of endless circling. The labyrinth from which none return. She falls into this labyrinth. Into the room of the dressing where the walls are covered with mirrors. Where mirrors are like eyes of men, and the women reflect the judgments of mirrors. Where the women stand next to each other, continue dressing next to each other, speak next to each other as if men were still with them. As if men could overhear their words. The room of the dressing where women sometimes speak in code. The room where each makes her own translation. The room where the women keep to themselves and she teaches her daughter to put on makeup. The room of the half real. Where the women partly see each other. Where the women partly laugh. Partly laugh at the shapes they see in the mirror and the girls once reflected there.

The room of the giggling girls. The room in which the girls whisper secrets about each other. Where one is said to have larger breasts. Where it is whispered she does not wear a bra. The room in which the girls run giggling to catch their friend with her breasts uncovered. The room of the disowned woman. The room where the women deny she is anything like them. Where they will not acknowledge the one who frightens them, the one who screams too loudly at her children, the one whose face is frozen to madness, who wears too many clothes.

The room in which the women fear time. In which she is afraid of becoming her mother. This labyrinth. The place that turns back on itself. The room in which the women grow up. In which they are no longer awkward in their clothing. In which they grow out of clumsiness. And where she blames herself for not gracing her clothes. The room in which women praise their clothing and sigh that they are no longer children. The room in which time is a mirror. The labyrinth in which the women fear aging.

She circles this maze of her fears, of her fear of seeing, of her fear of being revealed, of her fear of touching. The room of the dressing where the women are afraid to touch. Where the women are not close. Where the women keep themselves at a distance. Where the temptation to speak becomes large and the fear of speaking larger. Where all her words are dressed. And the mother teaches her daughter how to wear her hair. The room of the dressing in which the women shoulder all blame. In which the women agree that women are dangerous. The room in which women lament the darkness of women. And stories are told about women. The room in which the women cover themselves. And put each other at a distance. The room of the dressing where the women tell each other they are happy and in which the women look for secret unhappiness. This room where the women gossip. Where she carefully dresses all her words. And the mother teaches the daughter to pull up her slip. This room where they never touch. Where the women complain about each other. And say they cannot stand the company of women. The room of women who laugh at women. The room of women who know about each other. Whose looks are painful to each other. The room of women who have never really spoken. Who cannot be close. Where the sins of the father are visited upon the mother. And she looks at herself with his eyes. Where her daughter turns from her, though she carries her mother's knowledge in her bones, and will pass this on. The room where the daughter denies she is anything like her mother. The room of the dressing in which the women do not trust each other. The room where she finds herself in danger from herself.

And she says she is suffocating. And she says the horizon is a lie. And the air is filled with stories about her. And she says space denies her. The room in which the women are lost. The labyrinth from which they do not escape. Which keeps them going around in circles. The room in which the women lose their way and are no longer anywhere. The room where women die. The labyrinth where she is afraid of perishing.

The Room of the
Undressing

I go where I love and where I am loved.
H.D., "The Flowering of the Rod"

Startracks. *Spiral nebulae.* *Craters of the moon.* She lets herself fall. She falls into the room of her wants. The room where the demands of women are endless. Where her voice has endlessly demanded her to go. This room which reveals her. Where she is clumsy again. Where she is awkward in her grown-up clothing. Where she aches. This room of the revelation of all she thought horrible, and of her endlessly demanding body. Of all she shrank from in herself. This room filled with herself. She fell into this room. This room of outcasts. *Where we uncover our bodies. Where we meet our outcast selves.* The room in which she does not mock herself. This room filled with darkness. *Where we go into darkness. Where we embrace darkness. Where we lie close to darkness, breathe when darkness breathes and find darkness inside ourselves.* The room of the darkness of women. *Where we are not afraid. Where joy is just under the surface. Where we laugh. Where laughter fills us utterly when we see what we thought was horrible. Where our demands are endlessly received. Where revelation fills us with glee.* The room which she said she needed. The room without which she was sure she would perish. The first room in which she experienced space. This place where she could finally breathe. The place where she breathed out the stories she had not believed. *The room where we confess we never believed those stories were about us.* The room where she cast those stories from her forever. *Where we began to feel the atmosphere wants us.* Where she began to believe the horizon. This room of her wants. Of her desiring. This room of her desiring to live. This place which allows her to exist. Where the women stare into each other's eyes. Where the daughter feels the life of the mother. *Where our words are undressed. And we touch. This room of our touching where the mother teaches her daughter to face her secret feel-*

ings. The labyrinth of her knowledge. Where she has her own reasons. *The coral skeleton. The crystals of frost.* Of her knowing. This place of her wandering. *The circles of the tree's growth. The beehive.* The room of her first wandering and of her finding. This place where she finds her way.

THE CAVE

Above all, there was the sensation of moving physically over the contours of fulnesses and concavities, through hollows and over peaks—feeling, touching, seeing, through mind and hand and eye. This sensation has never left me. I, the sculptor, *am* the landscape. I am the form and the hollow, the thrust and the contour.

BARBARA HEPWORTH, *A Pictorial Autobiography*

The shape of a cave, we say, or the shape of a labyrinth. The way we came here was dark. Space seemed to close in on us. We thought we could not move forward. We had to shed our clothes. We had to leave all we brought with us. And when finally we moved through this narrow opening, our feet reached for ledges, under was an abyss, a cavern stretching farther than we could see. Our voices echoed off the walls. We were afraid to speak. This darkness led to more darkness, until darkness leading to darkness was all we knew.

The shape of this cave, our bodies, this darkness. This darkness which sits so close to us we cannot see, so close that we move away in fear. We turn into ourselves. But here we find the same darkness, we find we are shaped around emptiness, that we are a void we do not know.

The shape of a cave, this emptiness we seek out like water. The void that we are. That we wash into as sleep washes over us, and we are blanketed in darkness. We see nothing. We are in the center of our ignorance. Nothingness spreads around us. But in this nothing we find what we did not know existed. With our hands, we begin to trace faint images etched into the walls. And now, beneath these images we can see the gleam of older images. And these peel back to reveal the older still. The past, the dead, once breathing, the forgotten, the secret, the

161

buried, the once blood and bone, the vanished, shimmering now like an answer from these walls, bright and red. Drawn by the one who came before. And before her. And before. Back to the beginning. To the one who first swam from the mouth of this cave. And now we know all she knew, see the newness of her vision. What we did not know existed but saw as children, our whole lives drawn here, image over image, past time, beyond space.

The shape of a cave, the bud, the chrysalis, the shell, what new form we seek in this darkness, our hands feeling these walls, here wet, here damp, here crumbling away; our hands searching for signs in this rock, certain now in this darkness, what we seek is here, warm and covered with water, we sweat in this effort, piercing the darkness, laying our skin on the cool stone, tracing the new image over the old, etching these lines which become clear to us now, as what we have drawn here gleams back at us from the walls of the cave, telling us what is, now, and who we have become.

This round cavern, motion turned back on itself, the follower becomes the followed, moon in the sky, the edge becoming the center, what is buried emerges, light dying over the water, what is unearthed is stunning, the one we were seeking, turning with the ways of this earth, is ourselves.

This cave, the shape to which each returns, where image after image will be revealed, and painted over, painted over and revealed, until we are bone. Where we touch the ones who came before and see their visions, where we leave our mark, where, terrified, we give up ourselves and weep, and taken over by this darkness, are overwhelmed by what we feel: where we are pushed to the edge of existence, to the source which sounds like a wave inside us, to the path of the water which feeds us all.

The way of the water we follow, which has made this space, and hollowed the earth here, because the shape of this cave is a history.

The shape of this cave is a history telling us with each echo of the sound of each wave rushing against its sides: "I was not here before; my shape changes daily. I was sand. I was mountain. I was stone. I was water. I was shellfish and sea anemone and sea snail, I was fish, eel, urchin. I was plankton. I was seaweed and sea grass. Here I am black and polished and round, here I am yellow, here I am covered with moss, here I gleam with a purple reflection when the light lies across me, here I curve outward, here I sink back.

"When the water approaches me, the shape of the wave is changed. And when the tide ebbs, you will see, I, too, have changed."

The shape of the labyrinth. The shape of the cave. Space divided and not divided. Space mutable, we say, separation becoming union. Space changing. The new shape. Melting and transformation, the crystal and the seed, the endless possibility of form, as in the metal measuring rod, which changes its shape at the speed of light, we say.

The Hexenhaus destroyed (the witches reborn) the zoological garden opened (the reappearance of species) the prison razed (crime renamed) acoustics transformed (madness released) the buried (plants to flesh to earth) uncovered.

The rectangular shape of his book of knowledge, bending. The shape of our silence, the shape of the roofs of our mouths. Darkness.

BOOK
FOUR

HER VISION

Now She Sees

Through

Her Own Eyes

THE SEPARATE REJOINED

Out of my flesh that hungers
and my mouth that knows
comes the shape I am seeking
for reason.

AUDRE LORDE,
"On a Night of the Full Moon"

MYSTERY

> . . . healing must be sought in the blood of the wound itself. It is
> another of the old alchemical truths that "no solution should be
> made except in its own blood."
>
> NOR HALL, *Mothers and Daughters*

*Why is she lying so still there? And what is she dreaming? We ask,
here, in the center of this darkness. We not so different from darkness,
not seen but known as darkness itself, and dark to ourselves. She
sleeps. Her sleep is like death. And what is she, in this night, becoming? Buried from the light like the soil under the ice frozen solid. In
this dark and cold season, this wintering time, when the moon becomes smaller (just a shadow of herself) and her heart beats slower, we
touch the coldness of her skin. This sleeping body, we whisper. Out of
the light we can feel this body, hear the air enter her, and our hands
ask what is she dreaming in this darkness? What is she, in this night,
becoming? And we are darkness. Like the carbon from the air which
becomes the body of the plant and the body of the plant buried in the
earth becoming coal or the body of the plant in her mouth becoming
her own dark blood and her blood washing from her like tides (and the
sea drawing into itself, leaving the bodies of fish, coral spines, the
reef). This place. This place in which she breathes and which she takes
into herself and which is now in her, sleeping inside her. What sleeps
inside her? Like a seed in the earth, in the soil which becomes rich
with every death, animal bodies coming apart cell by cell, the plant
body dispersing, element by element, in the bodies of bacteria, pla-
naria, and back to the seed, this that grows inside her and that we cannot see. What does this body hold for us? (What we feel in this
darkness that seems like stillness to us.) And what made us feel that*

*every day was like another? Why did we no longer bother to draw
back the curtains? No longer bother to make the beds? Why did we
leave scraps of meat out on the tables? Leave our hair wild and un-
combed? Refuse any longer to speak? Draw into ourselves and ask?
And ask. What this body holds, now. What will come out of this earth.
The earth turning and we not feeling any movement. But moving.
Spinning through the stars. The moonlight. Turning in our sleep.
What was it she remembers? Why did she sit up in her sleep as if waking. What thought seized her? To cry out like a child. What child still
in her? Like the sunlight trapped in the leaf which becomes part of the
ground, of the sea, the body of the fish, body of animal, soil, seed.
What is growing inside and will pierce the surface, if she awakens with
this memory: what she was before. And light touches her eyelids,
warmth touches her skin, like the plankton thrown into the light by the
turbulence of the sea and the spore carried by the wind, her body
changes. And what does she feel in this morning? What does she see
now? If she opened the window, what new air does she breathe?
(Opens the window, combs her hair, washes her face, stares out at the
world and speaks.)*

 *The moon swells and tides wash over the rock; granite and shell be-
come sand; the roots of trees are polished and the cell divides every
day. Every day we move closer to the sun. Each day she is closer to
herself. And to this child within her, growing inside her. She remembers, what she might have been (as oxygen from the plant goes into the
flame, into ash). And she puts these pieces together. What is left after
the years and what will come together still, like the edges of tissue
grafting one to the other: blood cleanses the wound, and this place is
slowly restored. (And the forest reclaims what was devastated, and her
body heals itself of the years.) So we say, finally, we know what happens in this darkness, what happens to us while we sleep, if we allow
the night, if we allow what she is in the darkness to be, this knowledge,
this that we have not yet named: what we are. Oh, this knowledge of
what we are is becoming clear.*

THE OPENING

We Enter a
New Space

The new space . . . has a kind of invisibility to those who have
not entered it.

MARY DALY, *Beyond God the Father*

Space filled with the presence of mothers, and the place where
everyone is a daughter. *Space which does not exist without matter.* The
place where she predominates. *Space which is never separate from
matter.* The space shaped by the movements of white-haired women
and ringing with the laughter of old lady friends. The world seen on the
faces of middle-aged women. The place filled with the love of women
for women. Space shaped by the play of the littlest girls.

The stone dropped in water. Space that knows her. *Starlight in darkness.* Space lit up with her thoughts. *The circle in space.* Space dancing under her broom. Space transformed in her kitchen. In which her
pots and pans are foremost and the diapers of her children dominate
the landscape. Space charged with the cleaning out of tubs, the
threading of needles, the storage of leaves in jars. Space she has
cooked and scrubbed clean. Space shaped by her anger. The place
made by the one who tends to needs. Her feeling of having room. The
space she fills. *A motion circling the void. The electron a movement in
space.* Space freed from her not being. The place where she is recognized. And where she can see herself.

Space the shape of experience: the form of motion. Space full of curiosity about her, and the place which records her image. Space which she
embroiders. Space which she covers in quilts. Space which she makes

171

into lace. Space which she weaves. Where she builds the house of her culture. Where her breast is a self-reflection. This space which she paints.

Space filled with her paintings. Where she paints THE FITTING, where she draws THE COIFFURE, where she sets on her canvas the YOUNG WOMAN DRESSED IN BLACK, and paints her DREAM OF HAPPINESS, and the BROKEN MIRROR, and sets down the MOTHER ABOUT TO WASH HER SLEEPY CHILD, and paints the KNITTER, WOMAN SPINNING AND WEAVING, THE SELLER OF TISANE, where she records the OLD WOMAN FROM THE POORHOUSE, and the WORKING WOMAN, and records the LETTER OF REJECTION and sets down PORTIA WOUNDING HER THIGH, where she gives a shape to THE SUICIDE OF GENEVIEVE BRIBERT.

Space in which there is no center. Space filled with her disintegration. *Where all certainties change.* Space in which she feels she is coming apart. *Space where nothing is ever still and motion always changes shape.* The place where she holds on to nothing. *The stone dropped in the water* Space electrified by her feelings. *comes back to us in waves.* Space shaped about her. *Our movements rush the air* by the force of what she feels. *and penetrate the stone.* Where she makes out the invisible, where she touches the real.

Where she sees BISONS FLEEING A FIRE, where she paints WILD HORSES IN THE FAR WEST, where she makes out the shape of METAMORPHOSIS OF A FROG and creates STUDY OF A WOMAN FROM NATURE and sets down COW'S SKULL WITH CALICO ROSES and where she imagines THE PHENOMENON OF WEIGHTLESSNESS, where she extends into space WRAPPED IN SILENCE, and she shapes DEATH SNATCHING A CHILD, and she gives a form to NEVER AGAIN WAR, and she makes the motion of LIFT EVERY VOICE AND SING, she paints STRUGGLE OF OBJECTS FOR SUPREMACY, and she draws SELF-PORTRAIT WITH A PENCIL; she makes the shape of CONFESSION FOR MYSELF, and she sets down on canvas MOTHER RECEIVING THE CONFIDENCES OF HER DAUGHTER, and she paints PORTRAIT OF A WOMAN PLAYING A PRELUDE ON THE PIANO, and she makes the image of YOUNG WOMAN READING; where she paints the FEMALE LIFE CLASS; ILLUMINATIONS, DARK; SKY CATHEDRAL; MEDITATIONS; HOMAGE TO MY YOUNG BLACK SISTER, and ACTIVATED CIRCLES, and PELVIS WITH BLUE, and SYMPHONY FOR WOMEN, and CAPILLARY ACTION, and she paints GREAT LADIES TRANSFORMING THEMSELVES INTO BUTTERFLIES.

Her space *The cosmos* flooded with *The earth* her vision. The space where her feelings pulled her apart and what was inside her was revealed. And this lit her way.

Space where, in her circling motion, she found an opening.

We Enter a
New Time

The center of the new time is on the boundary of patriarchal time. What it is . . . is women's *own* time. It is our *life*time. . . .
MARY DALY, *Beyond God the Father*

One of the tasks of women's history is to call into question accepted schemes of periodization.
JOAN KELLY-GADOL, "Did Women Have a Renaissance?"

We say we are brilliant with light from the stars that began millennia ago and now burn in our minds.

Andromeda (*The Chained Princess*) The time when she was chained. The age in which the most significant event was her loss of her own name. The millennium that began on the day that the first rape of a woman took place. The day that settled in when the rape of a woman went unavenged. The age of laws which declared her unfit to govern. The age that was shaped by the fact that she was not taught to read. The centuries that did not declare her rights. The period that declared her unfit to practice medicine. The years in which she could not own property. The time during which her word could not stand alone in court. The age that was colored by the fact that she was home all day taking care of children. The period filled by the isolation of women. The time for which the most significant evidence is her invisibility.

Hydra (*The Dragon*) The century during which Ales Manfield was called a witch. The age when Katherine Kepler was tortured. The year when Ales Newman, Alice Nutter and Alizon Device were accused of belonging to a coven. The week when Anne Redferne, Anne Whittle, Elizabeth Demidyke, Jeanet Hargreaves, Katherine Hewit and Jeanet Preston were burned at the stake. The time that was governed by fire.

Canis Major (The Greater Dog) The period known for the daring of Judith who cut off the head of Holofernes and thus saved the city. The age typified by the courage of Alice Knyvet who kept the king from taking her castle by force. The decade known for the ferocity of Joan of Flanders. The time called the Years of Jacoba after the healing genius of Jacoba Felicie. The age famous for having prohibited Jacoba Felicie from practicing medicine.

We say there is no end to any act. The rock thrown in the water is followed by waves of water, and these waves of water make waves in the air, and these waves travel outward infinitely, setting particles in motion, leading to other motion and motion upon motion endlessly. We say the water has noticed this stone falling and has not forgotten. And in every particle every act lives, and the stars do not frighten us, we say, starlight is familiar to us.

Monocerous (The Unicorn) The age that began when Caroline Herschel looked at the stars. The period during which Emilie du Chatelet stayed up late in the night writing of space, time and force. The period that ended when Emilie du Chatelet died in childbirth.

The Pleiades (The Seven Sisters) The age in which those women who were virgins supported themselves by their nursing, weaving and making lace. The age in which they pooled their earnings and lived together.

Taurus (The Bull) The decade ruled by Reine Louise Audre, Queen of the Markets. The time in which she led a march of eight hundred women to Versailles. The year during which women demanded that the grain speculators be punished, demanded that conditions at the marketplace be made better, that priests be able to marry, that women receive better education, that male midwifery be put to an end; the year in which these women asked for an end to all privilege, demanded that husbands stop dissipating the dowries of their wives, that women have control over their own property and their children, that women be given employment. The day of the month celebrated because that was when women brought down the Bastille.

Leo (The Lion) The period of time in American history known as the years of the slave rebellions (which were led by women).

Lyra (The Harp) That year when she spoke of a "vision of a woman, wild/ With more than womanly despair." The period beginning with the words of Marie de Ventadour that "a lady must honor her lover as a friend not as a master." That decade famous for her play about the rapist who mistook pots and pans for virgins, and fondled them all night. The year her play was performed by the other sisters of the convent. The year glorified by the laughter of the nuns. That age distinguished by her book called *The City of Women* in which she extolled the virtues of women. The great age that began when a young woman published the words "Of what materials can that heart be composed which can melt when insulted and instead of revolting at injustice, kiss the rod?"

The Magellanic Clouds. The Orion Nebula. Star Clouds in the Milky Way. We say our lives are part of nature. We say in every particle every act lives. The body of the tree reveals the past. That the waves from the stone falling into the water were frozen in the winter ice. That stars pull at the bodies of crabs, and oysters know the phases of the moon.

Delphinus (The Dolphin) The time of the visions of Hildegarde von Bingen, the mysteries of Margery Kemp, and the year of the establishment of a colony where Anne Hutchinson preached.

Perseus (The Hero) The Harriet Tubman Years. The Age of Sappho. The period shaped by the socialist movement begun by Flora Tristan called Tristanism. The century called the Swallow Period after Ellen Swallow (because she invented the word "ecology"). The day devoted to the memory of Elizabeth Blackwell (because she was the first woman to graduate from medical school). The Ma Rainey Era.

Lepus (The Hare) The years that might have been had she not been busy raising the children, keeping them alive, gathering food, stitching the holes, sweeping the floor, steaming the fish, keeping the coal in the stove. The years which could not have been had she not done these things. The ages which survived through her sympathy; the centuries subtly informed by her compassion.

Virgo (The One Who Is Inviolable) The eons of clear rivers. The millennia of brilliant skies. The time immemorial of dark forests. The past history of flowering. *Aquarius (The Water Carrier)* The age of dryness. The period of dark skies. The centuries during which forests turned to deserts. The age of grieving for the earth.

Argo Navis (The Ship) Her birth. The day she said her first word. The time of her growing awareness. The days of her bleeding. The years when she learned about death. The age she was when she accepted change. The time of her broadening. When she felt her body become strong. That time of her life when she learned reciprocity and the inviolability of the other. The year when her anger gave her clarity and all her weeping was filled with intelligence. The morning of her full powers. The celebration of her first gray hairs. The solemn recognition of her coming of age.

The elliptical orbit. The pull of gravity. The satellite motion. Time in space, we say, the half note pushing the air, the quarter note traversing the earth. The bud, the egg, the risen bread, the right time for things. The right time she says is now. She says our lives have been changed by what has gone before. Up until now we have been kept from our past by silence, but, she says, the time of our silence is over, and we will have *The Chrysalis* those years again *opening.*

Cassiopeia (The Queen's Chair) We say the ages when she knew her own power. The age when she kept her own name. The age when she revealed the secret of the wheel. The age when she learned to speak with the animals. The age when she discovered the seed. The age during which she wove truth about herself. The age when she joined forces with the earth. When she listened and was heard. The age when she knew she was not alone. The Age of her Resonance.

OUR DREAMS

WHAT LIES UNDER OUR STILLNESS

Whatever I have said about my deeds and words in this trial, I let it stand and wish to reaffirm it. Even if I should see the fire lit, the faggots blazing, and the hangman ready to begin the burning, and even if I were in the pyre, I could not say anything different.

JOAN OF ARC, 1431

"What is in those diaries then?"
"They aren't diaries."
"Whatever they are."
"Chaos, that's the point."

DORIS LESSING, *The Golden Notebook*

This above all, we have never denied our dreams. They would have had us perish. But we do not deny our voices. We are disorderly. We have often disturbed the peace. Indeed, we study chaos—it points to the future. The oldest and wisest among us can read disorder. From dreams, or the utterances of madness, the chance cracks on a tortoise shell, the fortunate shapes of leaves of tea, the fateful arrangements of cards, we can tell things. And some of us can heal. We can read bodies with our hands, read the earth, find water, trace gravity's path. We know what grows and how to balance one thing against another.

Many of us who practiced these arts were put on trial. We stood at the gates of change, but those who judged us were afraid. They claimed the right to order the future. They would have had all of us perish, and most of us did. But some kept on. Because this is the power of such things as we know—we kept flying through the night, we kept up our deviling, our dancing, we were still familiar with animals though we were threatened with fire and though we were almost to a woman burned. And even if over our bodies they have transformed this earth, we say, the truth is, to this day, women still dream.

Flying

... ye was taken out of bed to that meeting in a flight.

BESSIE HENDERSON, Crook of Devon, 1661

In those years, whatever we wanted it seemed we could not have. Nothing in our lives was ever fortunate. We had the meagerest portions of things, and when things were rare, we went without. That is our lot in life, we told ourselves. And we stopped wanting. Only we longed, and we grew so accustomed to the pain of longing that we called this our nature. We put this into our songs. We said disappointment was part of life. Even in our imaginations, all our attempts began to fail. But one day all this changed. On this day we met a woman who was used to getting what she wanted. She ate large portions and her body was big. She let us know there were other such women. We were bewitched. We began to dream we were like this woman. Her very smile invited us to be like her. And that is how we were finally initiated.

We began to think we might get what we want. Our longing turned into desire. Do you know how desire can run through the limbs? How wanting lets your eyes pierce space? How desire propels even the sleeping? How a resolve to act can traverse this atmosphere as quick as light? We were alive with desire. And we knew we could never go back to those years of longing. This is why, despite the threat of fire and our fear of the flame, we burst out through the roofs of our houses. Desire is a force inside us. Our mouths drop open in the rushing air. Our bodies float among stars. And we laugh in ecstasy to know the air has wishes; the stars want. "Yes," we call out, full of ourselves and delight. "Yes," we sing. "We fly through the night."

Deviling

If anyone at the kalends of January goes about as a stag or a bull; that is making himself into a wild animal, and putting on the heads of beasts; those who in such wise transform themselves into the appearance of a wild animal, penance for three years because it is devilish.

ARCHBISHOP OF CANTERBURY, 7th century

The Devil has the best Music.

JOHN MILTON

Yes we are devilish; that is true we cackle. Yes we are dark like the soil and wild like the animals. And we turn to each other and stare into this darkness. We find it beautiful. We find this darkness irresistible. We cease all hiding. Nothing is secret: we display what they call evil in us. Yes, we have horns on our heads, and our feet are cloven, and we are covered with fur and with feathers. And how we love this state of affairs. We practice butting with our horns; our feet carry us quickly through the forest. In our fur and feathers, we attempt to repeat all the lessons they tried to teach us. But this fur and these feathers mock their words. We begin to laugh. We cannot stop laughing. One of us imitates the sound of the voice that has lectured us. With her hoof, she gestures pompously at us. In her growls and guttural moanings she follows the rhythms of this speech, produces its tones. We are delighted. She has captured the lecturer in her animal body. We are hysterical with laughter and now we join her mocking. We insult this foreign presence in her. We cast a spell on her. We drag her from her pulpit. We kill that lecturer in her. Now we are triumphant. We light torches. We wear flames on our very heads, so that our bodies cast light all around us. Now when we kiss the very darkest parts of ourselves with this light, we are transformed: And sweet voices pour from our mouths.

Dancing

There was one of two things I had a *right* to, liberty, or death; if I could not have one, I would have the other; for no man should take me alive; I should fight for my liberty as long as my strength lasted. . . .

HARRIET TUBMAN

From the beginning I conceived the dance as a chorus. . . . I so ardently hoped to create an orchestra of dancers that, in my imagination; they already existed. . . .

ISADORA DUNCAN, *My Life*

*Yes, we are
dancing, oh yes, we are
dancing, oh yes, we
dance, whenever we
can. Now we
move together.*

Tambourine. *The joy.*
Tambourine and pipe.
The joy in me. Tambourine,
pipe and violin.
The joy in me that
I see in you. Tambourine,
tambourine, tambourine
and pipe. *And if we should*
falter, tambourine,
violin, tambourine,
violin, *if danger over*
takes us, tambourine
and pipe, *we must*
stay together, violin
and harp, *we must*
not forget. Violin, pipe,
tambourine and harp.
Now we move together.
Feeling dances through us.
We move our feet together.
We do this dance.
Tambourine, tambourine,
harp and violin.
We dance
to be free, harp,
harp and pipe, *free*
to live our lives,
tambourine and harp,
the way we dream.
Tambourine and
harp. *If*
one of us falters,
violin, violin, violin,
if
danger over takes
her, violin, violin,
we must not forget,
tambourine, tambourine,

what happens to one, pipe
and harp, *happens*
to us all. Now
we move together, this
music rushes through
us, we dance with
the wind, to the
singing of the trees.
Tambourine, violin,
violin and harp,
And now we sing
together, violin
and pipe,
we sing what we
all know, tambourine,
tambourine, tambourine
and pipe, *what we*
do will bring
us danger,
tambourine,
we are taking
great risks, violin
and pipe, violin
and pipe.
But now we
dance together. We
dance with the trees,
we dance with the wind,
singing this is
our choice,
tambourine and violin and tambourine
and harp, *singing this*
is what we choose,
tambourine and pipe.
Now
we move together.
Violin. *We move to the*
music,

violin and harp,
of the joy in me,
tambourine and pipe,
that I see in you.
Tambourine,
tambourine. *Oh yes,*
we dance,
violin, violin, violin
and harp,
whenever
we can.

Animals
Familiar

> The cobra was known as Eye, *uzait*, a symbol of mystic insight
> and wisdom.
>
> MERLIN STONE, *When God Was a Woman*

And yes we are close to animals. One of us, we admit, speaks with snakes. When she was a child this animal licked her ears clean. And that explains her to us. Because that deft tongue washed out what stops up most of our hearing, she can hear most clearly. She can even, yes, even hear what the birds say. (And the birds bring messages from the dead, and the dead bring messages from the universe.) This cleanness of her ears accounts for her wisdom. To speak with her is to be amazed, not only at the nature of this world, but at the sound of one's own voice. She hears what is said, and she also hears what is not said. Oh, she is a marvelous listener! Those of us who tell our stories to her seem to hear them ourselves for the first time. So clean are her ears. And we hold nothing back from her. We blurt out all we can remember. What we forget, or don't know, she tells us. Then, with the whole story given to us, we can usually figure things out. As for what will happen to us, that she does not hear, that she needs to see. For this, she tells us, for she too does not hold back, for this she eats the body of that animal, its flesh that has rubbed against the ground becoming part of her blood, and in that way she sees what could not otherwise be seen. She sees lives that ended before their time, and what those lives could have done. She sees possibility. She sees lives half lived becoming whole. She reads stories that have never been written. Sees whole cities grow up, and the new growth of forests that were razed long ago. She sees all kinds of marvels far beyond what we ask her to see, things, she says, we could not even dream. We would think her raving, but she speaks to us so sweetly of what she says can be, that we too begin to see these things. We know her clarity for our own, and as for the way things are now, we grow most impatient.

OUR ANCIENT RAGES

Turbulence

The biosphere does not end where the light gives out.

G. EVELYN HUTCHINSON, "The Biosphere"

You have sometimes wondered, my dear friend, at the extreme affection of my nature—But such is the temperature of my soul—It is not the vivacity of youth, the hey-day of existence. For years I have endeavoured to calm an impetuous tide—labouring to make my feelings take an orderly course—It was striving against the stream.

MARY WOLLSTONECRAFT, *Letters*

We heard of this woman who was out of control. We heard that she was led by her feelings. That her emotions were violent. That she was impetuous. That she violated tradition and overrode convention. That certainly her life should not be an example to us. (The life of the plankton, she read in this book on the life of the earth, depends on the turbulence of the sea) *We were told that she moved too hastily. Placed her life in the stream of ideas just born. For instance, had a child out of wedlock, we were told. For instance, refused to be married. For instance, walked the streets alone, where ladies never did, and we should have little regard for her, even despite the brilliance of her words.* (She read that the plankton are slightly denser than water) *For she had no respect for boundaries, we were told. And when her father threatened her mother, she placed her body between them.* (That because of this greater heaviness, the plankton sink into deeper waters) *And she went where she should not have gone, even into her sister's marriage. And because she imagined her sister to be suffering what her mother had suffered, she removed her sister from that marriage.* (And that these deeper waters provide new sources of nourishment) *That she moved from passion. From unconscious feeling, allowing deep and troubled emotions to control her soul.* (But if the plankton sinks deeper, as it would in calm waters, she read) *But we say that to her passion, she brought lucidity* (it sinks out of the light, and it is only the turbulence of the sea, she read) *and to her vision, she gave the substance of her life* (which throws the plankton back to the light). *For the way her words illuminated her life we say we have great regard. We say we have listened to her voice asking, "Of what materials can that heart be composed which can melt when insulted and instead of revolting at injustice, kiss the rod?"* (And she understood that without light, the plankton cannot live and from the pages of this book she also read that the animal life of the oceans, and hence our life, depends on the plankton and thus the turbulence of the sea for survival.) *By her words we are brought to our own lives, and are overwhelmed by our feelings which we had held beneath the surface for so long. And from what is dark and deep within us, we say, tyranny revolts us; we will not kiss the rod.*

Cataclysm

> we have given until we have no more to give;
> alas, it was pity, rather than love, we gave;
> now having given all, let us leave all;
> above all, let us leave pity
>
> and mount higher
> to love—resurrection.
>
> H. D., "The Flowering Rod"

> You call me a thousand names, uttering yourselves.
>
> Earthquake, I answer you, flood and volcano flow—the Warning.
> This to remind you that I am the Old One
> who holds the Key, the Crone to whom all things
> return.
>
> ROBIN MORGAN, "The Network of the Imaginary Mother"

This story is told to us about the mountain. That one day suddenly and with no cause fire began to pour from her. That those living trustingly at her sides were frozen in their steps by the hot ash which she gave off, that without any warning a terrible death issued from her and stopped a whole city. That at that moment when she chose to

strike, food was being set forth on tables and daily life continued inno-
cently. Thus when we are shown the form of the dog whose agony was
preserved forever in this ash, we see why she cannot be trusted.

They asked her to feel sorry for their plight. They told her how it
was hard for them to cry. How dominance had been expected of them.
They said that they knew no other life than the one that they were
taught. That hence they were not responsible for what they did or
said. They said that such changes as she was requiring of them were
impossible. That their bodies could not be otherwise. That one could
not change overnight. That these matters she spoke of so bluntly were
subtle and complex. That she must be more patient. That she made
them feel guilty. That guilt kept them from moving. She was bringing
them to tears, they said: "Pity us." Couldn't she see that they had
tried? Couldn't she see she was asking too much of them? Be fair:
"You are unreasonable," they told her. But she answered them, "You
have called me unreasonable before."

Yet beneath this layer of ash, which the rain made into mud, and
the sun dried for centuries, we find another story. We discover that
the ash did not come suddenly and all at one moment. But first a
black cloud appeared in the sky above the mountain. And that after-
ward ash fell over the city for two days, until the sky became darker
and darker, and the ash piled thicker and thicker. That those who
perished would not leave, but chose to stay in their houses, to guard
their possessions; that the dog who died in that agony was chained to
the door; that those who died, died struggling for breath poisoned
from her fumes, that only at the last moment must they have wanted
to flee, only then believed in the power of this mountain to change
their lives.

And she said she was tired of this old dialogue. Whenever she heard
that cry, she said, of guilt, whenever she heard them moan for patience, her jaw closed. She could feel her face redden, and the back of
her spine was rigid. She was certain she would explode. Yes, she said,
she had grown unreasonable. "And I don't want to hear," she barked,
"any more of your reasons." She had been patient, she growled, too
long. "Do you know what the cost of this patience has been?" she
yelled. This dialogue is over, she shouted, and she vowed the old
drama would not be played out again. "I will give you no pity," she
said. She did not feel pity now, she bellowed.

Searching beneath the volcano, beneath the ocean floor, tracing the movements and the history of the movements of the earth, we find cause for the fires. We say beneath the earth is a flowing rock. We say this flowing rock rises to the surface, and we say the rock on the surface sinks toward the core of the earth, becoming molten and then hard and then molten again in turn. And we say also that there are breaks in the surface of the earth, places where the depths are uncovered, and it is at these broken places that the rock is transformed, and the surface of the earth is made. Where change takes place, we say, and where the earth is replenished we find volcanoes.

And so her anger grew. It swept through her like a fire. She was more than shaken. She thought she was consumed. But she was illuminated with her rage; she was bright with fury. And though she still trembled, one day she saw she had survived this blaze. And after a time she came to see this anger-that-was-so-long-denied as a blessing.

And we learn also that the coral reefs were made by coral fixing themselves on the bases of old volcanoes, worn down by the sea. And the lava which flows from volcanoes, we say, becomes a rich soil where luxuriant forests grow.

Consequences (What Always Returns)

And I pray one prayer—I repeat it till my tongue stiffens—Catherine Earnshaw, may you not rest as long as I am living! You said I killed you—haunt me, then! . . . Be with me always—take any form—drive me mad! Only *do* not leave me in this abyss, where I cannot find you! Oh God! It is unutterable! I *cannot* live without my life! I *cannot* live without my soul.

EMILY BRONTË, *Wuthering Heights*

To have risked so much in our efforts to mold nature to our satisfaction and yet to have failed in achieving our goal would indeed be the final irony. Yet this, it seems, is our situation.

RACHEL CARSON, *Silent Spring*

We say you cannot divert the river from the riverbed. We say that everything is moving, and we are a part of this motion. That the soil is moving. That the water is moving. We say that the earth draws water to her from the clouds. We say the rainfall parts on each side of the mountain, like the parting of our hair, and that the shape of the mountain tells where the water has passed. We say this water washes the soil from the hillsides, that the rivers carry sediment, that rain when it splashes carries small particles, that the soil itself flows with water in streams underground. We say that water is taken up into roots of plants, into stems, that it washes down hills into rivers, that these rivers flow to the sea, that from the sea, in the sunlight, this water rises to the sky, that this water is carried in clouds, and comes back as rain, comes back as fog, back as dew, as wetness in the air.

We say everything comes back. And you cannot divert the river from the riverbed. We say every act has its consequences. That this place has been shaped by the river, and that the shape of this place tells the river where to go.

We say he should have known his action would have consequences. We say our judgment was that when she raised that rifle, looking through the sight at him, and fired, she was acting out of what had gone on before. We say every act comes back on itself. There are consequences. You cannot cut the trees from the mountainside without a flood. We say there is no way to see his dying as separate from her living, or what he had done to her, or what part of her he had used. We say if you change the course of this river you change the shape of the whole place. And we say that what she did then could not be separated from what she held sacred in herself, what she had felt when he did that to her, what we hold sacred to ourselves, what we feel we could not go on without, and we say if this river leaves this place, nothing will grow and the mountain will crumble away, and we say what he did to her could not be separated from the way that he looked at her, and what he felt was right to do to her, and what they do to us, we say, shapes how they see us. That once the trees are cut down, the water will wash the mountain away and the river be heavy with mud, and there will be a flood. And we say that what he did to her he did to all of us. And that one act cannot be separated from another. And had he seen more clearly, we say, he might have predicted his own death. How if the trees grew on that hillside there would be no flood. And you cannot divert this river. We say look how the water flows from this place and returns as rainfall, everything returns, we say, and one thing follows another, there are limits, we say, on what can be done and everything moves. We are all a part of this motion, we say, and the way of the river is sacred, and this grove of trees is sacred, and we ourselves, we tell you, are sacred.

THE LION IN THE DEN
OF THE PROPHETS

She swaggers in. They are terrifying in their white hairlessness. She waits. She watches. She does not move. She is measuring their moves. And they are measuring her. Cautiously one takes a bit of her fur. He cuts it free from her. He examines it. Another numbers her feet, her teeth, the length and width of her body. She yawns. They announce she is alive. They wonder what she will do if they enclose her in the room with them. One of them shuts the door. She backs her way toward the closed doorway and then roars. "Be still," the men say. She continues to roar. "Why does she roar?" they ask. The roaring must be inside her, they conclude. They decide they must see the roaring inside her. They approach her in a group, six at her two front legs and six at her two back legs. They are trying to put her to sleep. She swings at one of the men. His own blood runs over him. "Why did she do that?" the men question. She has no soul, they conclude, she does not know right from wrong. "Be still," they shout at her. "Be humble, trust us," they demand. "We have souls," they proclaim, "we know what is right," they approach her with their medicine, "for you." She does not understand this language. She devours them.

POSSIBILITY

Gravity

> . . . escape from necessity? like children? but one would lose the
> value of life—
>
> SIMONE WEIL, First and Last Notebooks

> And because Barnard College did not teach me necessity, nor
> prime my awareness as to urgencies of need around the world,
> nor galvanize my heart around the critical nature of conflicts be-
> tween the powerful and the powerless, and, because, beyond
> everything else, it was not going to be school, evidently, but life-
> after-school, that would teach me the necessities for radical
> change, revolution: I left; . . .
>
> And so I continue: a Black woman who would be an agent for
> change. . . .
>
> JUNE JORDAN, Notes of a Barnard Dropout

*We dealt with hunger. We dealt with cold. We were the ones who
held things together.* Knit one, purl two. *We were the ones who, after
working all day, made the meals.* And the beginning. *We made sure
everybody ate.* And the end. *We were the ones who, if the cupboard
was bare, faced the open mouths of our children. And the way we
thought grew from what we did.* And the end and the beginning. *We
were the ones who nursed the dying through death.* The wheel. *The
ones who birthed, who had blood on our hands, the ones who suckled. We fed the calves and milked the cows. We worked in the fields.
We wrung the neck of the chicken, and tended the fire that cooked
the stew.* The double ax. *These labors shaped our thinking. We were
the ones who watched the wearing down and the daily mending and
did what had to be done with the lost. We were the ones who knew
what it all meant. Each breath. The cost. The years. We knew the*

limits. Gravity. *And what had to be done. We knew the length of caring.* The weight. *We felt children come to life in our bodies; even if we had no children we knew what the necessities were.* The pull. *Our hands made decisions we knew had to be made* The motion. *when there was no more caring, when there was no more food.* The end and the beginning. *Our bodies knew loss.* The circle. *Our bodies knew limitation. We were weary.* The gravitational pull. *Our limbs made the decision to move. Day after day we kept things going.* Knit one, purl two. *We were the ones who held things together.* Purl two, knit one. *And we were the ones who unraveled the patterns. Who refused to move.* The centrifugal force. *We were the ones who resisted. We were the ones who decided this can go on no longer, and placed our bodies in the way.* The curve of light. *What we thought came out of what we did.* The lens. *And we learned by doing.* The focus. *Necessity forced us to act together.* The reflection. *And we were the ones who learned from closeness. We smoothed the way from one to another. We saw the pulling away and the cleaving. We balanced the weight of needs in our hands.* Knit one. *And we waited for the right time.* The bread rising. *So if one of us was brave* purl two *all of us were filled with courage.* The circle of motion. *We did what they called impossible.* The verb. *We existed in ways they called unreal.* The word. *But our ideas came from what we did. And that is how we imagined* The pull *what we could do. And doing made us imagine more. And so our thoughts were grave* the double ax *and yet we laughed together.* Knit one, purl two. *We were the ones* The beginning *who held the dying and the grieving* and the end *and the birthing and the born.* The weight *And this is why we hold each other.* The weight of this earth. *And this is how our thinking has formed.*

Numbers

We play with numbers. Charming and sweet, we play little games with them, these figures. They are pale reflections, without the gravity of being of the potato, the glacier, the growth of lichen, the feather of an egret, the flecks in the iris of an eye, cracks in the dried clay of soil or the shed shell of a turtle, all of which they quantify, from which all they derive, the material forms whose awesome processes these num-

bers merely imitate, making simpler dramas with which we rest our minds, and in this bloodless theater of mathematics our hearts are eased. We are able to see the inevitability of process, count the days until our deaths, number the generations before and after, calculate the future colors of the eyes of our progeny, for numbers allow us, for moments, to objectify our own existence, which we know we cannot do to the potato or the glacier or the egret, the turtle nor the eye that meets us like our own with all its beautiful and its terrible knowledge of survival, the eye attached by ganglia and arteries through the brain's cortex down the spine even to the flesh of a foot that edges bare over the earth, feeling the hard outline of a crack on the clay surface.

Naming

Behind naming, beneath words, is something else. An existence named unnamed and unnameable. We give the grass a name, and earth a name. We say grass and earth are separate. We know this because we can pull the grass free of the earth and see its separate roots—but when the grass is free, it dies. We say the inarticulate have no souls. We say the cow's eye has no existence outside ourselves, that the red wing of the blackbird has no thought, the roe of the salmon no feeling, because we cannot name these. Yet for our own lives we grieve all that cannot be spoken, that there is no name for, repeating for ourselves the names of things which surround what cannot be named. We say Heron and Loon, Coot and Killdeer, Snipe and Sandpiper, Gull and Hawk, Eagle and Osprey, Pigeon and Dove, Oriole, Meadowlark, Sparrow. We say Red Admiral and Painted Lady, Morning Cloak and Question Mark, Baltimore and Checkerspot, Buckeye, Monarch, Viceroy, Mayfly, Stonefly, Cicada, Leafhopper and Earwig, we say Sea Urchin and Sand Dollar, Starfish and Sandworm. We say mucous membrane, uterus, cervix, ligament, vagina and hymen, labia, orifice, artery, vessel, spine and heart. We say skin, blood, breast, nipple, taste, nostril, green, eye, hair, we say vulva, hood, clitoris, belly, foot, knee, elbow, pit, nail, thumb, we say tongue, teeth, toe, ear, we say ear and voice and touch and taste and we say again love, breast and beautiful and vulva, saying clitoris, saying belly, saying toes and soft, saying ear, saying ear, saying ear, ear and hood and hood and green and all that we say we are saying around that which cannot be said, can-

not be spoken. But in a moment that which is behind naming makes it-self known. Hand and breast know each one to the other. Wood in the table knows clay in the bowl. Air knows grass knows water knows mud knows beetle knows frost knows sunlight knows the shape of the earth knows death knows not dying. And all this knowledge is in the souls of everything, behind naming, before speaking, beneath words.

The Possible

> To a certain degree this is why pottery is so exciting to make; you are never absolutely sure how a pot is going to come out. Though you may think you know every angle of possibility, there are always new ones!
>
> MARGUERITE WILDENHAIN, *Pottery: Form and Expression*

> . . . For no actual process happens twice; only we meet the same sort of *occasion* again.
>
> SUZANNE K. LANGER, *Philosophy in a New Key*

This teacher tells us we must ride the unknown. She has made many pots. She says we cannot rely on a formula. She has made pot after pot over many years and she says she still rides the unknown. We must fol-low our hands, she says, the clay will speak to our hands; the clay has qualities of its own, and we must yield to the clay's knowledge. She says every rule we have memorized, the roughing and the wetting of edges, for instance, to where the clay will be joined, every law must yield to experience. She says we must learn from each act, and no act is ever the same.

And the clay will respond to events, she says. She presses the clay into a piece of charred wood. We see a history of flames. She rolls the clay over sandstone. We see the path of the wind. She says each act takes a particular form and the textures are limitless. She invites us to use shells, twigs, rope, bark, birch, straw, burlap. She invites us to use our own hands, the particular print of each palm.

As our hands become cold from the clay, she asks us do we feel the elements yield to each other? Do we feel our skin vanish? Does the clay enter us? But with our hands on this wheel, for a moment, we face nothingness. For an instant we must admit we do not know the future, and we are afraid. Yet our hands are wet and coated with clay and they continue to work, despite our fear, they continue and this partic-ular clay speaks to them. And now as our hands give us knowledge, fear becomes wonder: we are amazed at this shape we have never seen before which we hold now in our hands.

We must give this thing a surface, our teacher tells us, and we must carry our work through the fire. She says here, too, recipes are useless. These will achieve only the conventional, she says. But beauty demands a more arduous process. We must know these glazes intimately. We glaze small vessels with every color we possess. We try dilution and thickness. We try the pots at different stages of the fire; red-hot, we thrust them in leaves, in sawdust, in water; we let bubbles rise in them; we see them turn smooth like glass. Suddenly, we find we have a new language.

The possibilities, she has told us, are endless: Red drips over the lid of a jar glazed with gray and over its swelling sides. As the color flows, the pot is fired, and two running drops are caught in motion. The red, now thick, now a wash, is resolved in particles over pink, and then one large swatch of redness appears like the half moon on our thigh when we bleed.

Violet blue is glazed over turquoise, and countless other blues appear. Circles of black, sienna and ocher move in waves like light over water. A gray stream forks into two; red fills the joints of a lattice of cracks; whiteness sits in a fissure like a lens; ocher reflects the light as gold, and in one swatch of jade, a sudden parting reveals a jagged space between two halves. These shapes suggest our hearts, suggest flowers, faces, breath, suggest waves, the possibilities of clear rivers, the possibilities of our lives running true, the possibility that we may know these mysteries, the lattice of veins in the leaf, the air caught by the light over the horizon, in our hands. The possibilities, we see, never end. And when we take the vessel out of the fire, our teacher tells us, we will always be surprised.

TRANSFORMATION

We Visit Our
Fears

> Without words, it comes. And suddenly, sharply, one is aware of
> being separated from every person on one's earth and every ob-
> ject, and from the beginning of things and from the future and
> even a little, from one's self. A moment before one was happily
> playing; the world was round and friendly. Now at one's feet
> there are chasms that had been invisible until this moment. And
> one knows, and never remembers how it was learned, that there
> will always be chasms, and across the chasms will always be those
> one loves.
>
> LILLIAN SMITH, *The Journey*

The old woman who was wicked in her honesty asked questions of
her mirror. When she was small she asked, "Why am I afraid of the
dark? Why do I feel I will be devoured?" And her mirror answered,
"Because you have reason to fear. You are small and you might be devoured. Because you are nothing but a shadow, a wisp, a seed, and you
might be lost in the dark." And so she became large. Too large for devouring. From that tiny seed of a self a mighty form grew and now it
was she who cast shadows. But after a while she came to the mirror
again and asked. "Why am I afraid of my bigness?" And the mirror answered, "Because you are big. There is no disputing who you are. And
it is not easy for you to hide." And so she began to stop hiding. She announced her presence. She even took joy in it. But still, when she
looked in her mirror she saw herself and was frightened, and she
asked the mirror why. "Because," the mirror said, "no one else sees
what you see, no one else can tell you if what you see is true." So after
that she decided to believe her own eyes. Once when she felt herself

growing older, she said to the mirror, "Why am I afraid of birthdays?" "Because," the mirror said, "there is something you have always wanted to do which you have been afraid of doing and you know time is running out." And she ran from the mirror as quickly as she could because she knew in that moment she was not afraid and she wanted to seize the time. Over time, she and her mirror became friends, and the mirror would weep for her in compassion when her fears were real. Finally, her reflection asked her, "What do you still fear?" And the old woman answered, "I still fear death. I still fear change." And her mirror agreed. "Yes, they are frightening. Death is a closed door," the mirror flourished, "and change is a door hanging open."

"Yes, but fear is a key," laughed the wicked old woman, "and we still have our fears." She smiled.

Erosion

Ablation.   Abrasion.   Mountain of accumulation.   Aeolian deposits.   Afforestation.   *Testimonies. Over and over we examined what was said of us. Over and over we testify. The lies. The conspiracy of appearances.* There are Fissures. There are cracks in the surface. *We realize suddenly we are weeping.* I heard a wail, she said, my voice. Alluvial Cone. Alluvial Fan. (Sediment, Sand, Silt.) Arroyo. Ash Cone. Attrition. Avalanche. *We are shouting now. We believe nothing can stop us now. What is named will not be forgotten. We are carried along by these testimonies. (There is a roaring inside us.) We are frightened. We do not know where this will stop.* Backwash. Basalt. Basin. Bedrock. Blizzard. Butte. In the bath she sees suddenly that her legs are woman's legs. Her shoulders drop softly and infinitely. Her belly rounds into dark hair. She is moved to call herself beautiful, to see the abundance of her skin. I touch her breast. *We see only each other. This beauty blinds us. We were longing for this. We are filled with longing.* Calving. (The iceberg detaches from the glacier.) Canyon. (Formed by the river cutting through arid walls.) *Cave. Coral. Current. Cycle. With every attempt to merge we find ourselves free again. Every mystery turns and speaks to us.* Searching for you, I fell into myself. *We rediscover origin. We are moved.* Dam. Debacle. *What we thought we wanted turns against us.*

The sound of weeping still ringing in our ears. Drift. Dune. Dust.

Earth. Epoch. Erosion. *We can tell you our children were born help-less. We can tell you how we fed them and dressed them and how we watched. We can tell you of their infinite patience and of their scream-ing impatience. Of their struggle to learn. How they discovered their feet. How they crawled on their knees. How every muscle stretched toward movement. How they listened. How they struggled toward speech.*

Fold. Fossil. Glacier. Hoarfrost. Ice. Islet. Isthmus. *We can say how we try to love and how the old scars prevent us. How we try to deny what has happened to us. How we rage that the old still claims us.* Jet streams, Key, Lagoon, Lake, Lava, Magma, Metamorphosis, Meteor (shooting star). *We can tell you how words spoken in rage accumulate around us. How we make our home in this language.*

Monsoon Forest. Moraine. Nadir. Oasis. Plain. Planet. *Suddenly we find we are no longer straining against all the old conclusions. We are no longer pleading for the right to speak: we have spoken; space has changed; we are living in a matrix of our own sounds; our words resonate, by our echoes we chart a new geography; we recognize this new landscape as our birthplace, where we invented names for our-selves; here language does not contradict what we know; by what we hear, we are moved again and again to speech.*

Quartz, Quagmire, Radiation. Rain. River. Rock. *We learn to say each other's names. We see the way we are together. We admit we will not go on forever. We admit death.*

Sandstone. Schist. Shale. *Love bursts in us. We do not try to hold on to this. We shudder. We shake. We separate.*

Tide. Timber line. *We know there is no retreating.* Umbra (The shadow). Undertow (The returning wave). *We acknowledge every consequence.* Volcano (The magma forces its way to the surface). Weathering (Decay and disintegration). Wind. Wood. Year. Zenith. *We say that we are part of what is shaped and we are part of what is shaping. We sleep and we remember our dreams. We awaken. We tell you we feel every moment; we tell you each detail affects us. We allow ourselves to be overwhelmed. We allow ourselves ecstasy, screaming, hysteria, laughter, weeping, rage, wonder, awe, softness, pain, we are crying out. (There is a roaring inside us, we whisper.) WE ROAR.*

CLARITY

Vision

> It is a period I remember vividly, not only because I was begin-
> ning to accomplish something at last, but also because of the de-
> light I felt in being completely by myself. For those who love to
> be alone with nature I need add nothing . . . no words of mine
> could convey even in part, the almost mystical awareness of
> beauty and eternity that accompany certain treasured moments.
>
> JANE GOODALL, *In the Shadow of Man*

She hunkers. She sits in a hunkering attitude. *We learn the attitude
of not hunting.* The attitude of learning. The attitude of practice. After
weeks walking on treacherous slopes she became sure-footed. The attitude of alert waiting. The attitude of having to go through. Of not
avoiding. *We finally agree to make this passage. We force open our
eyes.* The attitude of disappointment. For a year she circled them. At
every approach they vanished; they went fleeing. Despondency. *We
find what we were not looking for. We do not take this seriously. Later
we reinterpret the gravity of these accidents. In what was impenetrable, we find a way.* She learns the name of the fruit tree they feed
from, to recognize it. Illness. Exhaustion. Backward movement. The
attitude of recovery. *We learn to beware of panic; to anxiety we sing
softly, calming words, over and over. We have learned this from our
infants, whose inarticulate cries demanded this knowledge of us.* The
attitude of singular discovery. The attitude of risk. When she was
alone, she discovered the animals came closer. The attitude of es-
chewing protection. The attitude of disarming. *Although we had
learned to defend ourselves, when we chose we could make ourselves
vulnerable. These moments are sacred, we acknowledge.* She watched

them make their nests. She saw him build an upright fork; bend small branches over the foundation; put leafy twigs at the rim. She saw her accumulate a mound of greenery before she curled up. Solitude. No words. The exquisite. (She wrote that the waters of the lake sighed.) The attitude of moving closer by slow inches by mutual consent. She came within sixty yards of them. She saw they were less afraid. She watched them gather food. She watched them passing the meat of a piglet back and forth. She watched one squat over a termite nest and push a long grass stem into the mound. The attitude of respect. The attitude of not yet knowing. The attitude of slow recognition. One with a deformed, bulbous nose. One with hairless shoulders. One with scars from his upper lip to his nose. The attitude of watching. The attitude of watching for eight days. The attitude of seeing the unexpected. She saw them bite the ends off a piece of vine, collect several stems, choose among them, make tools. In the heavy rain, she watched them leap from trees, tear off huge branches, charge without stopping, lightning shaking the sky. She saw this dance three times in ten years. The attitude of marvel. Awe. *We stare in almost disbelief. We do not rush to speech. We allow ourselves to be moved. We do not attempt objectivity.*

One from
Another (The Knowledge)

> We were considered very poor midwives if our women had any tears.
>
> ANNA MAY, retired midwife, Frontier Nursing Service

We said we had experienced this ourselves. I felt so much for her then, she said, with her head cradled in my lap, she said, I knew what to do. *We said we were moved to see her go through what we had gone through: We said this gave us some knowledge.* She said in the hospital these things happen all the time. She said the woman was fully dilated. She said they had numbed her feelings. She said therefore the woman had no experience of the movements of her uterus and had no desire to push. That the doctor on duty was sleeping and refused to come to her aid. That she lay there for three hours until the shift changed. That though labor was induced then the baby was born bluish and died on the tenth day. She said that the doctor always wanted to maintain control. That he wanted this birth to go according to schedule. She said that he went up inside the cervix before she was fully dilated and that he clamped the cord and the fetal heartbeat stopped and that was why they had to perform a Caesarian. She said they had taken her baby away from her for twelve hours, for twenty hours, for four hours.

We said we had learned from being there. We said we learned from watching what had happened each time. We said we used few tools. That our hands had knowledge of this act. That our hands would allow this birth to happen in its own time. We said when we asked the doctors to explain these births, they themselves knew very little. We said we had witnessed the complexities of these processes, how perfectly attuned to each other were these events. We respected the laboring of her body, we said, and we learned what not to do, and where not to intrude, and these births amazed us with their ease.

She said that the hospital was filled with noise. That women were moved from bed to bed. From room to room. That the lights were too bright. The chrome too shiny. That the place reeked with antiseptic. She said in this atmosphere, what she had seen before, what she had felt before attending a birth, this ghostlike presence, was not there. But she said despite all this activity, the woman lay alone. She lay alone in labor. And no one looked into her eyes. No one responded to the questioning of her murmurs. *We said our hands themselves responded. We said it was so clear to us where and how to touch her. We said that to hold back this caring would have been a violence to ourselves.*

She said after their training in the hospitals they came to us with doctors' faces. She said it took weeks for them to drop this impersonality. *We said that to be there for her, we said that to hear what her needs were, that to listen to her, we had to separate ourselves from the doctors. We had to deny their authority and place the authority in ourselves. We said it was not possible to hear both their voices and her voice.* When she attended the birth, she said, she did all she could to make her calm. Waiting out her labor with her, she answered each of her questions, "Am I all right? Is the baby all right?"

We said each of us in our own way had to learn to trust each other. We said what we had learned in the hospitals was not to trust these women. When the transition from labor to birth came, she said, she applied hot compresses to her belly, if the stress was there, or to her lower back, when she felt it there. She said she rubbed coconut oil into her skin.

We said in the hospitals they made us wear leggings, they had wrapped our bodies, they had claimed our bodies might infect our newborn children. And the room was cold, we said. And the chrome frightened us. So we delivered ourselves, we said, into their hands. She said the room was kept heated for the comfort of the child when it was to be born. She said the laboring woman, warm with her efforts, removed her clothing. *We said in the hospitals we would have liked to remove our clothing. We said when we chose to trust this woman to attend us, we ceased to believe our bodies would infect our infants. We said, as we trusted her more, we began to do what we had always wanted to do.*

She said though the infant's head had been turned upward, at the last minute it rotated perfectly by itself and slipped out toward her hands. She said she held it gently, making the passage slow, so a sudden burst would not tear the birthing woman's body. *We said we felt ourselves needing her presence, relying on the calmness of her voice. We said what we felt in our bodies no longer frightened us.*

She said that first the head slipped out and then the body, that this was a girl, remarkably clean, the cord wrapped loosely around her neck, her arm over her chest. She said she felt the fundus then to see if the placenta was clear of the abdomen. She said then that she helped the mother put the baby to her breast. And that the uterus began to work again and delivered the placenta with one strong contraction, she said. And then, she said, she made two stitches along the scar of the old episiotomy. *We said if there was tearing it was along the lines of the old wounds. We said we discovered we had trusted her wisely, that to yield to her was to yield to ourselves.*

Acoustics

The string vibrates. The steel string vibrates. The skin. The calfskin.
The steel drum. The tongue. The reed. The glottis. The vibrating ven-
tricle. Heartbeat. Wood. The wood resonates. The curtain flaps in the
wind. Water washes against sand. Leaves scrape the ground. *We stand
in the way of the wave. The wave surrounds us. Presses at our arms,
our breasts. Enters our mouths, our ears.* The eardrum vibrates.
Malleus, incus, stapes vibrate. *The wave catches us. We are part of the
wave.* The membrane of the oval window vibrates. The spiral membrane in the cochlea vibrates. *We are set in motion by what moves outside our bodies.* Each wave of a different speed causes a different
place in the cochlea to play. *We have become instruments.* The hairs
lining the cochlea move. *We hear.* To the speed of each wave the ear
adds its own frequency. *What is outside us becomes us.* Each cell
under each hair sends its own impulse. *What we hear we call music.
We believe in the existence of the violin. The steel string. The skin.
Tongue. Reed. Wood. The curtain flapping in the wind. We take these
sounds as testimony: violin, skin, tongue, reed exist. Our bodies know
these testimonies as beauty.*

Ma Ma.   Da Da.   La le la le.   Mo Mon Po pon mah bowl
ma ba ba me mommy me seepy ba now bye bye now baby now
mommy now baby bankie bottie ca ca gah gr gr gr ma ma me my ma
ma sleepy baby me sleep night night me baby mommy go bye bye say
bye bye me

When she hears this cry she remembers smallness. Smallness rises
up in her. Translucence of skin rises up in her. Her mother rises up in

her. The taste of salt rises up in her. The taste of sweetness rises up in her. She thinks of the fragility of the inner ear. She thinks of death. She pokes her finger delicately, carefully, into the corpse of her own aged body, into the future. She thinks of the odor of feces. Of decaying leaves, the cast-off shell of the crab. Of the red membrane. Of the red bottom. The pulse in the skull. The moisture running off the back. The child's whole body. Smallness. Fitting against her forearm. Hand the size of her finger joint. She thinks of the redness inside, the wetness inside. She lifts the child's wet body to her. Under the child's weight and heat, her own body is moist. On the top of her skull, she thinks, was a membrane. With her two hands she makes an opening in the body of her mind to reveal what is vulnerable in her. The sound of her blood resonates. The sound of air enlarges her. Presses against her womb, presses against her vulva. She is small. She is infinitesimal. She is a small speck in darkness. In wet darkness. The darkness undulates. The darkness is hot against her. The darkness is growing, pressing into her. She is the darkness. She is heat. She grows. She presses the child's face to her face. Smallness—she closes her eyes in the softness—rises up in her. The child's fingers enter her mouth. The child's eyes stare into her eyes. This child vibrates through her. She knows this child.

The group velocity of waves. The period between one wave and another. Waves of waves. *We turned back to our mothers. We listened for the stories of their lives. We heard old stories retold.* The pitch. The volume. The timbre. *We heard again the story of the clean house, we heard again the story of the kitchen, the story of mending, the story of the soiled clothes.* The bell ringing. The confluence of pitches in the ringing of the bell. The overtones *of the cries of birthing, the story of waking at night, the story of the shut door, the story of her voice raging, we heard again the stories of bitches.* Resonance, the fork of the same pitch humming in sympathy, the sympathetic wave.

We tried to recover them as girls. We sought them as daughters. We asked to be led into recesses, we wanted to revive what was buried, we sought our own girlhoods we had feared lost. The regular impulses, the steady pitch of the note. The octave. Harmony. *We heard the story for the first time that her mother's mother had brought her mother to a doctor, and we heard what the doctor had said to her mother, that this pain would teach her a lesson, we heard that before this her* mother's mother had gone off by herself, had given a stillbirth, we *heard the words* out of wedlock *we understood* Sound only a milder form of the shock waves made by explosions, by blasts. *why these stories had been kept from us* Sound one of the ways *we know how many stories* in which concentrated energy *are in this silence* diffuses itself about the world.

    We say we have lost some of our mothers forever to this silence. We say we have found hatred in the mother for the daughter and in the daughter for the mother. We say of our mothers that parts of them are lost to us, that our mothers come back to us dismembered, that in the effort Waves *to recover them* from the friction on the bow of the string vibrating *we stand in danger* in the maple bridge, vibrating down the sound post *of losing ourselves* in the chamber of the body *or parts of ourselves* through the cells of the surrounding plane wood *in this whirlpool* shaped by the shape of the body *in the inherent lie of silence* outward into the air *that such stillness is not stillness* to reverberate to the shapes of walls *that this stillness is treachery* to resonate in the surrounding trees *that even as we find our daughters return to us* The waves *we recite again their names* the waves in the atom *saying that we cannot be complacent* the atom vibrates *nor stand still, that we must name every movement* that the smallest particle of matter is a vibration *that we must let our voices live within us* that matter is a wave, *that we survive by hearing.*

Our Labor

> The news seems vague and far off, not as if it were really happening. It sits on us like an ache. We are trying to ignore it lest the pain become unbearable.   September 5, 1937
> *Hundreds and Thousands,* the journals of Emily Carr

    All around us, each way we look, we see only whiteness. And the sky itself is heavy with snow which keeps dropping silently, whiteness upon whiteness. The only sounds are the sounds of our voices, muffled and small. Yet we speak rarely. Our minds have become as plain as the landscape around us. And the rhythms of our bodies, moving steadily through these drifts, have become slow. Hour after hour things appear to be the same. Yet the drifts grow deeper. This landscape seems to be frozen still, and we cease to believe that under this ice there were ever leaves, ever a soil, that water ever ran, or that trees grow here still. No evidence of these beings can reach us. And our memories of this place are sealed from us by this winter; none of the sharp edges of existence reach us, the odors of this place, its taste, blunted. And even the snow itself becomes unreal. Our skin which at first was stung by the cold has now become so cold itself that it does not recognize coldness. Our feet and our hands which burned with pain are numb. Our vision seems half blinded by the relentless light from the snow. And we have come to believe there is nothing to taste; nothing to smell. We are certain that all that is around us and in us is absolute stillness. This has always been, we tell ourselves. Yet something in us is changing: our hearts beat slower and slower. And we who were so eager to go on think we want to rest here in this place. That it is best not to continue. Our bodies grow very heavy. Our eyes are almost closed. We would let ourselves sink into this snow. We would sleep. To end this struggle is mercy, we think. We marvel at how pain has left our bodies. We feel nothing. We dream that this is not really happening. And kindness we say is quietness. We would sleep. But some voice in us labors to wake, cries out so that we are startled, and we work to open our eyes. Our hands reach out into the snow and we wash this ice over our faces. As we awaken, our skin stings again. And as we push our bodies toward movement, we ache, and we feel pain again in our hands and our feet. We shiver. We are on the verge of crying that these chills are unbearable. But we do not sleep. We see clearly where we are now, and we know that it is winter. And suddenly, through this shocking cold, we remember the beauty of the forest lying under this whiteness. And that we will survive this snow if we are aware, if we continue. And now we are shouting with all our strength to the other sleepers, now we are laboring in earnest, to waken them.

MATTER REVISITED

I want nothing left of me for you, ho death
except some fertilizer
for the next batch of us
who do not hold hands with you
who do not embrace you
who try not to work for you
or sacrifice themselves or trust
or believe you, ho ignorant
death, how do you know
we happened to you?
                    JUDY GRAHN,
                    A Woman Is Talking to Death

THE YEARS

Her Body
Awakens

> . . . this we were, this is how we tried to love
> and these are the forces they had ranged against us,
> and these are the forces we had ranged within us,
> within us and against us, against us and within us.
>
> ADRIENNE RICH, *Twenty-one Love Poems*

Let go that which aches within you. She tells her. That which is stone within you. Which was once green in you. That has become hard within you, let go the years within you, she tells her. Her body. Her body holds. Her body has seized what had to be seized, what had to be learned, her body is a fortress, her body is an old warrior, how she has fought becomes clear, how she has known when to hold back becomes clear, how she has learned to grin becomes clear, how she has stayed on her feet becomes clear, how she has learned to keep secrets, learned to keep going, to preserve what was possible, learned every code, lived underground, lived on the barest means possible, her body, how she has hidden suffering, how she has worn, how she has kept going, how she was proud of her strength, of her indestructibleness, how she would keep going into battle, how she has worn muteness, how she kept on despite all odds, how she refused to admit defeat, how she wore muteness like a shield, how she denied sorrow, her body living its secret life, her body sheltering wounds, her body sequestering scars, her body a body of rage, her body a furnace, an incandescence, her body the exquisite fire, her body refusing, her body endlessly perceiving, her body growing huge, her body large and swollen, her body enormous and sagging, her body soft and flaccid, her body endlessly perceiving the absence, her body refusing to submit, her body continuing, her body consuming, her body sweating, her body rising and falling, her body beating, beating, flowing, throbbing, her body endlessly perceiving, endlessly perceiving the absence, her body refusing, her body refusing to submit, refusing, her body, her body, her body endlessly perceiving, endlessly perceiving, her body endlessly perceiving the absence, the absence of tenderness, her body refusing, her body refusing to submit, her body refusing to submit, to submit to lies, let go that which aches within you, she tells her, let go the years within you, she says.

The Anatomy Lesson (Her Skin)

> It is only real feelings that possess this power of transferring themselves into inert matter.
> SIMONE WEIL, *First and Last Notebooks*

From the body of the old woman we can tell you something of the life she lived. We know that she spent much of her life on her knees. (Fluid in the bursa in front of her kneecap.) *We say she must have often been fatigued, that her hands were often in water.* (Traces of calcium, traces of unspoken anger, swelling in the middle joints of her fingers.) *We see white ridges, scars from old injuries; we see redness in her skin.* (That her hands were often in water; that there must have been pain.) *We can tell you she bore several children. We see the white marks on her belly, the looseness of the skin, the wideness of her hips, that her womb has dropped.* (Stretching in the tissue behind the womb.) *We can see that she fed her children, that her breasts are long and flat, that there are white marks at the edges, a darker color of the nipple. We know that she carried weights too heavy for her back.* (Curvature of the spine. Aching.) *From the look of certain muscles in her back, her legs, we can tell you something of her childhood, of what she did not do.* (Of the running, of the climbing, of the kicking, of the movements she did not make.) *And from her lungs we can tell you what she held back, that she was forbidden to shout, that she learned to breathe shallowly. We can say that we think she must have held her breath. From the size of the holes in her ears, we know they were put there in her childhood. That she wore earrings most of her life. From the pallor of her skin, we can say that her face was often covered.* From her feet, that her shoes were small (toes bent back on themselves), *that she was often on her feet* (swelling, ligaments of the arch broken down). *We can guess that she rarely sat through a meal.* (Tissue of the colon inflamed.) *We can catalogue her being: tissue, fiber, bloodstream, cell, the shape of her experience to the least moment, skin, hair, try to see what she saw, to imagine what she felt, clitoris, vulva, womb, and we can tell you that despite each injury she survived. That she lived to an old age. (On all the parts of her body we see the years.) By the body of this old woman we are hushed. We are awed. We know that it was in her body that we began. And now we say that it is from her body that we learn. That we see our past. We say from the body of the old woman, we can tell you something of the lives we lived.*

History (Her Hair)

> We begin to see that so far from being inscrutable problems, requiring another life to explain, these sorrows and perplexities of our lives are but the natural results of natural causes, and that, as soon as we ascertain the causes, we can do much to remove them.
> CHARLOTTE PERKINS GILMAN, *Women and Economics*

> The history of mankind is a history of repeated injuries and usurpations on the part of man toward woman, having in direct object the establishment of an absolute tyranny over her. To prove this, let facts be submitted to a candid world.
> *Declaration of Sentiments and Resolutions,*
> Seneca Falls, 1848

Fine light hairs down our backbones. Soft hair over our forearms. Our upper lips. Each hair a precise fact. (He has never permitted her to exercise her inalienable right to franchise. He has compelled her to submit to laws, in the formation of which she had no choice.) *Hair tickling our legs.* The fact of hair against skin. The hand stroking the hair, the skin. Each hair. Each cell. (He has made her, if married, in the eye of the law, civilly dead.) *Our hair lying against our cheeks.* The assemblage of facts in a tangle of hair. (He has taken from her all right to property, even to the wages she earns. He has denied her the facilities for obtaining a thorough education, all colleges being closed against her.) *Hair rounding our vulvas.* How continual are the signs of growth. How from every complexity single strands can be named. (He has created a false public sentiment by giving to the world a different code of morals for men and women.) *Hair curling from under our arms.* How tangles are combed out and the mysterious laid bare. (He has usurped the prerogative of Jehovah himself . . .) *Hair which surprises us.* Each hair traces its existence in feeling. (. . . claiming it as his right to assign for her a sphere of action, when that belongs to her conscience and to her God.) *Which betrays our secrets.* The mysterious becomes the commonplace. Each hair in the profusion has its own root. (He has endeavored in every way that he could to destroy her confidence in her own powers . . .) *Hairs grow all over our bodies.* Profusion is cherished. Profusion is unraveled. Each moment acquires identity. Each fact traces its existence in feeling. (. . . to lessen her self-respect . . .) *We are covered with hair.* The past is cherished. (. . . and to make her willing to lead a dependent and abject life.) *We stroke our bodies; we remark to each other how we have always loved the softness of hair.*

Memory (The Breasts)

Because of my mother, who gave me definitions, I knew what I was committed to in life. . . . Mother, small, delicate boned, witty and articulate, turned out to be exactly my age. Owing to continuous bad health, she had barely any education, and so her spirit remained fervent and pure. She alone, with her modest but untroubled intuitions about books and painting, music and people, had been my education.

KAY BOYLE, *Being Geniuses Together*

Mrs. Willard did not return until I had been at the seminary some time. I remember her arrival and the joy with which she was greeted by teachers and pupils. . . . She was a splendid-looking woman, then in her prime, and fully realized my idea of a queen. . . . She gave free scholarships to a large number of girls . . . with a proviso that . . . they should in turn educate others.

ELIZABETH CADY STANTON, *Eighty Years and More*

They remember that she gave. What she made. What she did. *What we were to each other.* What she taught me. What I learned at her breast. That she made things. That she made words. That she fed me. Suckled me. Clothed me. Cradled me. Washed me. *We remember her labor.* She told us how she almost died. How she was weary. How her skin ached. What soreness she felt. What her mother's name was. How her mother made things. What her mother told her. How she was pushed away. How she was hated. How her milk was sour. What she wore at her wedding. Where she had dreamed of going. *What our first words were.* How she had quarreled with her sister. How they fought over a doll. How the other was prettier. How she pushed me away. How she hated me. How her milk was sour. *How we hated her. Her body. We remember our fear of becoming her. What we were to each other. What we learned.* What was said behind backs. Who had done what. What was revealed in dressing rooms. *How we saw each other naked. How there were some we trusted. How we showed our bodies to each other, how we held up our breasts to be seen, how we laid our heads, what we learned, what we knew, we remember, everything she said to us, when we must be careful, where we might go, what we might do, what we must not say, how we saw what she did, how we carried in our hearts, how we remembered there was one, how we re-peated to each other the name of the one who made her own way, who was alone, how we were in awe, how we marveled, how we paraded before the glass in her dressing gown, what we were to each other, how she told us what we suspected might be true, how she said she refused to be subjected, how she said all our efforts were marvelous.* How I re-alized I could not have gone on without her. How I was amazed by her knowledge. That she knew what was in me. How her sorrow shot through me. How I found myself weeping for her. How she told me her story, held her hands one on top of the other, her palms facing up, her fingers open, how her story, how I remembered that she held me, my face on her shoulder, how she told me what she remembered of how she was hated. How I was moved to. *What we were for each other. How we remembered.* How her memory brought me my mem-ory. How I knew what she knew, how her breasts felt then, her body, *how we were flooded with memory. How we loved in these moments: how telling these stories brought us here.*

Archives (Her Vulva)

> . . . We know that relying solely on argument we wandered for forty years politically in the wilderness. We know that arguments are not enough . . . and that political force is necessary.
> CHRISTABEL PANKHURST, speech delivered at
> Albert Hall, March 18, 1908

Who were those for whom we fought? I seemed to hear them in my cell, the defenseless ones who had no one to speak for their hungry need. The sweated workers, the mothers widowed with little children, the women on the streets, and I saw that their backs were bent, their eyes grown sorrowful, their hearts dead without hope. And they were not a few, but thousands upon thousands.

LADY CONSTANCE LYTTON, on her conviction for
"disorderly behavior with intent to disturb
the peace," 1909

We were never told of the existence of this movement. The existence of this movement was denied to us. We believed we were the first to want to act. We thought we were the first to refuse to submit. I remained there until the Wednesday evening, still being fed by force. I was then taken back to the same hospital cell, and remained there until Saturday, October 2, noon, feeding being continued in the same way. On Saturday, October 2, about dinnertime, I determined on stronger measures by barricading my cell. I piled my bed, table and chair by jamming them together against the door. They had to bring some men warders to get in with iron staves. I kept them at bay about three hours. *The denial of this movement was not called a lie. The denial of this movement was never spoken. No one ever spoke of this movement as existing or not existing.* I walked quietly onto the stage, took the placard out of the chair and sat down. A great cry went up from the women as they sprang from their seats and stretched their hands toward me. It was some time before I could see them for my tears, or speak to them for the emotion that shook me like a storm. *We are told that we are unique in history. That our history has been a history of passivity. We are to be blamed for our passivity, they say, we are our own oppressors. For our sufferings, they blame our passivity.* The women were treated with the greatest brutality. They were pushed about in all directions and thrown down by the police. Their arms were twisted until they were almost broken. Their thumbs were forcibly bent back and they were tortured in other nameless ways that make one feel sick at the sight. *We say we have discovered action in ourselves. We say we are determined, even if we are the first.* We have been prepared to sacrifice our safety of life and limb. We have been prepared to do these things because we believe in our cause. We say this not to boast of it, but to claim that we have the same spirit that the reformers of all ages have had to show before they could win success. *But we say we do not believe we were the first. We say this is not possible. We discover the old papers. We read the old accounts. These have been hidden from us, we see, for a reason.* I wrote on the wall:

> To defend the oppressed
> To fight for the defenseless
> Not counting the cost.

Letters (Her Clitoris)

> How do you do this year? I remember you as fires begin, and evenings open at Austin's, without the maid in black, Katie, without the Maid in black. Those were unnatural evenings—Bliss is unnatural—How many years, I wonder, will sow the moss upon them, before we bind again, a little altered it may be, elder a little it *will* be, and yet the same as suns, which shine, between our lives and loss, and violets, not last years, but having the Mother's eyes—
>
> EMILY DICKINSON, letter to Catherine Scott Turner, 1859

> Sarah Butler Wister first met Jeannie Field Musgrove while vacationing with her family at Stockbridge, Massachusetts, in the summer of 1849. Jeannie was then sixteen, Sarah, fourteen. During two subsequent years spent together in boarding school, they formed a deep and intimate friendship . . . their affection remained unabated throughout their lives, underscored by their loneliness and their desire to be together.
>
> CARROLL SMITH-ROSENBERG,
> "The Female World of Love and Ritual:
> Relations Between Women in Nineteenth Century America"

It was said of us that we had nothing of value to say. (Nothing has happened but loneliness perhaps too daily to relate, she wrote.) *That our lives were filled with gossip and trivia.* (Are you in danger, she wrote, I did not know that you were hurt. Will you tell me more?) *That it was difficult to imagine what we might say to each other.* (Every day life feels mightier, she wrote, and what we have the power to be, more stupendous.) *That left to our own devices we lack passion.* (She came to see us in May. I remember her frock, and how prettily she fixed her hair, and she and Vinnie took long walks and got home to tea at sundown.) *That we needed moreover to be protected from the harshness of life.* (And now remembering is all there is, and no more Myra. I wish 'twas plainer, Loo, the anguish in this world. I wish one could be sure the suffering had a loving side.) *It was said of us that we were narrow and could not see past our own small lives.* (O Matchless Earth—we underrate the chance to dwell in thee, she wrote.) *And that thus our capacity for love was dwarfed, as our minds were smaller.* (She wrote, Each of us gives or takes in corporeal person for each of us has the skill of life. I am pleased by your sweet acquaintance.) *They remarked on our prudery and our fear of sex.* (If the day should come when you failed me either through your fault or my own, she wrote her, I would foreswear all human friendship, thenceforth.) *They recorded that our vulvas would not permit entry.* (Gratitude is a word I should never use toward you, she wrote to her. It is perhaps a misfortune of such intimacy and love that it makes one regard all kindness as a matter of course, as one has always found it, as natural in the embrace of meeting.) *They say that reticence toward love of the body was natural in us. That modesty was natural in us.* (Dear darling Sarah! she wrote, How I love and happy I have been! You are the joy of my life. . . . I cannot tell you how much happiness you gave me. . . . My darling how I long for the time when I shall see you. . . .) *We asked them how they could be certain* (I want you to tell me in your next letter . . . that I am your dearest) *that they knew* (I will go to bed . . . I could write all night—a thousand kisses—I love you with my whole soul) *what was possible in us.* (my separation from you, grievous to be borne . . . Oh, Jeannie. I have thought and thought and yearned over you these two days. Are you married I wonder? My dearest love to wherever and *who* ever you are.) *What we could be.*

Records (Her Womb)

From the evidence adduced on trial, it appeared that Miss Ashe went to the establishment of Howard . . . about the middle of January 1858, for the purpose of having abortion procured, supposing herself pregnant, by a young farmer, by whom she had been employed during the previous summer; that a bargain was struck between the reputed father of the child and Howard, by which he was to perform the desired service for the sum of $100.

Report of a trial for criminal abortion,
C. P. Frost, M.D., of St. Johnsbury, Vermont

The "immorality" of women, favorite theme of misogynists, is not to be wondered at; how could they fail to feel an inner mistrust of the presumptuous principles that men publicly proclaim and secretly disregard? They learn to believe no longer in what men say

Her sister swore that she witnessed every operation. She testified
that the doctor operated three times with instruments. (She could not
describe the instruments minutely. She did not know how many there
were.) She said water discharged from her sister's body (for two or
three hours, she said). She said on the next day, he operated again.
(She said he used two or three instruments.) She said her sister did
not cry out, but gave other evidence, she said, of considerable pain.
There was now a discharge of blood, she said. On the night of the
same day, Saturday, she reported, he operated again. After this, her
sister did not sit up, she said. He used instruments again, she said, and
also his hand. This time a child was delivered about two-thirds grown,
she said. She said her sister continued to bleed for a few days. That
she lived from that Saturday to the next Friday evening, that the last
two or three days of her life she was delirious and picked at her
clothes. It is said from the body of the dead woman no proof of innocence or guilt can be issued. *We go back. We ask what happened then.
We find no mention. No reference. No books. Books out of print. Lost,
destroyed. Pages torn away. Days missing. We find documents.* She
finds letters. Diaries. Stories are repeated. *We discover* she was operated on four times before she died, *we discover* a hairpin was removed
from her bladder, *we read* they took salts of lead, copper, zinc and
mercury, *we read* they let themselves fall down staircases, *we read* she
injected vinegar into the bladder, *we read* her womb was perforated
by a knitting needle, by a probe, *we read hemorrhage, we read in-
flammation, we read that she drank a solution of soap and then ran for
a quarter of an hour, we read* she remained for four days in her room
bathed in her own blood with no food and no water *we read that the
doctors would do nothing for her pain we read that she gave birth
alone that the infant was found dead beside her nearly dead body that
she was sentenced to death, we read pain, we read illness. We can tell
you something of what they went through, we say.* Standing in the
pharmacy, she was afraid they would know she was hemorrhaging.
From the records, we say, we can guess what she felt. So that her

screaming would not give her away, she began to sing. *From the records* She spent the night on the floor rocking in agony, biting her teeth into the flesh of her palm so she would not awaken them *we can tell you what we know. The past is a hard stone within us. On this subject we have become unmovable, implacable. There is no way of convincing us otherwise, we say, and what is stone becomes wood that ages and resonates: we know what we know.*

OUR NATURE

WHAT IS STILL WILD IN US

Now we will let the blood of our mother sink into this earth. This is what we will do with our grieving. We will cover her wounds with mud. We will tear leaves and branches from the trees and together pile them over her body. The sky will no longer see her fallen thus. We will pull grass up by the roots. We will cover her. Thus, as we do this, we know her body will melt away. And only her bones will remain. But these we will take. Still feeling her absence, we will cradle her tusks in our trunks, and carry them to another ground. And thus will this soil be absolved of her death, and the place of her dying be innocent again, and thus her bones will no longer be chaffed by the violence done there. But though all traces of her vanish, we will not forget. In our lifetimes we will not be able to forget. Her wounds will fester in us. We will not be the same. The scent of her killer is known to us now. We cannot turn our backs at the wrong moment. We must know when to trumpet and charge, when to recede into denser forest, when to turn and track the hunter. We feel the necessity of these acts in us. We will pass this feeling to our young, to those who follow in our footsteps, who walk under our bodies, who feel safe in our presence, who did we not warn them, did we not teach them this scent, might approach this enemy with curiosity. Who imitate our movements and rely on our knowledge; we will not allow them to approach their enemies easily. They will learn fear. And when we attack in their defense, they will watch and learn this too. From us, they will become fierce. And so a death like this death of our mother will not come easily to them. This is what we will do with our grieving. They will know whom to beware and whom to fear. And this hatred that began to grow in us when we saw her body fall will become their hatred and no man will approach

them safely. No man will come near them and live. We will not forget and this memory will protect them. What they have learned from us, all that we have taught them so that they can survive, how to suck up water into their trunks, how to pull down leaves from trees, how to lift with their tusks, and dig holes by the river with their feet, all this they will pass on, and generation after generation will remember the scent of this enemy. This is how long our grieving will last. And only if the young of our young or the young of their young never know this odor in their lifetime, only if no hunter approaches them as long as they live, and no one with this scent attempts to capture them, or use them to his purpose, only then will the memory of this death pass from our hide. Only then will those with the scent of her killer be absolved, as the soil is absolved, of her blood. Only then, when no trace is left of this memory in us, will we see what we can be without this fear, without this enemy, what we are.

THIS EARTH

WHAT SHE IS TO ME

> One should identify oneself with the universe itself. Everything
> that is less than the universe is subjected to suffering . . .
>
> SIMONE WEIL, *Notebooks*

As I go into her, she pierces my heart. As I penetrate further, she
unveils me. When I have reached her center, I am weeping openly. I
have known her all my life, yet she reveals stories to me, and these stories are revelations and I am transformed. Each time I go to her I am
born like this. Her renewal washes over me endlessly, her wounds ca-
ress me; I become aware of all that has come between us, of the noise
between us, the blindness, of something sleeping between us. Now
my body reaches out to her. They speak effortlessly, and I learn at no
instant does she fail me in her presence. She is as delicate as I am; I
know her sentience; I feel her pain and my own pain comes into me,
and my own pain grows large and I grasp this pain with my hands, and
I open my mouth to this pain, I taste, I know, and I know why she goes
on, under great weight, with this great thirst, in drought, in starvation,
with intelligence in every act does she survive disaster. This earth is
my sister; I love her daily grace, her silent daring, and how loved I am
*how we admire this strength in each other, all that we have lost, all
that we have suffered, all that we know: we are stunned by this beauty,*
and I do not forget: what she is to me, what I am to her.

FOREST

THE WAY WE STAND

> The poor little working-girl who had found strength to gather up the fragments of her life and build herself a shelter with them seemed to Lily to have reached the central truth of existence.
>
> EDITH WHARTON, *The House of Mirth*

> The bank was dense with magnolia and loblolly bay, sweet gum and gray-barked ash. . . . He went down to the spring in the cool darkness of the shadows. A sharp pleasure came over him. This was a secret, lovely place.
>
> MARJORIE KINNAN RAWLINGS, *The Yearling*

The way we stand, you can see we have grown up this way together, out of the same soil, with the same rains, leaning in the same way toward the sun. See how we lean together in the same direction. How the dead limbs of one of us rest in the branches of another. How those branches have grown around the limbs. How the two are inseparable. And if you look you can see the different ways we have taken this place into us. Magnolia, loblolly bay, sweet gum, Southern bayberry, Pacific bayberry; wherever we grow there are many of us; Monterey pine, sugar pine, white-bark pine, four-leaf pine, single-leaf pine, bristlecone pine, foxtail pine, Torrey pine, Western red pine, Jeffry pine, bishop pine. And we are various, and amazing in our variety, and our differences multiply, so that edge after edge of the endlessness of possibility is exposed. You know we have grown this way for years. And to no purpose you can understand. Yet what you fail to know we know, and the knowing is in us, how we have grown this way, why these years were not one of them heedless, why we are shaped the way we are, not all straight to your purpose, but to ours. And how we are each purpose, how each cell, how light and soil are in us, how we are in the soil, how we are in the air, how we are both infinitesimal and great and how we are infinitely without any purpose you can see, in the way we stand, each alone, yet none of us separable, none of us beautiful when separate but all exquisite as we stand, each moment heeded in this cycle, no detail unlovely.

THE WIND

Ask who keeps the wind
Ask what is sacred

MARGARET ATWOOD, "Circe Poems"

Yes, they say our fate is with the wind. The wind? Yes, they say when the wind blows this way one thing will happen, and when it blows the other way, something else will be. Something else will be? Yes, these are the questions. Does the wind blow for us? This is what we must ask. Are we ready for this wind? Do we know what this wind will bring us? Will we take what the wind gives, or even know what is given when we see it? Will we see? Will we let the wind blow all the way through us? Will the wind know us? These are the questions to ask. Will we let the wind sing to us? Do our whole bodies listen? When the wind calls, will we go? Will this wind come inside us? Take from us? Can we give to the wind what is asked of us? Will we let go? Are we afraid of this wind? Will we go where we are afraid to go? Will the wind ask us? This is the question. Are we close to the wind? Will the wind ask much of us, and will we be able to hear the wind singing and will we answer? Can we sing back, this we ask, can we sing back, and not only sing, but in clear voices? Will this be, we ask, and will we keep on answering, keep on with our whole bodies? And do we know why we sing? Yes. Will we know why? Yes.

MATTER

Because we know ourselves to be made from this earth. See this grass. The patches of silver and brown. Worn by the wind. The grass reflecting all that lives in the soil. The light. The grass needing the soil. With roots deep in the earth. And patches of silver. Like the patches of silver in our hair. Worn by time. This bird flying low over the grass. Over the tules. The cattails, sedges, rushes, reeds, over the marsh. Because we know ourselves to be made from this earth. Temporary as this grass. Wet as this mud. Our cells filled with water. Like the mud of this swamp. Heather growing here because of the damp. Sphagnum moss floating on the surface, on the water standing in these pools. Places where the river washes out. Where the earth was shaped by the flow of lava. Or by the slow movements of glaciers. Because we know ourselves to be made from this earth, and shaped like the earth, by what has gone before. The lives of our mothers. What she told me was her life. And what I saw in her hands. The calcium in the joints, the aching as she hemmed my dress. These clothes she made for me. *The pools overgrown by grass, reed, sedge, the marsh over time, becoming dry, over centuries, plankton disappearing, crustaceans gone, clams, worms, sponges, what we see now floating in these pools, fish, birds flying close to the waters. This bird with the scarlet shoulders. This bird with the yellow throat. And the beautiful song. The song like flutes. Like violoncellos in an orchestra. The orchestra in our mind. The symphony which we imagine. The music which was our idea. What we wanted to be. The lives of our grandmothers. What we imagined them to be.* She told me what she had wanted to be. What she had wanted to do. That she wanted to act on the stage. To write. She showed me the stories she wrote before she was married. Before I was born. *Why we were born when we were, as we were, we imagined. We imagined what she imagined then, what lay under the surface, this still water, the water not running over rocks, lacking air, the bacteria, fungi, dwelling at the bottom, without light, no green bodies, freeing no air, the scent of marsh gas, this bog we might lose ourselves in, sink in, the treachery here, our voices calling for help and no one listening, the silence, we made from this earth, returning to earth, the mud covering us, we giving ourselves up to this place, the fungi, bacteria, fish, everything struggling for air in this place, beetles capturing air bubbles on the surface of the pond, mosquitoes reaching with tubes to the surface of the water, fish with gills on the outsides of their bodies, fish gulping air at the surface, air captured in small hairs on the bodies of insects, stored in spaces in the stems of plants, in pockets in the tissue of leaves, everything in this place struggling for light, stems and leaves with thin skins, leaves divided into greater surfaces, numerous pores, tall plants in shallow water, open to the light; a jungle of growth in the shallow water at the edge, interwoven stems, matted leaves, places for wrens to hide, for rails, bitterns, for red-winged blackbirds to protect their nests. Fish hiding in plants underwater, insects' and snails' eggs, pupa cases, larvae and nymphs and crayfish. Sunlight pouring into plants, ingested into the bodies of fish, into the red-winged blackbird, into the bacteria, into the fungi, into the earth itself, because we know ourselves to be made of this earth, because we know sunlight moves through us, water moves through us, everything moves, everything changes, and the daughters are returned to their mothers. She always comes back. Back from the darkness. And the earth grows green again. So we were moved to feel these things. The body of the animal buried in the ground rotting feeds the seed. The sheaf of grain held up to us silently.* Her dreams, I know, she said, live on in my body as I write these words. *This proof. This testimony. This shape of possibility. What we dreamed to be. What we labored for. What we had burned desiring. What always returns. What she is to me. What she is to me, we said, and do not turn your head away, we told them, those who had tried to name us, those who had tried to keep us apart, do not turn your head away when we tell you this, we said,* how she was smaller than I then, *we try to tell you,* what tenderness I then felt for her, *we said,* as if she were my daughter, as if some part of myself I had thought lost forever were returned to me, *we said,* and then held her fiercely, *and we then made you listen, you turning your head away, you who tried to make us be still, you dividing yourself from this night we were turning through, but we made you listen, we said, do not pretend you do not hear what we say to each other, we say,* when she was returned to me and I to her that I became small to her, that my face became soft against her flesh, that through that night she held me, as if part of herself had returned, like mother to daughter *because we know we are made of this earth, and we know these meanings reach you, we said, the least comment of the stare, we said, the barely perceptible moment of despair,* I told her, *the eloquence of arms, those threaded daily causes, the fundaments of sound, cradling the infant's head, these cries,* the crying I heard in her body, *the years we had known together,* I know these meanings reach you, *we said, and the stars and their light we hold in our hands, this light telling the birds where they are, the same light which guides these birds to this place, and the light through which we imagine ourselves in the bodies of these birds, flying with them, low over the grass, weaving our nests like hammocks from blade to blade, from reed to reed. We standing at the edge of the marsh. Not daring to move closer. Keeping our distance. Watching these birds through the glass. Careful not to frighten them off. As they arrive. First the males, jet black, with a flash of red at their shoulders, a startling red which darts out of their blackness as they spread their wings. First the males and then the females flying together in the winter, now joining the males. The females with yellow throats, their wings brown and black, and light around their eyes. Now all of them calling. Calling or singing. Liquid and pleasant. Like the violoncello. We imagine like the violoncello, the cello we have made in our minds, the violin we have imagined, as we have imagined the prison, as we have made up boundaries, or decided what the fate of these birds should be, as we have invented poison, as we have invented the cage, now we stand at the edge of this marsh and do not go closer, allow them their distance, penetrate them only with our minds, only with our hearts, because though we can advance upon the blackbird, though we may cage her, though we may torture her with our will, with the boundaries we imagine, this bird will never be ours, he may die, this minute heart stop beating, the body go cold and hard, we may tear the wings apart and cut open the body and remove what we want* to see, but still this blackbird will not be ours and we will have nothing. And even if we keep her alive. Train her to stay indoors. Clip her wings. Train her to sit on our fingers, though we feed her, and give her water, still this is not the blackbird we have captured, for the blackbird, which flies now over our heads, whose song reminds us of a flute, who migrates with the stars, who lives among reeds and rushes, threading a nest like a hammock, who lives in flocks, chattering in the grasses, this creature is free of our hands, we cannot control her, and for the creature we have tamed, the creature we keep in our house, we must make a new word. For we did not invent the blackbird, we say, we only invented her name. And we never invented ourselves, we admit. And my grandmother's body is now part of the soil, she said. Only now, we name ourselves. Only now, as we think of ourselves as passing, do we utter the syllables. Do we list all that we are? That we know in ourselves? We know ourselves to be made from this earth. We know this earth is made from our bodies. For we see ourselves. And we are nature. We are nature seeing nature. We are nature with a concept of nature. Nature weeping. Nature speaking of nature to nature. The red-winged blackbird flies in us, in our inner sight. We see the arc of her flight. We measure the ellipse. We predict its climax. We are amazed. We are moved. We fly. We watch her wings negotiate the wind, the substance of the air, its elements and the elements of those elements, and count those elements found in other beings, the sea urchin's sting, ink, this paper, our bones, the flesh of our tongues with which we make the sound "blackbird," the ears with which we hear, the eye which travels the arc of her flight. And yet the blackbird does not fly in us but is somewhere else free of our minds, and now even free of our sight, flying in the path of her own will, she wrote, the ink from her pen flowing on this paper, her words, she thought, having nothing to do with this bird, except, she thought, as she breathes in the air this bird flies through, except, she thought, as the grass needs the body of the bird to pass its seeds, as the earth needs the grass, as we are made from this earth, she said, and the sunlight in the grass enters the body of the bird, *enters us,* she wrote on this paper, and the sunlight is pouring into my eyes from your eyes. Your eyes. Your eyes. The sun is in your eyes. I have made you smile. Your lips part. The sunlight in your mouth. Have I made the sun come into your mouth? I put my mouth on yours. To cover that light. To breathe it in. My tongue inside your mouth, your lips on my tongue, my body filled with light, filled with light, with light, shuddering, you make me shudder, you make the movement of the earth come into me, you fill me, you fill me with sound, is that my voice crying out? The sunlight in you is making my breath sing, sing your name, your name to you, beautiful one, I could kiss your bones, put my teeth in you, white gleam, whiteness, I chew, beautiful one, I am in you, I am filled with light inside you, I have no boundary, the light has extinguished my skin, I am perished in light, light filling you, shining through you, carrying you out, through the roofs of our mouths, the sky, the clouds, bursting, raining, raining free, falling piece by piece, dispersed over this earth, into the soil, deep, deeper into you, into the least hair on the deepest root in this earth, into the green heart flowing, into the green leaves and they grow, they grow into a profusion, moss, fern, and they bloom, cosmos, and they bloom, cyclamen, in your ears, in your ears, calling their names, this sound from my throat echoing, my breath in your ears, your eyes, your eyes continuing to see, continuing, your eyes telling, telling the light, the light. And she wrote, when I let this bird fly to her own purpose, when this bird flies in the path of his own will, the light from this bird enters my body, and when I see the beautiful arc of her flight, I love this bird, when I see, the arc of her flight, I fly with her, enter her with my mind, leave myself, die for an instant, live in the body of this bird whom I cannot live without, as part of the body of the bird will enter my daughter's body, because I know I am made from this earth, as my mother's hands were made from this earth, as her dreams came from this earth and all that I know, I know in this earth, the body of the bird, this pen, this paper, these hands, this tongue speaking, all that I know speaks to me through this earth and I long to tell you, you who are earth too, and listen *as we speak to each other of what we know: the light is in us.*

NOTES

In these notes, the following symbols are used for the following texts.

AM   *The Architecture of Matter,* by Stephen Toulmin and June Goodfield.
CD   *Civilization and Its Discontents,* by Sigmund Freud.
DC   *Darwin's Century,* by Loren Eiseley.
DPT   *The Development of Physical Theory in the Middle Ages,* by James A. Weisheipl.
DS   *The Dangerous Sex,* by H. R. Hays.
EV   *The Evolution of Physics,* by Albert Einstein and Leopold Infeld.
HH   *The Horrors of the Half-Known Life,* by G. J. Barker-Benfield.
HS   *A History of Science,* by W. C. Dampier.
MES   *Medieval and Early Modern Science,* by A. C. Crombie.
MFM *The Metaphysical Foundations of Modern Science,* by E. A. Burtt.
NGI   *Not in God's Image,* edited by Julia O'Faolain and Lauro Martines.
NIL   *New Introductory Lectures on Psychoanalysis,* by Sigmund Freud.
PA   *Patriarchal Attitudes,* by Eva Figes.
PSV   *The Physician and Sexuality in Victorian America,* by John S. and Robin M. Haller.
SE   "The Spermatic Economy: A Nineteenth-Century View of Sexuality," by Ben Barker-Benfield.
TH   *The Troublesome Helpmate,* by Katherine M. Rogers.
TP   *The Tao of Physics,* by Fritjof Capra.
UE   *The Universe and Dr. Einstein,* by Lincoln Barnett.

The citations below are provided so that the reader may identify sources for my parody of the patriarchal voice and my telling of the history of patriarchal thought regarding woman and nature. (Here and there, for the sake of humor or style, I take liberty with language, but still the essential arguments of patriarchy are not distorted.) Complete bibliographical information for these citations can be found in the Bibliography.

The notes for the rest of the book are not complete. It would have been tedious and probably impossible to list all the sources used for each section. Those texts which are listed are given to indicate the actual phenomenon or historical occurrences of which the writing is a reflection (for example in "Turbulence," I cite an article on "The Biosphere" which explores the necessity of the turbulence of the sea to all life), and also to give credit to the thinking of others.

BOOK ONE

7   *that matter is transitory and illusory:* see *The Republic of Plato,* "Allegory of the Cave," trans. Francis Macdonald Cornford.

   Sic transit: see Thomas à Kempis, *Imitatione Christi,* trans. Anthony Hoskins.

   Matter . . . allegory for the next: see MES, vol. 1, p. 15. Crombie describes science before the twelfth century: "The study of nature was not expected to lead to hypotheses and generalisations of science but to provide vivid symbols of moral realities."

   Matter . . . passive and inert: see Aristotle, *The Physics,* bk. 7, trans. Wicksteed and Cornford, vol. 2. Everything that is moved, he posits, must be moved by something. See also MES, vol. 1, p. 71. According to Crombie, Aristotle's idea of substance was the basis of "all natural explanation" from the thirteenth through the seventeenth centuries.

   soul is the cause: see the Platonists of Chartres, as cited in MES, vol. 1, p. 30.

8   *the existence of God can be proved:* see Thomas Aquinas, *Summa Theologica,* and HS, p. 86.

   reason exists to: see the "later scholastics," as cited in HS, p. 86.

   God is unchangeable . . . Logos: see Origen, as cited in HS, p. 64.

   "And I do not know": see St. Augustine, *De Libero Arbitrio,* as cited in MES, vol. 1, p. 14.

   that Genesis: see Thierry of Chartres, *De Septem Diebus et Sex Operum Distinctionibus,* cited in MES, vol. 1, p. 27.

   "He who does not know mathematics": see Roger Bacon, *Opus Majus,* trans. Robert Belle Burke, vol. 1, p. 116.

   all truth: Bacon was influenced by the thought of Pythagoras.

   true explanation: see Robert Grosseteste, *Summary of Philosophy,* as cited in DPT, p. 52.

   That there are three degrees: see Robert Kilwardby, *De Ortu Scientiarum,* as cited in DPT, pp. 52–4.

   science might be able . . . made without limit: see Roger Bacon, *Epistola de Secretis Operibus,* as cited in MES, vol. 1, p. 55.

9   *that vision takes place:* see Plato, *Timaeus,* as cited in MES, vol. 1, p. 31.

   that God is primordial light: see Robert Grosseteste, *op. cit.,* as cited in DPT, pp. 51–2.

   waters of the firmament: see Bede, as cited in MES, vol. 1, pp. 19–20.

   the space above is: see E. M. Tillyard, *The Elizabethan World Picture,* p. 37.

the earth is a central sphere: see Plato, *Timaeus,* as elaborated by the Platonists of Chartres, cited in MES, vol. 1, pp. 27–30. Plato and Eudoxus both favored perfect circles.

all bodies: see Aristotle, *The Physics, op. cit.,* vol. 1, pp. 188–9. See also MES, vol. 1, pp. 75–8.

"is so depraved": see Pierre Boistuau, *Théâtre du Monde,* as cited in E. M. Tillyard, *op cit.,* p. 39.

"shineth night and day": see *Mirror of the World,* as cited in Tillyard, *ibid.* p. 39.

"the good angels": see St. Augustine, *The City of God,* ed. David Knowles (Baltimore: Penguin, 1972), p. 367.

10 *"the Devil's Gateway":* see Tertullian, *De Cultu Feminarum,* and NGI, pp. 132–3.

That regarding: see Heinrich Kramer and James Sprenger, *Malleus Maleficarum,* pp. 115–17. The phrase "intellectually like children" is quoted by Kramer and Sprenger from Terence.

Frailty, thy name is woman: see William Shakespeare, *Hamlet.*

the word woman: see Kramer, *op cit.,* pp. 115–16. "Wherefore in many vituperations that we read against women, the word woman is used to mean lust of the flesh." (The brothers were fond of quoting authorities on the evil of women.)

woman, whose face is a burning wind: ibid., p. 122 (here citing St. Bernard).

female provides the matter: see Aristotle, *Generation of Animals,* trans. A. L. Peck, p. 185, and MES, vol. 1, p. 152.

in the bestiary: see *Bestiary,* as cited in HS, p. 66.

Vital Heat: see Albertus Magnus, *De Animalibus,* as cited in MES, vol. 1, p. 152.

monstrosities: ibid. vol. 1, p. 152.

semen: see Aristotle, *Generation, op. cit.,* pp. 163, 175 "Semen, then, is a compound of *pneuma* and water (*pneuma* being hot air) . . ." And "The reason is that the female is as it were a deformed male; and the menstrual discharge is semen, though in an impure condition i.e. it lacks one constituent, and one only, the principle of Soul." See also MES, vol. 1, p. 153.

spontaneous generation: Albertus Magnus, *De Animalibus,* as cited in MES, vol. 1, p. 153.

"In the middle": see Copernicus, *On the Revolution of the Celestial Orbs,* as cited in J. D. Bernal, *The Scientific and Industrial Revolutions,* p. 408.

11 *the Sun is God:* see Johannes Kepler, *Astronomia Opera Omnia,* as cited in MFM, p. 60.

"all things decay": see Edmund Spencer, *The Faerie Queene*, bk. 3, canto 6.

the face of the earth: see Loren Eiseley, *The Firmament of Time*, for a discussion of catastrophism.

"the world is the Devil": Martin Luther, as cited in Norman O. Brown, *Life Against Death*, p. 212.

power of the devil . . . in the privy parts: see Kramer, *op. cit.*, as cited in PA, p. 59.

women under the power: see Francesco Maria Guazzo, *Compendium Maleficarum*, as cited in DS, chap. 15. See also Pennethorne Hughes, *Witchcraft*.

"Lucifer before his Fall": see Thomas Nash, *Pierce Pennilesse, His Supplication to the Divell*.

"Virgin's urine": see Michael Scot, *Physionomia*, and NGI, p. 142.

12   *no wickedness to compare*: see Kramer, *op. cit.*, pp. 114–15.

a virtuous wife: see Ephesians 5:22–33.

"tongues in trees": see William Shakespeare, *As You Like It*.

immutable laws: see Descartes's metaphysics as discussed in MFM, p. 114 and passim.

planetary orbits . . . six planets: see Johannes Kepler, *Mysterium Cosmographicum*, as cited in MES, vol. 2, p. 180.

music of the spheres: see Kepler, *Harmonice Mundi*, as cited in MFM, p. 63.

cause of the universe: see Kepler, *Astronomia Opera Omnia*, as cited in MFM, pp. 64–5.

all shapes . . . single figure: see MFM, pp. 44–6. (This geometrical compass was devised by Galileo.)

heliocentric systems: see Nicolaus Copernicus, *De Revolutionibus*, as cited in MFM, p. 38. See also MES, vol. 2, pp. 176–7.

13   *"Nature"*: see Galileo, *Dialogue Concerning the Two Chief World Systems*, trans. Stillman Drake, p. 117.

"Nature is not": see MFM, p. 39.

"Nature is pleased": see Isaac Newton, *The Mathematical Principles of Natural Philosophy*, cited in MFM, p. 218.

"Vain pomp and glory": see William Shakespeare, *Henry VIII*.

"inordinate affections and passions": see Kramer, *op. cit.*, p. 119.

women's sorrows: see *Politeuphia, Wits Commonwealth*, ed. Nicholas Ling, as cited in TH, p. 107.

"are made of blood": see John Marston, *Works*, cited in TH, p. 125: "Women are made/ of blood, without souls . . ."

"shifts oft like the inconstant": see John Gay, "Dione": "Woman's mind/ oft' shifts her passions, like th' inconstant wind."

"all witchcraft": see Kramer, *op. cit.,* p. 122.

sin originated: see Justin of Rome, *Dialogue in Trypho,* as cited in George H. Tavard, *Women in Christian Tradition,* p. 69.

that angels are thin: see Nash, *Pierce Pennilesse.*

nature can be understood only: see Nicholas of Cusa: "Knowledge is always measurement," and Kepler: "Nothing can be known completely except quantities or by quantities," as cited in MFM, pp. 53, 68. (The language "understood only by reduction" is mine.)

without mathematics: see Galileo, *Opere Complete,* as cited in MFM, p. 75.

that which cannot be measured: see MFM, p. 93, on Galileo. See also MFM, p. 88, citing the famous passage of Galileo that all qualities outside of number depend on sense perception and are therefore not real. St. Augustine in *On the Free Choice of the Will* argues even that "the truth of numbers belongs not to the senses of the body . . ."

14   *whether or not motion is real . . . motion is real:* see William of Ockham, who considered motion as well as quantity to be unreal (his absolutes were substance and quality), and Brawardine, who considered motion "a real geometrical structure," as cited in DPT, pp. 62–88.

all motion: see *The Works of Honorable Robert Boyle,* vol. 1, p. 2: "The Origin of Motion in Matter Is from God." See also Kepler, *Astronomia Opera Omnia,* as cited in MFM, p. 59, and Newton, as cited in MFM, p. 289. See also René Descartes, *Principles of Philosophy,* pt. 2, prin. 64, and see Aristotle, *Physics,* bk. 3, chap. 1, where he argues that "Nature is the principle of movement and change," and he defines change as the passage from potential to actual, thus laying the basis for a first mover who is immovable.

all motion results: see Descartes, as cited in HS, p. 136. See also Newton: "No man endowed with a competent faculty of thinking will grant that a body can act where it is not." Newton, however, knew that a body could act so. See Giorgio de Santillana, *Reflections on Men and Ideas,* p. 26.

God alone sees: see Sir Isaac Newton, *Opticks,* pp. 345, 379.

position of . . . particles: see Laplace, as cited in MFM, p. 96.

sensation of color: see René Descartes, *Principles,* as cited in MFM, p. 120, and Newton, *Opticks,* p. 328.

women exist for pleasure: see Erasmus, *Colloquies* (Erasmus posed this argument as a devil's advocate), as cited in NGI, p. 182.

"How fair": see Song of Songs 7:6.

human mind: see Kepler, *Opera,* as cited in MFM, p. 68.

what is there: see Kepler, letter to Herwart von Hohenburg, 1599 as cited in MES, vol. 2, p. 188.

one authentic and the other bastard: see Democritus, as cited in AM, p. 58.

15   *women are the fountain:* see the Seven Sages of Rome, as cited in TH, p. 97.

defective rib: see Kramer, *op. cit.,* p. 117.

one would follow: see John Lyly, *Euphues,* as cited in TH, p. 111.

sensations are confused: see Descartes, *Principles,* as cited in MFM, p. 116.

"hysterical": see *Oxford English Dictionary.*

dramatic poetry: see Plato, *The Republic,* pp. 337, 338, 83.

"inordinate affections": see Kramer, *op. cit.,* p. 119.

"dangerous effect": see Fénelon, *Traité de l'education des filles,* as cited in NGI, pp. 249–50.

husbands should not: see L. B. Alberti, *The Family in Renaissance Florence,* as cited in NGI, p. 188.

"Who, moving" see William Shakespeare, sonnet 2.

woman "is not fully": see Martin Luther, in a letter written to three nuns, August 6, 1524, in NGI, p. 196.

where there is death: see St. John Chrysostom, *Della Verginata,* in NGI, p. 138.

16   *God does not . . . He will not die:* see Newton, *Principles,* as cited in MFM, p. 259, and Newton, *Opticks,* p. 379. (This is essentially my parody.)

God is a mathematician: see Hans Jonas, *The Phenomenon of Life,* on Kepler and Galileo's notion of divine geometry and for his brilliant argument against this.

"these the Divine Wisdom": see Galileo, *Two Great Systems,* as cited in Hugh Kearney, *Science and Change, 1500–1700,* p. 146.

God has allowed us: see Kepler, letter to Herwart von Hohenburg, 1599, as cited in MES, vol. 2, p. 188.

"not the woman": see St. Augustine, *On the Holy Trinity,* in NGI, p. 130. See also Aquinas, *Summa,* in NGI, p. 131.

"the image of God": see Gratian, *Decretum,* in NGI, p. 130.

God is the principle: see Aquinas, *Summa,* in NGI, p. 131.

the minds of women: see Malebranche, in NGI, p. 246.

All abstract knowledge: see Immanuel Kant, as cited in H. J. Mozans, *Woman in Science,* p. 136.

controversy: see NGI, pp. 247–8.

to the woman who owns: see Molière, *Les Femmes Savantes,* trans. Curtis Page.

"but a brute thing": see *The Works of Honorable Robert Boyle,* as cited in MFM, p. 183.

no intellect: ibid.

17 *nature should:* see Immanuel Kant, *Critique of Pure Reason,* as cited in MES, vol. 2, pp. 329–30.

She is asked why she wears male: Questions asked of Joan of Arc during her trial as a witch. See Margaret Murray, *The Witch-Cult in Western Europe,* pp. 271–6, and Rossell Hope Robbins, *The Encyclopedia of Witchcraft and Demonology,* pp. 282–7.

He says that nature ... must be examined ... bound into service ... put on the rack: see Francis Bacon, as cited in Carolyn Iltis, *Nature and the Female in the Scientific Revolution,* and William Leis, *The Domination of Nature,* p. 57 and passim.

18 *She is asked if she signed the devil's book ... How she was able to fly:* see Robbins, *op. cit.,* pp. 106, 175–7, 180, 410.

19 *the rational soul:* see Robert Boyle, *op. cit.,* as cited in MFM, p. 183.

Adam is soul: see Hubmaier, *On Free Will,* in NGI, p. 202.

animals do not think ... oysters, sponges": see René Descartes, letter to Marquis of Newcastle, in *Descartes Selections,* ed. Ralph H. Eaton, pp. 355–7.

20 *souls of women:* see Samuel Butler, *Miscellaneous Thoughts:* "The souls of women are so small/ That some believe they've none at all."

universe acts: see MES, vol. 2, p. 164: "It was the most fundamental general conclusion of Descartes's mechanistic philosophy that all natural phenomena could eventually when sufficiently analyzed be reduced to a single kind of change, local motion; and that conclusion became the most influential belief of 17th century science."

secret of the universe: see MFM, pp. 98–9, on Galileo's positivism, and p. 226 on Newton: "The ultimate nature of gravity is unknown, it is not necessary for science that it be known, for science seeks to understand how it acts, not what it is."

That the particular: see MFM: "It is possible to have a correct knowledge of the part without knowing the nature of the whole." pp. 227–8.

"celestial machine": see Kepler, letter to Herwart von Hohenburg, 1605, in MES, vol. 2, p. 196.

maker of the universe: see Newton, *Opera Quae Exstant Omnia,* as cited in MFM, p. 290.

"was the eye contrived": see Newton, *Opticks,* p. 344.

"heart of animals": see William Harvey, *On Circulation,* trans. Leake, p. 71.

21   *That God is skilled:* see Newton, *(Opera quae exstant Omnia)* as cited in MFM, pp. 289–91.

    Everything in the universe: see Newton, as cited in HS, pp. 170–1. Newton believed there was a general law but could not solve the problem of gravity, which he did not accept as innate.

    God constructed his clock: see Newton, as cited in HS, pp. 74–5, and MFM, pp. 293–5. Newton believed the clock to need adjustments; however, Leibnitz and Huygens thought God acted only at creation. See MFM, pp. 101, 292.

    God does not learn . . . choose to respond: see Newton, *Opticks,* p. 379. "God is able to . . . vary the laws of Nature and make Worlds of several sorts in several parts of the Universe." The language in the text is my parody of this image of an autistic God created by seventeenth-century intellect.

    "a God without dominion": see Newton, *Principles,* as cited in MFM, p. 294.

    we adore: ibid.

    "My author": see John Milton, *Paradise Lost,* 4.

    "Women should be": see Gratian, *Decretum,* in NGI, p. 130.

    women not be allowed: see John Calvin, *Institutes of the Christian Religion,* in NGI, pp. 202–3.

    "not in the character of": see Immanuel Kant, *Critique,* as cited in MES, vol. 2, p. 329.

22   *women . . . ovaries:* see I. de Valverde, *Historia de las composicion del cuerpo humano,* in NGI, p. 122.

    human knowledge . . . "womb of nature": see Francis Bacon, *The New Organon,* bk. 1, aphorisms 1, 109.

    "it is annoying": see Boccaccio, *Concerning Famous Women,* cited in PA, p. 22.

    in the inferior world: see Matthew Hale, *The Primitive Origination of Mankind,* as cited in Leis, *op. cit.,* p. 33.

    power in words: see Ficino, as cited in Leis, p. 37.

    he who calls: see Francis Bacon, *Valerus Terminus,* as cited in Leis, p. 51.

    man fell: see Francis Bacon, as cited in Leis, p. 49.

    "knowing the force": see René Descartes, as cited in Bernal, *The Scientific and Industrial Revolutions,* p. 447.

    it is predicted: see Francis Bacon, *Atlantis,* as cited in Lewis Mumford, *The Myth of the Machine,* p. 117.

23   two spaces: see Newton's theology and the divine sensorium, as described in MFM, pp. 244–55. (Newton makes clear, however, in *Opticks,* p. 379, that God has no need·of the universe as an organ:

Page

"God has no need of such organs . . ."). See also MFM, pp. 143–50, on Henry More's concept of "Space as the divine presence."

the vulgar: see Newton, *Principia,* p. 78. See also MFM, p. 245.

"Man has been": see Adam Sedgwick, *Discourse on the Studies of the University,* as cited in Gertrude Himmelfarb, *Darwin and the Darwinian Revolution,* p. 235.

changes: see Loren Eiseley, *The Firmament of Time,* and DC.

And the sun will soon: see Lord Kelvin: "inhabitants of the earth cannot continue to enjoy the light and heat essential to their life . . ." as cited in DC, p. 238.

last of a series: see Louis Agassiz, *An Essay in Classification,* as cited in DC, p. 97. According to the progressionists, the link between species was of "a higher and immaterial nature." See Hugh Miller, *The Testimony of the Rocks.*

appearance of man: see Sedgwick, "Presidential Address before the Geological Society of London, 1831," as cited in DC, p. 266.

in this universe a stair: see Sir Thomas Browne, *Religio Medici,* as cited in DC, p. 7.

And woman is "the idlest part": see Earl of Rochester, as cited in TH, p. 162.

"fair Aurelia's womb": ibid.

24 *that savage races:* see Hugh Miller, *op. cit.,* pp. 229–31.

All nature . . . designed to benefit: see Rev. William Buckland, *The Bridgewater Treatises* vol. 1, p. 524. See also William Paley, *Natural Theology.*

Animals run: see DC, p. 177.

teeth were created: see Richard Westfall, *Science and Religion in Seventeenth-Century England,* p. 50, and his discussion of the virtuosi.

"exist solely": see Arthur Schopenhauer, *Parerga and Paralipomena,* "On Women," as cited in DS, p. 199.

nature has made it natural: see Henry A. Jones, *The Case of Rebellious Susan,* as cited in TH, p. 217. Sir Richard, in this nineteenth-century play, urges Elaine, a New Woman, to cook her husband a good dinner, etc. He says, "It's Nature that is so ungallant and unkind to your sex," and later: "Nature's darling woman is a stay-at-home woman."

"a monster more horrible": see James McGrigor Allan, "The Real Differences," as cited in p. 220.

nature has closed: see *Saturday Review of Literature,* September 12, 1857, editorial ridiculing the attempts of Barbara Leigh Smith and Bessie Parkes, who worked for "widened professional and educational opportunities for women," as cited in TH, p. 211.

24　*"Nature is the art":* see Browne, *op. cit.,* in DC, p. 13.

secret cabinet: see Linnaeus, as cited in DC, p. 23.

we are assured: see Paley, *op. cit.,* as cited in DC, p. 176.

But still: see DC, p. 178.

doubt . . . rocks of the earth: see James Hutton: "Thus . . . from the top of the mountain to the shore of the seas . . . everything is in a state of change," in DC, pp. 69–75.

"nature lives in motion": see Hutton, as cited in Eiseley, *The Firmament,* p. 25.

"traces of vanished": see DC, p. 196.

"undermine": Charles Darwin, as cited in DC, p. 172.

25　*teeth appear:* see Charles Darwin, *Foundations of the Origin of the Species,* ed. Frances Darwin, as cited in DC, p. 196.

"it is derogatory": ibid., DC, p. 193.

nature makes nature: see DC, p. 198.

bones of animals: see Darwin, *Journal of Researches,* as cited in DC, p. 162.

in 1852: see Vinzenz Ziswiler, *Extinct and Vanishing Animals.*

"immanent purpose": see Lamarck, as cited in DC, pp. 50–1.

oranguntan: ibid.

nature evolves species: see Ernst Haeckel, *The Evolution of Man,* as cited in DC, p. 334.

forces of nature . . . blind will: see Arthur Schopenhauer, *The World as Will and Representation,* trans. E. F. J. Payne.

merciless and insatiable: see Karl Stern, *The Flight from Woman,* p. 119, for his discussion of Schopenhauer and the Marquis de Sade.

red in tooth and claw: see Alfred Lord Tennyson, *In Memoriam.*

nature lives and breathes: see Marquis de Sade, *Justine,* as cited in Stern, *op. cit.,* pp. 113–15.

26　*woman's nature is more natural:* see Friedrich Nietzsche, *Beyond Good and Evil,* p. 169.

Woman!: see Robert Gould, *A Satyr Against Wooing,* as cited in TH, p. 164.

opposed to the will: see Schopenhauer, *The World.*

evolution of the brain: see "Wallace and the Brain," in DC, pp. 290–324.

only through reason: see Schopenhauer, *The World.*

"the genitals are the real focus": ibid., p. 330.

organs compete: see Wilhelm Roux, *Der Kampf der Theile Organismus,* as cited in DC, p. 335.

woman's generative: see Dr. Charles Meigs, as cited in SE, p. 347.

woman is what she: see Dr. Horatio Storer, as cited in SE, p. 347.

"degraded to the level": see Augustus Kinsley Gardner, *Conjugal Sins,* as cited in SE, p. 347.

"ovarian neuralgia": see A. L. Smith, "Are Modern School Methods in Keeping with Physiological Knowledge?" as cited in PSV, p. 59.

the thinking woman: see Barbara Cross, *The Educated Woman in America,* as cited in Adrienne Rich, "The Theft of Childbirth," *New York Review of Books,* October 2, 1975.

27 *And the young:* see Sylvanus Stall, *What a Young Man Ought to Know,* as cited in PSV, p. 219.

Higher education: see A. L. Smith, "Higher Education of Woman and Race Suicide," as cited in PSV, p. 61.

Woman's greatest: see Joseph A. Conwell, *Manhood's Morning,* as cited in PSV, p. 83.

"All corporeal": see Charles Darwin, *The Origin of Species,* p. 450.

"The brain": see Louis Agassiz, *The Structure of Animal Life,* as cited in DC, p. 97.

woman is less evolved: see PSV, pp. 57–8, 61.

Men and women differ: see Hegel, *Grundlinien der Philosophie des Rechts,* as cited in NGI, p. 290.

her evolution resulted: see PSV, pp. 57–8.

that the later development of the: see Pfitzner, cited in a refutation by Havelock Ellis in *Man and Woman,* as cited in PA, p. 117.

28 *woman's brain mass:* see PSV, pp. 56–7, 66–7. See also Ellis, in PA, p. 116, and James McGrigor Allan, "The Real Differences," as cited in TH, pp. 220–1 *n.*

lacking in reason; see Schopenhauer, "On Women," as cited in PA, p. 121.

in the womb: see Meckel, as cited in HS, p. 260.

mentally women: see Allan, *op. cit.,* in TH., p. 219.

thoughts of women: see Herbert Spencer, *Principles of Psychology,* as cited in PSV, p. 63. See also Hegel, *Philosophy of Right,* as cited in PA, pp. 120–1.

"Science offends the modesty": see Nietzsche, *Beyond Good and Evil,* p. 87.

that abstract thought: see Sir Almroth E. Wright, *The Unexpurgated Case Against Women Suffrage,* as cited in TH, p. 221 *n.*

female organism transmits: see William K. Brooks, "The Condition of Women from a Zoological Point of View," as cited in PSV, p. 69.

"the male": see Remy De Gourmont, *The Natural Philosophy of Love,* p. 52.

28   *"Undergo . . . a severe":* see Charles Darwin, *The Descent of Man in Relation to Sex,* as cited in PA, p. 113.

29   *without the male:* see De Gourmont, *op. cit.,* p. 52.

mankind has evolved: see DC, pp. 337–9, on Condorcet and others regarding the scale of being. See also Himmelfarb, *op. cit.,* p. 230, on Tennyson: "evolution . . . becomes . . . the promise of salvation."

arise and fly: see Alfred Lord Tennyson, *In Memoriam.*

all animals are merely: see Oken, as cited by Alexander Gade von Aesch, *Natural Science in German Romanticism,* in DC, p. 95.

And striving: see Emerson, as cited in DC, p. 52.

Man is an animal, and he is the most: Eiseley puts the date of the recognition that man is an animal at 1859, the date of the publication of the *Origin,* as cited in DC, p. 255. See also DC, p. 97, citing Luis Agassiz, *An Essay in Classification:* "that man is the last of a term of a series, beyond which there is no material progress possible . . ." and DC p. 287–324.

according to the laws of survival: see Lamarck and Erasmus Darwin, as discussed in DC, p. 51. (Note: Lamarck meant unconscious volition, but the popular nineteenth-century view was that the conscious will shaped evolution.)

"What was her": see Charles Kingsley, *Yeast,* as cited in TH, p. 192.

"stronger and . . . better equipped": see Lamarck, *Zoological Philosophy,* as cited in DC, p. 52.

women were not meant: see Marquis de Sade, *La Nouvelle Justine,* as cited in DS, p. 83.

That woman is as: ibid.

that the able: see Charles Darwin, *Origin,* pp. 95–100.

the wolf . . . victor . . . allowed to breed: ibid, p. 96 and passim.

30   *That the species are shaped:* ibid., p. 450: "Thus, from the war of nature, from famine and death, the most exalted object which we are capable of conceiving, namely the production of the higher animals, directly follows."

"vast wilderness": see John Todd, *The Students Manual* and *The Young Man, Hints Addressed to Young Men of the United States;* and George Rogers Taylor, *The Transportation Revolution,* as cited in SE, pp. 366–7.

sons be raised: see Isaac Ray, *Mental Hygiene,* and Amariah Brigham, *Remarks on the Influence of Mental Cultivation and Mental Excitement on Mental Health,* as cited in SE, p. 337.

that the young man must be constantly seeking: see Todd, *Students Manual,* as cited in SE, p. 339.

education he must sacrifice: see Brooks, "Women from the Standpoint of a Naturalist," as cited in PSV, p. 71.

That in evolution: see Hardaker, "Science and the Woman Question," and Grant Allen, "Women's Place in Nature," in PSV, p. 66.

That as the male brain became: see Spencerians, as cited in PSV, pp. 66–7.

Women are the weaker: see Herbert Spencer, *The Study of Sociology,* as cited in PSV, pp. 62–3.

And that because . . . "For, as nature": see Schopenhauer, "On Women," as cited in Karl Stern, *op. cit.,* p. 112.

those women who: see Spencer, *The Study,* as cited in PSV, p. 62.

nature has provided men: see Schopenhauer, *The World,* vol. 2, p. 335.

women skilled in intuition: see Spencer, *The Study,* as cited in PSV, p. 63.

girls should: see Brooks, "Women from the Standpoint of a Naturalist," as cited in PSV, p. 71.

nature endows: see Schopenhauer, "On Women," as cited in PA, p. 123.

31   *beauty vanishes:* see Schopenhauer, "On Women," as cited in DS, p. 199.

men do not like: see *Saturday Review* editorial, as cited in TH, p. 211.

society can be thankful: see Woods Hutchinson, "The Economics of Prostitution," as cited in PSV, p. 56.

ovum is passive: I owe this language to Carolyn Iltis, who cited Edmund Cope, "The Two Perils of the Indo European: What Evolution Teaches."

That in sperm . . . semen est: see Gardner, *Our Children,* as cited in SE, p. 341. *"Totus homo,"* etc., is "an expression of Feruel."

runts, feeble: see Gardner, *op. cit.,* as cited in SE, p. 342.

sperm functions: see Brooks, "The Condition of Women," as cited in PSV, p. 69.

ovum transmits: ibid.

sperm . . . newer variations: ibid.

That the male mind: see Brooks, "The Condition of Women," as cited in PSV, p. 69.

"All organic beings": see Darwin, *Foundations,* as cited in DC, p. 101.

all creatures are pressed: see Darwin, *Origin,* p. 29: "In the next chapter the Struggle for existence amongst all organic beings throughout the world, which inevitably follows from the high geometrical rate of their increase, will be considered. This is the doctrine of Malthus applied to the whole animal and vegetable kingdom."

all the plants: see Condolle, as cited in DC, p. 101.

tendency of all beings: see Comte de Buffon, as cited in DC, p. 40. See also Thomas Malthus, "An Essay on the Principle of Population as It Affects the Future Improvement of Society," included in *The Autobiography of Science,* ed. Moulton and Schifferes: ". . . I say that the power of population is indefinitely greater than the power in the earth to produce subsistence for man."

the human race tends: see Malthus, *Essay,* as described in HS, p. 275. (Actually, Malthus, in his essay, lists other boundaries, such as "failure of agricultural enterprise.")

natural government: see John Hunter, *Essays and Observations,* as cited in DC, p. 329.

war serves: see Sir Arthur Keith, Darwin's official biographer, as cited in Himmelfarb, *op. cit.,* p. 417.

32 *history of human society:* see Karl Marx and Friedrich Engels, *The Communist Manifesto.* (When Marx read the *Origin,* he saw it as "a basis in natural science for the class struggle in history." See Himmelfarb, *op. cit.,* p. 421, citing Marx.)

development of large: see John D. Rockefeller, as cited in Himmelfarb, *op. cit.,* p. 420.

each organism: see Thomas Huxley, as cited in DC, p. 335.

human body: ibid.

"milk-white": see John Keats, *Poetical Works.*

"every woman is always": see Allan, "The Real Differences," as cited in TH, p. 220.

during menses: ibid.

pity is the offspring: see Jean Jacques Rousseau, "Discourse on the Origin and Foundations of Inequality," *First and Second Dialogues,* pp. 130–2.

poets . . . learned: see Nietzsche, *Beyond Good and Evil,* p. 219.

women appear: see Darwin, *Descent,* as cited in PA, p. 112.

pity . . . closer to the state: see Rousseau, "Discourse," pp. 130–3.

"the sick are": see Nietzsche, *A Genealogy of Morals,* as cited in PA, p. 127.

a man whose house: see T. W. H. Crosland, *Lovely Woman,* as cited in TH, pp. 222–3.

men must work: see Reverend Charles Kingsley, "Three Fishers Went Sailing," song with accompaniment for pianoforte; music by J. Hullah.

who would sympathize: see Schopenhauer, "On Women," as cited in DS, p. 200.

surface . . . Australian: see R. Sweichel, as cited in DC, p. 277.

33 *all the stages:* see Auguste Comte, "The Science of Society," included in *Varieties of Classic Social Theory,* ed. Hendrik Leek, p. 68.

That the struggle . . . face of the earth: see Darwin, *Life and Letters of Darwin,* as cited in DC, p. 283.

gloom of the forest: see Henry Piddington, *Journal of the Asiatic Society of Bengal,* as cited in DC, p. 262.

Hottentots: see DC, p. 260–1, citing accounts of voyagers of the late seventeenth and eighteenth centuries.

tribes in South America: see *Science Progress,* 1914, as cited in DC, p. 290.

Negroes . . . like orang-utans: see Carl Vogt, *Lectures on Man,* as cited in DC, pp. 262–3.

among the lower races: ibid.

And woman . . . like the Negro: see PSV, p. 57.

intellectual faculties: see Carl Vogt, *Lectures on Man,* as cited in PSV, p. 51.

woman's brain . . . "lower races": see Allan, "The Real Differences," as cited in TH, pp. 220–1 *n.*

"approach to the animal type": see Vogt, *op. cit.,* as cited in DC, p. 263.

From voyages: see Geoffrey Atkinson, *The Extraordinary Voyage in French Literature before 1700,* as cited in DC, p. 28.

Slavery . . . a condition: see Nietzsche, *Beyond Good and Evil,* p. 169. Nietzsche draws the analogy here between woman's condition and slavery.

A woman should be: see John Cordy Jeaffreson, *A Woman in Spite of Herself,* as cited in TH, p. 194.

"I am a woman": ibid. (These words and the words above are put into the mouth of a woman.)

both the emancipated: see PSV, pp. 57–8.

34 *"the generous sentiments":* see George Fitzhugh, *Sociology for the South,* as cited in TH, p. 190 *n.*

But as to women and men: see DC, chap. 8.

struggle for existence: see A. von Humboldt, *Personal Narrative of Travels,* as cited in DC, p. 183.

theory of mutation may make it possible: see Thomas Case, *Science,* 1905, as cited in DC, p. 250.

"animals our fellow": see Charles Darwin, *Life and Letters,* as cited in DC, p. 352. (These are the words of Darwin as a young man.)

The redder blood: see J. D. Bernal, *Science and Industry in the Nineteenth Century,* p. 59, referring to Julius Robert Mayer's observations relevant to the equivalence of heat and motion.

Heat and motion: ibid, pp. 63–4.

The engineer: see Freidrich Engels, *Dialectics of Nature,* as cited in Bernal, *Science,* p. 42: ". . . the practical mechanics of the engineer arrives at the concept of *work* and forces it on the theoretician."

Heat, energy and work: see Bernal, *Science,* on the work of Joule, p. 43. See also EV, p. 49.

"Where are the limits . . . their breathing and in their movement": see Marc Sequin, *Traité sur l'influence des chemin de fer,* as cited in Bernal, *Science,* pp. 53–5. (Sequin was a "pioneer of railway construction in France" and an "enthusiast for the Industrial Revolution.")

36 *The energy of a man:* see Gardner, *Old Wine,* as cited in SE, p. 358.

And the train: see George Stephenson, as cited in Bernal, *Science,* p. 50. (Stephenson was an engineer who developed workable railroad tracks.)

animal heat: see Lavoisier, as cited in Bernal, *Science,* p. 43. *Both the sexes:* see M. A. Hardaker, as cited in PSV, p. 65.

Rules for mobilizing: see Ben Franklin, as discussed in Meyer, *Positive Thinkers,* cited in HH, p. 72.

"are naturally": see Todd, *Students Manual,* as cited in SE, p. 338.

Cures . . . "torpid": see Ray, *Mental Hygiene,* as cited in HH, p. 73.

Women are not: ibid., p. 74.

men should concentrate: ibid., p. 73.

Under proper control: see Gardner, as cited in HH, pp. 182–3.

men who lose: see W., "Insanity Produced by Masturbation," *Boston Medical and Surgical Note,* as cited in HH, p. 180.

entropy, the amount: see Dietrich Schroeer, *Physics and Its Fifth Dimension: Society,* pp. 127–8.

the earth cannot: ibid., p. 130, citing the calculations of Lord Kelvin.

"The energies of our": see Arthur James Balfour, *The Foundations of Belief* as cited in *The Oxford Dictionary of Quotations.*

promiscuous intercourse: see Dr. Benjamin Rush, *Medical Inquiries and Observations upon Diseases of the Mind,* as cited in HH, p. 76.

"generative energy": see H. D. Thoreau, *Walden,* as cited in HH, p. 182.

young man who: see PSV, p. 219.

37   *Through those two:* see Charles Baudelaire, "Sed Non Satiata."
      sturdy manhood: see W., *op. cit.,* as cited in SE, p. 342.
      Alas and dissolute: see Baudelaire, *op. cit.*
      victim of masturbation: see W., *op. cit.,* as cited in HH, p. 180.
      to break: see Baudelaire, *op. cit.*
      until all powers of the system: see W., *op. cit.,* as cited in HH, p. 180.
      I shall go . . . dazzling dream: see Baudelaire, "La Chevelure."
      practice of building . . . allowing the thoughts . . . dissipation: see Todd, *Students Manual,* as cited in HH, p. 176.
      I shall plunge: see Baudelaire, "La Chevelure."
      no nation has ever: see Todd, *Students Manual,* as cited in HH, p. 187.
38   *Only lust:* see Orson Fowler, *Creative and Sexual Sciences,* as cited in PSV, p. 201.
      "Prostitution": see Baudelaire, "Le Crépuscle du soir."
      the soldier: see *A message to the soldiers of the British Expeditionary Force, 1914, to be kept by each soldier in his Active Service Pay-Book,* as cited in *The Oxford Dictionary of Quotations.*
      "Only science": see Ivan P. Pavlov, *Lectures on Conditioned Reflexes,* p. 41.
      behavior of dogs: see Pavlov, *Conditioned Reflexes.*
      Of charges of electricity . . . history that can be determined: see EV, "Field, Relativity," and on Faraday's discoveries and Maxwell's equations, pp. 125–64.
      All kinds of stimuli: see Pavlov, *Conditioned Reflexes,* and J. B. Watson and behaviorism as discussed in HS, pp. 345–5.
39   *All matter:* see AM, p. 229 and passim. See also atomic table in HS, p. 385. See also Thomas S. Kuhn, *The Structure of Scientific Revolutions,* pp. 134–5: "Chemists could not, therefore, simply accept Dalton's theory on the evidence, for much of that was still negative. Instead even after accepting the theory, they had still to beat nature into line. . . . When it was done, even the percentage composition of well-known compounds was different. The data themselves had changed."
      hard, impenetrable: see Isaac Newton, as cited in TP, p. 56.
      ultimate reality: see Alfred North Whitehead, *Science and the Modern World,* p. 17: "There persists, however, throughout the whole period the fixed scientific cosmology which presupposes the ultimate fact of an irreducible brute matter." See also AM, p. 270.
      Movements of molecules: see EV, pp. 59–62, on Brownian movement.

nothing in this world: see CD, p. 3. Freud is the one, of course, who challenges this certainty, saying, "This is a deceptive appearance."

X-rays: see Robert Reid, *Marie Curie,* p. 58: "He gave the rays the name X because this was the physicists' usual symbol for an unknown.

Radium is isolated: ibid., pp. 85–7.

Radioactivity: ibid., p. 96. (When Frederick Soddy, on discovering the spontaneous disintegration of the atom, called this "transmutation," Rutherford answered, "For Mike's sake, Soddy, don't call it *transmutation.* They'll have our heads off as alchemists.")

The unconscious is discovered . . . at any given moment: see NIL, "Dissection of the Personality."

From the phosphorescent: see HS, pp. 371–6.

The energy of the self: see NIL, "Dissection," p. 73. Freud, *Psychopathology of Everyday Life.* Passim. Freud, *The History of the Psychoanalytic Movement,* p. 62. Freud and Breuer, *Studies on Hysteria.* Passim.

40   *women have a weaker:* see Freud, "Civilized Sexual Morality and Modern Neurosis" ("Woman is endowed with a weaker sexual instinct"), as cited in Kate Millett, *Sexual Politics,* p. 192. See also NIL, "Femininity," p. 131: "Furthermore it is our impression that more constraint has been applied to the libido when it is pressed into the service of the feminine function."

self is made: see NIL, "Dissection," p. 72.

less superego: see Freud, "Some Psychological Consequences of the Anatomical Distinction Between the Sexes," in *Sexuality and the Psychology of Love,* p. 193: "Their super-ego is never so inexorable, so impersonal, so independent of its emotional origins as we require it to be in men." See also NIL, "Femininity," p. 129. See also Freud, *Totem and Taboo* (Freud compares the psychology of "the primitive races" with the psychology of the neurotic). And in NIL, "Dissection," p. 75, Freud describes the id as "primitive."

less ego: This formulation in language is my parody of Freud's view of the feminine. (Always less.) See "Femininity," passim, for his description of the female ego as being formed essentially from a sense of mutilation. See also "Anatomical Distinction," p. 193 ("They are less ready to submit to the great necessities of life"), and CD for Freud's notion that it is men who cope with reality and build civilization. Of his eventual wife, Martha Bernays, Freud wrote: "Am I to think of my delicate sweet girl as a competitor?" see *Letters of Sigmund Freud,* as cited in Mary Ellmann, *Thinking About Women,* p. 88.

women are less objective: see Freud, "Anatomical Distinction," *op. cit.,* p. 193.

men are responsible: see CD, p. 50 and passim.

Small boys: see Erik Erikson, "Womanhood and the Inner Space," as cited in Millett, *op. cit.,* p. 214. See also Helene Deutsch, *The Psychology of Women,* vol. 1, p. 282.

enclosures: ibid.

to be female: see CD, p. 50.

man is confined: see EV, p. 155: "Unfortunately we cannot place ourselves between the sun and the earth, to prove there the exact validity of the law of inertia and to get a view of the rotating earth . . . the earth is our co-ordinate system."

that confinement: see EV, p. 155: "All our experiments must be performed on the earth on which we are compelled to live."

A group of scientists: see EV, "Outside and Inside the Elevator," pp. 214–16.

electromagnetic field: see EV, p. 145.

41 *velocity of the earth:* see EV, pp. 155–6.

a single event: see TP, p. 62.

near the speed of light: see EV, p. 186.

The elevator . . . true absolutely: see EV, pp. 214–16.

Time and space: see EV, "Field, Relativity."

heartbeat of a man: see Einstein, as cited in UE, p. 65.

simultaneous: see TP, p. 62. See also Ernst Cassirer, *Substance and Function and Einstein's Theory of Relativity,* p. 381.

"two frightening ghosts": see EV, p. 238.

The idea of time: see NIL, "Dissection," pp. 74–6.

A young woman . . . free to drink: see Freud and Breuer, *Hysteria,* pp. 55–83. See also Freud, *The Origin and Development of Psychoanalysis,* p. 7.

In the dream: see Freud: *ibid.,* p. 40.

42 *trip backward . . . wishes and memories still:* see Freud, *Psychoanalytic Movement,* pp. 44–5. See also NIL, "Dissection," p. 74.

Space and time: see UE, p. 21.

Gravity: see HS, pp. 407–10.

universe is shaped: see UE, pp. 103, 91.

empty space: see UE, p. 50, and TP, p. 64.

universe is curved: see EV, p. 237.

Matter . . . an event: see Whitehead, *Science and the Modern World.* See also EV, pp. 241–2.

Mass changes . . . matter is a form: see EV, pp. 241–3, 196–7. See also AM, p. 280.

The distinction: see UE, p. 70.

no real: see EV, p. 242.

the id, the ego: see NIL, "Dissection," p. 79.

before the emergence: see NIL, "Dissection," p. 63 and passim, and "Femininity," passim.

43 *she seeks to merge:* see NIL, "Dissection," p. 63.

thoughts of women are formless: see Ellmann, *op. cit.,* p. 55 and passim.

"and it was": see James Joyce, *Ulysses.*

impossible to picture: see Sir James Jeans, as cited in UE, p. 30, and TP, pp. 208–23.

women show a bias: see Bacofen, as cited in Deutsch, *op. cit.,* vol. 1, p. 284.

Discontinuity . . . wave and a particle: see EV, p. 249 and passim.

A duality: see UE, p. 30.

"as meaningless as": see UE, p. 30.

"the riddle": see NIL, "Femininity," p. 116.

Häupter . . . Menschenhäupter: see NIL, "Femininity," p. 113, citing Heine, *Nordsee.*

behavior of the ovum: see NIL, "Femininity," p. 114.

female must: ibid., pp. 118–28.

44 *passivity now has:* ibid., p. 128: "Passivity now has the upper hand."

what a woman wants: see letter from Freud to Marie Bonaparte in Ernest Jones, *The Life and Work of Sigmund Freud,* p. 377.

what is known: see Irwin Schrodinger, "Our Image of Matter," in Heisenberg, Born, Schrodinger and Auger, *On Modern Physics,* p. 46. See also UE, p. 24, and Werner Heisenberg, "The Uncertainty Principle," in Moulton and Schifferes, *The Autobiography of Science,* p. 56. (In EV, p. 31, Einstein compares the universe to a pocket watch which is forever closed.)

nature of the universe: see UE, p. 78.

nature of the psyche: see NIL, "Dissection," p. 69.

Under the gaze: see UE, pp. 30–4.

absolutely: ibid., p. 37.

science will never know: see UE, p. 37: "One by-product of this surrender is a new argument for the existence of free will."

behavior of the single: see EV, p. 285.

quality of nature: see AM, p. 290.

memories of women: see NIL, "Femininity," p. 120.

if the universe . . . all the choir: see Einstein quoting Berkeley, as cited in UE, p. 21.

Still, prediction: see EV, p. 27. See also De Santillana, *op. cit.,* "Necessity, Contingency and Natural Law."

electrons will be studied: see AM, p. 289, and EV, p. 249 and passim.

45 *in the year 1950:* see Talcott Parsons and Robert F. Bales, *Family Socialization and Interaction Process,* p. 14.

domestic pattern: see Parsons, *Essays in Sociological Theory,* p. 224.

Waves of probability: see EV, pp. 288–9.

impossible to find: ibid., and Heisenberg et al., *op. cit.*

"tendencies to exist": see TP, p. 68.

The universe . . . finite . . . void: see UE, pp. 110–18.

small boys: see CD and Freud, *Totem and Taboo,* and NIL, pp. 85–6.

re-creation of the father: see CD, p. 13.

from the love: see NIL, pp. 85–6, 129.

to abate . . . nature: see CD, p. 18.

46 *girls . . . born castrated:* see Freud, "Female Sexuality," in *Sexuality,* p. 202.

"momentous": see Freud, "Anatomical Distinction" as cited in Millett, *op. cit.,* p. 181.

wound . . . all women, ibid., p. 183.

women invented: see NIL, "Femininity," p. 132.

woman . . . debased: see Freud, "Femininity," as cited in Millett, *op. cit.,* p. 185.

clitoris is a prototype: see Freud, "Fetishism," in *Sexuality,* p. 219: "just as the normal prototype of an organ felt to be inferior is the real little penis of the woman, the clitoris."

small girls develop: see NIL, "Femininity," pp. 124–35.

illnesses of the mind: see Freud, *Origin,* p. 16.

ego is split: see NIL, "Dissection," p. 59.

A young woman: see Breuer, *Hysteria,* "Case Histories: Fräulein Anna O."

Antimatter . . . supernova: see AM, p. 294.

47 *An instinct . . . power over nature;* see CD, pp. 70–4.

in woman her body: see NIL, "Femininity," p. 116. The suppression of aggression, Freud writes, is imposed both "constitutionally" and by society. "Thus," he writes, "masochism . . . is truly feminine."

a new fantastic toilette . . . carriage flies along like mad: see Sacher-Masoch, *Venus in Furs,* as cited in Gertrud Lenzer, "On Masochism: A Contribution to the History of a Phantasy and Its Theory." (Sacher-Masoch's work was "the principal source of Krafft-Ebing's description and definition of masochism.")

the female cell: see Marie Bonaparte, *Female Sexuality,* as cited in Millett, p. 204.

the infant girl: ibid., p. 205.

young girls dream: see Deutsch, *op. cit.,* vol. 1, p. 255.

women have a lust: see Freud, "The Economic Problems of Masochism," as cited in Millett, op. cit., p. 195.

when a woman steps: see Deutsch, *op. cit.,* vol. 1, p. 285.

the meson: see AM, p. 294.

lambda . . . kaon: see table in TP, p. 227.

structure invisible: see Geoffrey Chew, as cited in TP, p. 274: "A truly elemental particle—completely devoid of internal structure—could not be subject to any forces that would allow us to detect its existence."

48   *Every question:* see EV, p. 292: "Every important advance brings new questions. Every development reveals . . . new and deeper difficulties." See also Einstein, as cited in TP, p. 41: "As far as the laws of mathematics refer to reality, they are not certain; and as far as they are certain, they do not refer to reality."

spectators and part: see Niels Bohr, as cited in UE, p. 127.

amorphous: see UE, p. 92.

time does not: see TP, p. 62.

absolute space . . . Solid elements: ibid., pp. 61–2.

LAND

Territory: These are the names of places passed through by Lewis and Clark. Their trip through this territory made the western expansion possible. See Bernard de Voto in his Introduction to *The Journals of Lewis and Clark:* ". . . it satisfied desire and it created desire: the desire of the westering nation."

The Struggle: See Francis Parkman, *The Oregon Trail.*

The Abyss: See John James Audubon, "The Lost One," in *The Delineations of American Scenery and Character,* as quoted by Annette Kolodny, *The Lay of the Land.*

Guide: See Grace Raymond Hebard, *Sacajawea: A Life of the Indian Guide,* and *The Journals of Lewis and Clark.*

Possession: See Louis B. Wright and Elaine Fowler, *The Moving Frontier.*

Use: See Barry Commoner, *The Closing Circle,* on single-crop land usage and the effects of inorganic nitrogen fertilizer. See also Murray Bookchin, *Our Synthetic Environment:* "In many areas of the United States the land has been turned into an early lifeless, inorganic medium that must be nursed along like an invalid at the threshold of death." See also in Bookchin, reference to the theory of Justus von Liebig that the soil was essentially dead. In fact, as Bookchin writes: "The soil," in a natural state, "is a highly differentiated world of living and inanimate things . . . always in the process of formation."

Exploration: This description of taking a soil sample from Mars was taken from a story in the San Francisco *Chronicle,* August 9, 1976.

TIMBER

See Ellis Lucas, *The Big Woods,* on the beginnings of the lumber industry on the West Coast. For advice such as: "The forest should be close to the sawmill," see various forest management texts, for example, *Managing the Small Forest* (U.S. Dept. of Agriculture) or A. J. Panshin and E. S. Harrar and W. J. Baker and P. B. Proctor, *Forest Products.* For comments on the management of office labor and on labor management in general, see tests such as Henry and M. C. H. Niles, *The Office Supervisor,* or Leffingwell and Robinson, *Textbook of Office Management.* "Production (Current of the Years)" is my description of a photograph of a giant redwood felled with hand tools, the crew posed around it, taken on the Mendocino coast in the 1930s.

WIND

This description of how to control hurricanes is drawn from a scientific speculation by Dr. Roger Revelle, "A Long View from the Beach," in *The World in 1984,* a book of predictions about future and possible accomplishments of science. The story of the woman who attempts to escape from an asylum was taken from Lara Jefferson's account in *These Are My Sisters.*

COWS

See Nevens, *Dairy Cattle Selection and Feeding.* ("Animals with well-shaped udders are in demand"), or Petersen, *Dairy Science,* for information relevant to the raising of dairy cattle. For a more general discussion of factory farming, see Harrison, "On Factory Farming," in *Animals, Men and Morals,* ed. Godlovitch and see Peter Singer, *Animal Liberation.* For a history of the worship of the Virgin Mary, see Warner, *Alone of Her Sex.* My comments on modern childbirth came from my own experience and those of my friends. See also Suzanne Arms, *Immaculate Deception,* and Kathleen Barry, "The Cutting Edge." I thought the two following quotations relevant here. From Charles Darwin, *The Variation of Plants and Animals under Domestication:* "When we compare highly improved stall-fed cattle with the wilder breeds, or compare mountain and lowland breeds, we cannot doubt that an active life, leading to the free use of limbs and lungs, affects the shape and proportions of the whole body." And from Charlotte Perkins Gilman, *Women and Economics:* ". . . look at the relative condition of a wild cow and a 'milk cow,' . . . the wild cow is a female. She has healthy calves, and milk enough for them; and that is all the femininity she needs. . . . She is a light, strong, swift, sinewy creature, able to run, jump and fight if necessary. We, for economic uses, have artificially developed the cow's capacity for producing milk. She has become a walking milk-machine, bred and tended to that express end, her value measured in quarts."

THE SHOW HORSE

For descriptions of the training and education of show horses and short treatises on their natures, see such books as Alois Podhajsky, *The Riding Teacher;* Captin Elwyn Hartley Edwards, *From Paddock to Saddle;* Noel Jackson, *Effective Horsemanship.*

HER BODY

For extensive descriptions of the fear of the female body in this culture, see Neumann, *The Great Mother;* H. R. Hays, *The Dangerous Sex;* Lederer, *The Fear of Women.* In *"Skin," "Hair," "Womb"* and *"Breast,"* the operations described are procedures in use in this century and were taken from various medical texts such as John Conley, *Face Lift Operation;* Cohen, *Abdominal and Vaginal Hysterectomy: New Techniques Based on Time and Motion Studies;* Danforth, *Textbook of Obstetrics and Gynecology.* Also, Franklyn's *Beauty Surgeon* was consulted. The surgeries described in *"Clitoris"* and *"Vulva"* were popular in the nineteenth century. See Barker-Benfield, "The Spermatic Economy," in *Feminist Studies,* and Angus McClaren, "Medicine and Morality in France 1800–1850," also in *Feminist Studies,* citing Louis Huart: "The lady's doctor has in our days replaced the confessor; and he has gone further than the confessor, because he is the sovereign director of the body and the soul of his client." See also Carol Smith Rosenberg, "Puberty and Menopause: The Cycle of Femininity in 19th Century America," in *Clio's Consciousness Raised.* For a description of clitoridectomy by the man who developed the surgical technique and was a zealous practitioner of it, see Isaac Bauer Brown, *On Surgical Diseases of Women.* For operations of the vulva performed for frigidity and "hyperaesthesia," see T. Galliard Thomas, *A Practical Treatise on the Diseases of Women.* See also Seale Harris, *Women's Surgeon: The Life of Marion J. Sims.*

BOOK TWO

WHERE HE BEGINS

Separation: For proscriptions regarding the clean and the unclean, see Maimonides, *The Code: Book X: The Book of Cleanness.* See also Leviticus, and see Paul Ricoeur, *The Symbolism of Evil.* For the story of Maria Goretti's sainthood after her rape and murder, see Brownmiller, *Against Our Will.* For different tellings of the Kore-Demeter myth, see Nor Hall, *Mothers and Daughters;* C. Kerenyi, *Eleusis;* Jane Ellen Harrison, *Mythology.* Also consulted for this section were Robert Graves, *The Greek Myths,* vols. 1 and 2; Bulfinch's *Mythology: The Age of Fable; The Homeric Hymns* (trans. Apostolos W. Athanassakis); *Larousse World Mythology.* See also Fred Hess, *Chemistry Made Simple; Handbook of Chemistry and Physics,* 52d ed.

The Image: The paintings named in this section are all by Pablo Picasso. See *Homage to Picasso for His Ninetieth Birthday.* "She Was a Phantom of Delight" is by William Wordsworth. The lines "my wife with the hourglass waist," etc., were taken and only slightly changed from the poem "Free Union" by André Breton, as translated by Kenneth White.

Marriage: See James L. Christensen, *The minister's marriage handbook.* See also Genesis, Deuteronomy and Leviticus. See Rosemary Reuther, *Religion and Sexism.* For a discussion of plastics, see Herman Mark, *Giant Molecules,* and Carl R. Theiles, *Men and Molecules.* (Plastics are not biodegradable and their molecular structure has been altered. In this way they are outside life, at least they cease to partake of the normal rhythms of the biosphere.)

HIS POWER

The Hunt: This story of the deer and her fawn being shot was taken from an account published in the *New York Times* by Ruth C. Adams, November 1, 1975. For stories such as the breaking of the back of the hare (a practice of English schoolboys), see Maureen Duffy, "Beasts for Pleasure," in *Animals, Men and Morals.* For a description of methods of hunting elephants, see Iain and Oria Douglas-Hamilton, *Among the Elephants.* For lists of extinct and vanishing species, see Ziswiler, *Extinct and Vanishing Animals.*

The Garden: This is a true story.

HIS VIGILANCE

Space Divided: These measurements were taken from such sources as Alfred Hopkins, *Prisons and Prison Building,* and Sasaki, Walker and Associates, *St. Louis Zoological Garden Development Program, 1962.* The description of the Hexenhaus was taken from Grillot DeGivry: *Witchcraft, Magic and Alchemy.* See also "On Trial for Biocide: 2,4,5-T and 2,4-D."

Science: See Dorothea Lange's photograph "Child and Her Mother, Wapato, Yakima Valley, Washington, 1939."

HIS KNOWLEDGE

What He Sees: See the account of this event by a visitor to Audubon's home in *John James Audubon and His Journals,* ed. Maria Audubon. See also Alice Ford, *John James Audubon.*

Acoustics: See Babcock, Freedman, Norton and Ross, *Sex Discrimination and the Law,* citing from "United States vs. Wiley." See also Susan Brownmiller, *Against Our Will,* especially with regard to rape during war. See also George Berkeley, *Three Dialogues Between Hylas and Philonous,* and David Hume, *A Treatise of Human Nature.* See also "Images of Women in the Talmud," in Ruether, *Religion and Sexism:* "women were not trained in Jewish law; it was inconceivable that they should be able to sit in judgement . . . a woman could not give testimony." Mary Daly has pointed out that the root of the word "testimony" is "testes," because men covered their testicles while swearing in court.

The Argument: See J. Paul Pundel, *Histoire de l'opération Césarienne,* for the arguments of the doctors of theology of the Faculty of Paris. (For aid in translating these arguments I am grateful to Monique Wittig.) I observed strip-mining operations and their effects in East Kentucky. See also John F. Stacks, *Stripping.*

HIS CONTROL

Burial: See George G. Berg, "Hot Wastes from Nuclear Power," in *Nuclear Power Economics and the Environment,* and Wesley Marx, *The Frail Ocean.* Marx reveals that whole movie sets are dumped into the Pacific Ocean off Hollywood, and that the Los Angeles Police Department dumps confiscated revolvers, brass knuckles and sawed-off shotguns into the sea. (The quotations here from Dostoyevsky's *Crime and Punishment* do not appear in the same sequence in which they occur in the novel.)

HIS CERTAINTY

Quantity: The examples of quantification in this section were drawn from various sources, including Hermàn Kahn, *On Thermo-Nuclear Warfare;* Ralph E. Lapp, *Kill and Overkill;* "Mathematics, Population and Food," in Newman, *The World of Mathematics.*

Probability: See Amitai Etzioni, *The Genetic Fix.* See also U.C. Clip Sheet, December 2, 1975, April 6 and November 2, 1976. See also Pierre Simon de Laplace, "Concerning Probability," and Gregor Mendel, "Mathematics of Heredity," in Newman, *The World of Mathematics.*

HIS SECRETS

Dream Life (Marie Curie): See Eve Curie, *Madame Curie;* Robert Reid, *Marie Curie;* Marie Curie, *Pierre Curie* and *Autobiographical Notes of Marie Curie.*

    (Sigmund Freud): See *Bergasse 19: Sigmund Freud's Home and Offices, Vienna, 1938, Photographs by Edmund Engelmann.* See also Ernest Becker, *The Denial of Death;* Sigmund Freud, *The Interpretation of Dreams;* Freud, "Thoughts on War and Death" in *Creativity and the Unconscious.* See also *Sigmund Freud,* ed. Paul Roazen; Freud, *A General Introduction to Psychoanalysis;* C. G. Jung, *Critique of Psychoanalysis.*

    (René Descartes): See Karl Stern, *The Flight from Woman,* chapter on Descartes, for description of Descartes's dream. See also René Dubos, *So Human an Animal.*

    (Isaac Newton): See Augustus de Morgan, *Essays on the Life and Work of Newton,* and J. W. N. Sullivan, *Isaac Newton.* See also Andradne, "Isaac Newton," and John Maynard Keynes, "Newton, the Man," in James R. Newman, *The World of Mathematics;* Giorgio de Santillana, *Reflections on Men and Ideas,* "Newton the Enigma."

    (Charles Darwin): See Gertrude Himmelfarb, *Darwin and the Darwinian Revolution,* for a description of Darwin's daily schedule. See also Herbert Wendt, *Before the Deluge,* and Charles Darwin, *The Origin of Species.*

    (Johannes Kepler): See Arthur Koestler, *The Watershed.*

    (Linnaeus): See Loren Eiseley, *Darwin's Century.*

TERROR

See Herbert S. Zim, *The Universe,* for various measurements of size and distance. See also Hans Jonas, *The Phenomenon of Life:* "it appears that waiving the intelligibility of life—the price which modern knowledge was willing to pay for its title to the greater part of reality—renders the world unintelligible as well." See also Hannah Arendt, *The Origins of Totalitarianism,* especially for her discussion of state terrorism, which she associates with theories of natural and social inevitability.

The Cave: For discussions of caves and labyrinths and their significance in neolithic religion, see Gertrude Rachel Levy, *The Gate of Horn.* See also John Mitchell, *The Earth Spirit,* and John Sharkey, *Celtic Mysteries.* The sea cave described here is located on the northern California coast near Gualala.

BOOK FOUR

MYSTERY

See Gay Gaer Luce, *Biological Rhythms in Human and Animal Physiology,* for observations such as that fiddler crabs "exhibit both solar and lunar rhythms" or that geomagnetic fields influence the movements of earthworms and snails. See also *The Biosphere.*

THE OPENING

We Enter a New Space: The paintings named in this section are all by women. See Ann Sutherland Harris and Linda Nochlin, *Women Artists: 1550–1950;* Karen Petersen and J. J. Wilson, *Women Artists;* Judy Chicago, *Through the Flower.* For a discussion of how events are repeated throughout space, see Itzhak Bentov, *Stalking the Wild Pendulum.*

OUR DREAMS

See Pennethorne Hughes, *Witchcraft;* Margaret A. Murray, *The Witch-Cult in Western Europe;* I. M. Lewis, *Ecstatic Religion.* Regarding powers of serpents, see Merlin Stone, *When God Was a Woman:* "Cassandra was left overnight at the shrine of Delphi as a very young child. When her mother . . . Hecuba arrived . . . she is said to have found the child surrounded by the sacred snakes that were kept in the shrine. They were licking Cassandra's ears. This experience is offered as the explanation of how Cassandra gained the gift of prophecy."

OUR ANCIENT RAGES

Turbulence: On the role of turbulence in the sea in maintaining the biosphere, see G. Evelyn Hutchinson, "The Biosphere," in *The Biosphere.* See also various biographies of Mary Wollstonecraft.

Cataclysm: See Peter Francis, *Volcanoes,* and in particular his account taken from Pliny and modern archaeological evidence of the eruption of Vesuvius.

Consequences: See Peter Marshall, "Streaming Wisdom," and Robert B. Curry, "Watershed Form and Process, The Elegant Balance," in *The Co-Evolution Quarterly* (Winter 1976–77). This was also written from my observation of the effects of strip mining in the East Kentucky Cumberland Mountains, and from my knowledge of the Inez Garcia case. (Inez Garcia was acquitted of the charge of murder after she shot one of two men who participated in her rape.)

POSSIBILITY

The Possible: See Marguerite Wildenhain, *Pottery: Form and Expression;* M. C. Richards, *Centering* and *The Crossing Point;* Hal Riegger, *Raku, Art and Technique;* F. Carlton Ball and Janice Lovoos, *Making Pottery Without a Wheel.*

CLARITY

Vision: See Jane Goodall, *In the Shadow of Man.* I found this quotation from Simone Weil's *First and Last Notebooks* relevant here: "To contemplate what cannot be contemplated (the affliction of another), without running away, and to contemplate the desirable without approaching—that is what is beautiful [many forms of running away]."

One from Another: See Suzanne Arms, *Immaculate Deception,* for accounts of modern midwives and nurses. For a history of the suppression of midwifery, see Thomas Rogers Forbes, *The Midwife and the Witch;* and Barbara Ehrenreich and Deirdre English, *Witches, Midwives and Nurses: A History of Woman Healers;* and see Adrienne Rich, *Of Woman Born.*

Acoustics: See Pete H. Lindsay and Donald A. Nouman. *Human Information Processing: An Introduction to Psychology,* Academic Press (San Diego) 1972, on acoustics and the shape of the ear. (That the sensual is a reality in itself, created by two beings, a dialogue between tree and eye, ear and wood, occurred to me while listening to a concert at 1750 Arch Street.) See also Guy Murchie, *Music of the Spheres,* on the acoustical atom.

THE YEARS

History (Her Hair): See *Declaration of Sentiments and Resolutions,* Seneca Falls, 1948 ("He has never permitted her to exercise her inalienable right to franchise"), as published in *Feminism: The Essential Historical Writings,* ed. Miriam Schneir.

Archives (Her Vulva): See Midge MacKenzie, *Shoulder to Shoulder,* a documentary of the movement for suffrage in England, for the words of Constance Lytton, Emmeline Pankhurst and others.

Letters (Her Clitoris): Quotations in this section are from *The Letters of Emily Dickinson,* ed. Thomas H. Johnson and Theodora Ward ("She came to see us in May"), and from letters written between close women friends in the nineteenth century ("My darling how I long for the time when I shall see you"), as quoted in Carroll Smith-Rosenberg's "The Female World of Love and Ritual: Relations Between Women in Nineteenth Century America."

Records (Her Womb): The record of this event—Report of a trial for criminal abortion—was given to me by Carroll Smith-Rosenberg. I also consulted her paper "H. R. Storer and the Crazy Kangaroo." See also Walter Coles, "Abortion—Its Cause and Treatment," *St. Louis Medical and Surgical Journal,* June 1975, and Simone de Beauvoir's *The Second Sex.* (In the trial for abortion referred to here, the jury found the defendant guilty of performing an abortion but not guilty of manslaughter. He was sentenced to two years in the state prison. Other accounts of abortions in this writing come from my own experience and the experience of my friends.)

OUR NATURE

Elephants do cover their dead with leaves, and are known to remove bones. They teach their young to beware of certain enemies. See Iain and Oria Douglas-Hamilton, *Among the Elephants.*

Matter: For a description of the habitat of red-winged blackbirds in California, see Elna Bakker, *An Island Called California.* Also see the fields around Point Reyes. In her journal Emily Carr writes: "and the blackbird's song permeates your whole you."

BIBLIOGRAPHY

Anderson, Ruth I. *Secretarial Careers.* New York: Henry Z. Walck, 1961.

Anthony, H. D. *Sir Isaac Newton.* New York: Abelard-Schuman, 1960.

Arendt, Hannah. *The Origins of Totalitarianism.* Cleveland: World, 1958.

Ariès, Philippe. *Western Attitudes Toward Death from the Middle Ages to the Present.* Baltimore: Johns Hopkins University Press, 1974.

Aristotle. *Generation of Animals.* Translated by A. L. Peck. Cambridge, Mass.: Harvard University Press, 1963.

Aristotle. *The Physics.* Vols. 1 and 2. Translated by Philip H. Wicksteed and Francis M. Cornford. New York: Putnam, 1929.

Arms, Suzanne. *Immaculate Deception.* Boston: Houghton Mifflin, 1975.

Armstrong, Edward A. *The Way Birds Live.* New York: Dover, 1967.

Audubon, John James. *John James Audubon and His Journals.* Edited by Maria Audubon. New York: Putnam, 1900.

Austin, Mary. *The Land of Little Rain.* Albuquerque: University of New Mexico Press, 1974.

Bachelard, Gaston. *The Poetics of Space.* Translated by Maria Jolas. Boston: Beacon, 1969.

Bacon, Francis. *The New Organon.* Indianapolis: Bobbs-Merrill, 1960.

Bacon, Roger. *Opus Majus.* Vol. 1. Translated by Robert Belle Burke. Philadelphia: University of Pennsylvania Press, 1928.

Bailey, Cyril. *The Greek Atomists and Epicurus.* Oxford: Clarendon Press, 1928.

Bakker, Elna. *An Island Called California.* Berkeley: University of California Press, 1971.

Ball, F. Carlton, and Lovoos, Janice. *Making Pottery Without a Wheel.* New York: Reinhold, 1965.

Barker-Benfield, Ben. "The Spermatic Economy: A Nineteenth-Century View of Sexuality." *Feminist Studies,* Vol. 1, no. 2 (Fall 1972).

Barker-Benfield, G. J. *The Horrors of the Half-Known Life.* New York: Harper & Row, 1976.

Barnett, Lincoln. *The Universe and Dr. Einstein.* New York: New American Library, 1955.

Barry, Kathleen. "The Cutting Edge." Unpublished.

———. "The Judgment of Patricia Hearst." *Chrysalis,* no. 1 (1977).

Bates, Marston. *The Forest and the Sea.* New York: Time-Life Books, 1964.

Bear, Firman E. *Theory and Practice in the Use of Fertilizers.* New York: John Wiley, 1938.

Becker, Ernest. *The Denial of Death.* New York: Free Press, 1973.

Bell, Susan Groag, ed. *Women: From the Greeks to the French Revolution.* Belmont, Cal.: Wadsworth, 1973.

Bentov, Itzhak. *Stalking the Wild Pendulum.* New York: Dutton, 1977.

Bergasse 19: Sigmund Freud's Home and Offices, Vienna, 1938. Photographs by Edmund Engelmann. Introduction by Peter Grey. New York: Basic Books, 1972.

Bernal, J. D. *Science and Industry in the Nineteenth Century.* Bloomington: Indiana University Press, 1970.

———. *The Scientific and Industrial Revolutions.* Vol. 2. Cambridge, Mass.: M.I.T. Press, 1971.

Bernikow, Louise, ed. *The World Split Open.* New York: Random House, 1974.

The Biosphere: A Scientific American Book. San Francisco: W. H. Freeman, 1970.

Bleibtreu, John N. *The Parable of the Beast.* New York: Macmillan, 1967.

Bohr, Neils. *Essays 1958–1962 on Atomic Physics and Human Knowledge.* New York: Random House, 1966.

Bookchin, Murray. *Our Synthetic Environment.* New York: Harper & Row, 1974.

Born, Max. *Experiment and Theory in Physics.* New York: Dover, 1956.

Boyle, Robert. *The Works of Honorable Robert Boyle in six volumes.* London: W. Johnston, 1772.

Bridenthal, Renate, and Koonz, Claudia. *Becoming Visible: Women in European History.* Boston: Houghton Mifflin, 1977.

Bridgewater Treaties: Geology and Mineralogy considered with reference to Natural Theology. Vols. 1 and 2, Rev. William Buckland. London: William Pickering, 1836.

Brockman, C. Frank. *Trees of North America.* New York: Golden Press, 1968.

Brown, Dee. *Bury My Heart at Wounded Knee.* New York: Holt, Rinehart and Winston, 1971.

———. *The Gentle Tamers.* New York: Putnam, 1958.

Brown, Isaac Baker. *On Surgical Diseases of Women.* London: J. W. Davies, 1861.

Brown, Nelson C. *Lumber*. New York: John Wiley, 1947.

Brown, Norman O. *Life Against Death*. New York: Random House, 1959.

———. *Love's Body*. New York: Random House, 1966.

Brownmiller, Susan. *Against Our Will*. New York: Simon & Schuster, 1975.

Budge, E. A. Wallis. *The Egyptian Book of the Dead*. New York: Dover, 1967.

Bulfinch, Thomas. *The Age of Fable*. New York: New American Library, 1962.

Jacob Burckhardt. *The Civilization of the Renaissance in Italy*. New York: Random House, Modern Library, 1954.

Burtt, E. A. *The Metaphysical Foundations of Modern Science*. Garden City, N.Y.: Doubleday, 1954.

Calder, Nigel. *The World in 1984*. Vol. 1. Baltimore: Penguin, 1965.

Capra, Fritjof. *The Tao of Physics*. Berkeley: Shambhala, 1975.

Carr, Emily. *Hundreds and Thousands: The Journals of Emily Carr*. Toronto: Clark, Irwin, 1966.

Carson, Rachel. *Silent Spring*. New York: Fawcett, 1962.

———. *Under the Sea Wind*. New York: New American Library, 1941.

Cassirer, Ernst. *The Problem of Knowledge*. Translated by William Woglom and Charles Hendel. New Haven, Conn.: Yale University Press, 1974.

———. *Substance and Function and Einstein's Theory of Relativity*. Translated by William and Marie Swaboy. New York: Dover, 1953.

Chesler, Phyllis. *Women and Madness*. Garden City, N.Y.: Doubleday, 1972.

Chicago, Judy. *Through the Flower*. New York: Doubleday, 1975.

Christensen, James L. *The Minister's Marriage Handbook*. Westwood, N.J.: Fleming H. Revell, 1966.

Clark, Ronald W. *Einstein: The Life and Times*. Cleveland: World, 1971.

The Code of Maimonides. Book 10: The Book of Cleanness. New Haven, Conn.: Yale University Press, 1944.

The Co-Evolution Quarterly, no. 12 (Winter 1976–77).

Collingwood, R. G. *The Idea of Nature*. New York: Oxford University Press, 1960.

Commoner, Barry. *The Closing Circle*. New York: Alfred A. Knopf, 1971.

Cottrell, Dorothy, and Novick, Sheldon, eds. *Our World in Peril: An Environment Review*. New York: Fawcett, 1971.

Crombie, A. C. *Medieval and Early Modern Science*. Vols. 1 and 2. Garden City, N.Y.: Doubleday, 1959.

Cropper, Elizabeth. "On Beautiful Women, Parmigianino, *Petrarchismo* and the Vernacular Style," *Art Bulletin*, vol. 58, no. 3.

Crop Quality as Affected by Fertilizers. Review of American Literature, 1929.

Curie, Eve. *Madame Curie.* Garden City, N.Y.: Doubleday, 1937.

Curie, Marie. *Pierre Curie and Autobiographical Notes of Marie Curie.* New York: Dover, 1963.

Dagmann, Raymond F. *The Conservation Alternative.* New York: John Wiley, 1975.

Daly, Mary. *Beyond God the Father.* Boston: Beacon, 1973.

———. *The Church and the Second Sex.* New York: Harper & Row, 1968.

Dampier, W. C. *A History of Science.* New York: Cambridge University Press, 1971.

Danforth, David N. *Textbook of Obstetrics and Gynecology.* New York: Harper & Row, 1971.

Darwin, Charles. *The Origin of Species.* New York: New American Library, 1958.

———. *The Variation of Plants and Animals Under Domestication.* Vol. 1. New York: Appleton, 1896.

———. *The Voyage of the Beagle.* New York: Bantam, 1972.

De Beauvoir, Simone. *The Coming of Age.* New York: Putnam, 1972.

DeGivry, Grillot. *Witchcraft, Magic and Alchemy.* New York: Dover, 1971.

de Gourmont, Remy. *The Natural Philosophy of Love.* New York: Collier Books, 1960.

De Morgan, Augustus. *Essays on The Life and Work of Newton.* London: Open Court Publishing Co., 1914.

De Rougemont, Denis. *Love in the Western World.* Translated by Montgomery Belgion. New York: Pantheon, 1956.

De Santillana, Giorgio. *Reflections on Men and Ideas.* Cambridge, Mass.: M.I.T. Press, 1968.

Descartes, René. *Descartes Selections.* Edited by Ralph Eaton. New York: Scribner, 1927.

Deutsch, Helene. *The Psychology of Women.* Vols. 1 and 2. New York: Grune & Stratton, 1944.

De Voto, Bernard, ed. *The Journals of Lewis and Clark.* Boston: Houghton Mifflin, 1953.

Dostoyevsky, Fyodor. *Crime and Punishment.* New York: Random House, Vintage, 1950.

Douglas-Hamilton, Iain and Oria. *Among the Elephants.* New York: Viking, 1975.

Dubos, René. *So Human an Animal.* New York: Scribner, 1968.

Edwards, Elwyn Hartley. *From Paddock to Saddle.* New York: Scribner, 1972.

Ehrenreich, Barbara, and English, Deirdre. *Complaints and Disorders.* Old Westbury, N.Y.: Feminist Press, 1973.

———. *Witches, Midwives and Nurses.* Oyster Bay, N.Y.: Glass Mountain Pamphlets.

Einstein, Albert. *Relativity.* Translated by Robert W. Larson. New York: Crown, 1961.

Einstein, Albert, and Infeld, Leopold. *The Evolution of Physics.* New York: Simon & Schuster, 1938.

Eiseley, Loren. *Darwin's Century.* Garden City, N.Y.: Doubleday, 1961.

———. *The Firmament of Time.* New York: Atheneum, 1974.

Eliade, Mircea. *Myths, Rites, Symbols.* Edited by Wendell C. Beane and William G. Doty. 2 vols. New York: Harper & Row, 1976.

Ellmann, Mary. *Thinking About Women.* New York; Harcourt, Brace & World, 1968.

Etzioni, Amitai. *The Genetic Fix.* New York: Harper & Row, 1973.

Euripides. *The Bacchae.* Translated by Geoffrey Kirk. New York: Prentice-Hall, 1970.

Fairbrother, Nan. *Men and Gardens.* New York: Alfred A. Knopf, 1956.

Farb, Peter. *The Forest.* New York: Time-Life Books, 1963.

Feminism. The Essential Historical Writings. Edited by Miriam Schneir. New York: Random House, Vintage Books, 1972.

Feminist Studies, vol. 1, no. 2 (Fall 1972).

Figes, Eva. *Patriarchal Attitudes.* New York: Fawcett, 1970.

Findhorn Community. *The Findhorn Garden.* New York: Harper & Row, 1975.

Fishbein, Anne Mantel. *Modern Woman's Medical Encyclopedia.* New York: Avon, 1968.

Flexner, Eleanor. *Century of Struggle.* New York: Atheneum, 1968.

Forbes, Thomas Rogers. *The Midwife and the Witch.* New Haven, Conn.: Yale University Press, 1966.

Ford, Alice. *John James Audubon.* Norman: University of Okalhoma Press, 1964.

Fox, Helen M. *Andre Le Nôtre, Garden Architect to Kings.* New York: Crown, 1962.

Francis, Peter. *Volcanoes.* Baltimore: Penguin, 1976.

Fremantle, Anne. *The Age of Belief.* New York: New American Library, 1955.

Freud, Sigmund. *Civilization and Its Discontents.* Translated by Joan Riviere. Garden City, N.Y.: Doubleday, n.d.

———. *Creativity and the Unconscious.* New York: Harper & Row, 1958.

———. *Dora: An Analysis of a Case of Hysteria.* Edited by Philip Rieff. New York: Collier, 1963.

———. *A General Introduction to Psychoanalysis.* Translated by Joan Riviere. New York: Simon and Schuster, 1963.

———. *The History of the Psychoanalytic Movement.* Edited by Philip Reiff. New York: Collier, 1972.

————. *The Interpretation of Dreams*. Edited by James Strachey. New York: Science Editions, 1961.

————. *Leonardo da Vinci and a Memory of His Childhood*. Translated by Alan Tyson. New York: Norton, 1964.

————. *Moses and Monotheism*. Edited by Katherine Jones. New York: Random House, Vintage Books, 1967.

————. *New Introductory Lectures on Psychoanalysis*. Translated by James Strachey. New York: Norton, 1964.

————. *The Origin and Development of Psychoanalysis*. Gateway, 1967. Henry Regnery Co.

————. *Psychopathology of Everyday Life*. Translated by A. A. Brill. New York: New American Library, n.d.

————. *Sexuality and the Psychology of Love*. Edited by Philip Rieff. New York: Collier, 1963.

Freud, Sigmund, and Breuer, Josef. *Studies on Hysteria*. Translated by James Strachey in collaboration with Anna Freud. New York: Avon, 1966.

The Freud Journal of Lou Andreas-Salomé. Translated by Stanley A. Leavy. New York: Harper & Row, 1964.

Frome, Michael. *Whose Woods These Are: The Story of the National Forests*. Garden City, N.Y.: Doubleday, 1962.

Galileo. *Dialogue Concerning the Two Chief World Systems—Ptolemaic and Copernican*. Translated by Stillman Drake. Berkeley: University of California Press, 1953.

Gardiner, Muriel, ed. *The Wolf-Man by the Wolf-Man* with *The Case of the Wolf-Man* by Sigmund Freud. New York: Basic Books, 1971.

Gilman, Charlotte Perkins. *Women and Economics*. New York: Harper & Row, 1966.

Godlovitch, Stanley, Godlovitch, Roslind, and Harris, John, eds. *Animals, Men and Morals*. New York: Grove, 1971.

Goodall, Daphne Machin. *Know Your Pony*. Cranbury, N.J.: A. S. Barnes, 1972.

Goodall, Jane van Lawick. *In the Shadow of Man*. New York: Dell, 1971.

Goodell, W. *Lessons in Gynecology*. Philadelphia: D. G. Brinton, 1887.

Graves, Robert. *The Greek Myths*. Baltimore: Pelican, 1955.

Gray, Dorothy. *Women of the West*. Millbrae, Cal.: Les Femmes, 1976.

Guttmacher, Alan Frank. *Into This Universe*. New York: Viking, 1937.

Haggard, H. W. *Devils, Drugs and Doctors*. New York: Harper, 1929.

Hahn, Emily. *Animal Gardens*. Garden City, N.Y.: Doubleday, 1967.

Hall, Nor. *Mothers and Daughters*. Minneapolis: Rusoff Books, 1976.

Haller, John S. and Robin M. *The Physician and Sexuality in Victorian America*. Urbana: University of Illinois Press, 1974.

Handbook of Chemistry and Physics. 52d ed. Cleveland: Cleveland Chemical Rubber Publishing Co., n.d.

Handbook of Correctional Institution Design and Construction. Washington, D.C. U.S. Bureau of Prisons, 1949.

Harris, Ann Sutherland, and Nochlin, Linda. *Women Artists: 1550–1950.* New York: Alfred A. Knopf, 1976.

Harrison, Jane Ellen. *Mythology.* New York: Harcourt, 1924.

Hartman, Mary, and Banner, Lois W., eds. *Clio's Consciousness Raised.* New York: Harper & Row, 1974.

Harvey, William. *Exercitatio Anatomica de Motu Cordis et Sanguinis in Animalibus.* Translated by Chauncey Leake. Springfield: C. C. Thomas, 1941.

Hawkes, Jacquetta. *Dawn of the Gods.* New York: Random House, 1968.

Hays, H. R. *The Dangerous Sex.* New York: Pocket Books, 1972.

H.D. *Tribute to Freud.* New York: McGraw-Hill, 1974.

Hebard, Grace Raymond. *Sacajawea: A Life of the Indian Guide.* Glendale: Arthur A. Clark, 1933.

Heisenberg, Born, Schrodinger and Auger. *On Modern Physics.* New York: Collier, 1962.

Heisenberg, Werner. *Physics and Beyond.* Translated by Arnold J. Pomerans. New York: Harper & Row, 1971.

Hepworth, Barbara. *A Pictorial Autobiography.* New York: Praeger, 1970.

Herrick, Francis. *Audubon the Naturalist.* Vol. 1. New York: Appleton, 1917.

Hess, Fred C. *Chemistry Made Simple.* Garden City, N.Y.: Doubleday, 1955.

Himmelfarb, Gertrude. *Darwin and the Darwinian Revolution.* Garden City, N.Y.: Doubleday, 1962.

Homage to Picasso for his Ninetieth Birthday. Exhibition for the benefit of the American Cancer Society. Printed in the Netherlands by Joh. Enschedt en Zonen Haarlem, 1971.

The Homeric Hymns. Translated by Apostolos N. Athanassakis. Baltimore: Johns Hopkins University Press, 1976.

Hopkins, Alfred. *Prisons and Prison Building.* New York: Architectural Book Publishing Co., 1930.

Hughes, Pennethorne. *Witchcraft.* Baltimore: Penguin, 1965.

Hyams, Edward. *A History of Gardens and Gardening.* New York: Praeger, 1971.

———. *Soil and Civilization.* New York: Harper & Row, 1976.

Hypatia's Sisters. Seattle: Feminists Northwest, 1975.

Iltis, Carolyn. *Nature and the Female in the Scientific Revolution.* Unpublished.

International Symposium on Man's Role in Changing the Face of the Earth. Edited by William L. Thomas. Chicago: University of Chicago Press, 1956.

Itard, Jean. *The Wild Boy of Aveyron*. New York: Monthly Review Press, 1972.

Jackson, Noel. *Effective Horsemanship*. New York: Arco, 1967.

Jebb, Major J. *Modern Prisons: Their Construction and Ventilation*. London: John Weale, 1844.

Jefferson, Lara. *These Are My Sisters*. New York: Doubleday, 1975.

Jonas, Hans. *The Phenomenon of Life*. New York: Dell, Delta Books, 1966.

Jones, Ernest. *The Life and Work of Sigmund Freud*. New York: Harper, 1961.

Jones, Howard Mumford. *The Age of Energy*. New York: Viking, 1971.

Joyce, James. *Ulysses*. New York: Random House, Modern Library, 1961.

Jucius, James Michael. *Personnel Management*. Homewood, Ill.: R. D. Irwin, 1967.

Jung, C. G. *Critique of Psychoanalysis*. Princeton, N.J.: Princeton University Press, 1975.

Jungk, Robert. *Brighter Than a Thousand Suns*. New York: Grove, 1958.

Kahn, Herman. *On Thermo-Nuclear Warfare*. Princeton, N.J.: Princeton University Press, 1961.

Kaufmann, William W. *The McNamara Strategy*. New York: Harper & Row, 1964.

Kearney, Hugh. *Science and Change, 1500–1700*. World University Library Series. New York: McGraw-Hill, 1971.

Kerényi, C. *Eleusis*. New York: Schocken, 1977.

Kirchshofer, Dr. Rosl, ed. *The World of Zoos*. New York: Viking, 1966.

Klaits, Joseph and Barrie, eds. *Animals and Man in Historical Perspective*. New York: Harper & Row, 1974.

Koestler, Arthur. *The Watershed: A Biography of Johannes Kepler*. Garden City, N.Y.: Doubleday, 1960.

Kolodny, Annette. *The Lay of the Land*. Chapel Hill: University of North Carolina Press, 1975.

Koyré, Alexandre. *From the Closed World to the Infinite Universe*. Baltimore: Johns Hopkins University Press, 1968.

Kramer, Heinrich, and Sprenger, James. *Malleus Maleficarum*. Translated by Montague Summers. London: Arrow, 1971.

Kübler-Ross, Elisabeth. *On Death and Dying*. New York: Macmillan, 1970.

Kuhn, Thomas S. *The Structure of Scientific Revolutions*. Chicago: University of Chicago Press, 1970.

Lambridis, Helle. *Empedocles, a Philosophical Investigation*. University, Ala.: University of Alabama Press, 1976.

Lane, Margaret. *The Tale of Beatrix Potter*. New York: Fredrich and Co., 1946.

Langer, Suzanne. *Philosophy in a New Key.* Cambridge, Mass.: Harvard University Press, 1973.

Lapp, Ralph E. *Kill and Overkill: The Strategy of Annihilation.* New York: Basic Books, 1962.

————. *The Weapons Culture.* New York: Norton, 1968.

Lederer, Wolfgang. *The Fear of Women.* New York: Grune & Stratton, 1968.

Leffingwell, William H., and Robinson, Edwin. *Textbook of Office Management.* New York: McGraw-Hill, 1950.

Leis, William. *The Domination of Nature.* New York: Braziller, 1972.

Lenzer, Gertrud. "On Masochism: A Contribution to the History of a Phantasy and Its Theory." *Signs,* vol. 1, no. 2.

Lerner, Gerda. *Black Women in White America.* New York: Random House, 1972.

Levy, Gertrude Rachel. *The Gate of Horn.* London: Faber and Faber, 1948.

Lewis, I. M. *Ecstatic Religion.* Baltimore: Penguin, 1971.

Lindsay, Peter H., and Norman, Donald A., eds. *Human Information Processing: An Introduction to Psychology.* New York: Academic Press, 1972.

Lippard, Lucy R. *From the Center.* New York: Dutton, 1976.

Lucas, Ellis. *The Big Woods.* New York: Doubleday, 1975.

Luce, Gay Gaer. *Biological Rhythms in Human and Animal Physiology.* New York: Dover, 1971.

Lurie, Nancy Oestreich, ed. *Mountain Wolf Woman.* Ann Arbor: University of Michigan Press, 1966.

Managing the Small Forest. Farmer's Bulletin No. 1989. U.S. Dept. of Agriculture. Washington, D.C.

MacKenzie, Midge. *Shoulder to Shoulder: A Documentary.* New York: Alfred A. Knopf, 1975.

Mark, Herman F. and Time-Life Editors. *Giant Molecules.* New York: Time-Life Books, 1968.

Marx, Wesley. *The Frail Ocean.* New York: Ballantine, 1970.

Measuring and Marketing Timber. Farmer's Bulletin No. 1210. U.S. Forest Service, Dept. of Agriculture. Washington, D.C.

Mellaart, James. *Catal Hüyük: A Neolithic Town in Anatolia.* London: Thames and Hudson, 1967.

Meyerhoff, Hans. *The Philosophy of History in Our Time.* Garden City, N.Y.: Doubleday, 1959.

Michelet, Jules. *Satanism and Witchcraft.* Translated by A. R. Allinson. New York: Citadel, 1939.

Miller, Hugh. *The Testimony of the Rocks.* Edinburgh: William P. Nimmo, 1869.

Millett, Kate. *Sexual Politics.* New York: Avon, 1970.

Mitchell, John. *The Earth Spirit.* New York: Avon, 1975.

Molière, *Les Femmes Savantes.* Translated by Curtis Page. New York: Putnam, 1908.

Moore, Honor. Introduction to *The New Women's Theatre.* New York: Random House, 1977.

Moore, Patrick, and Nicolson, Iain. *Black Holes in Space.* New York: Norton, 1976.

Moore, W. G. *A Dictionary of Geography.* Baltimore: Penguin, 1974.

Moravia, Alberto. *Man as an End.* New York: Farrar, Straus & Giroux, 1966.

Morgan, Robin, ed. *Sisterhood Is Powerful.* New York: Random House, 1970.

Moulton, Forest, and Schifferes, Justus, eds. *The Autobiography of Science.* Garden City, N.Y.: Doubleday, 1945.

Mozans, H. J. *Woman in Science.* Cambridge, Mass.: M.I.T. Press, 1974.

Mumford, Lewis. *The Myth of the Machine.* New York: Harcourt Brace, 1970.

———. *Technics and Civilization.* New York: Harcourt Brace, 1963.

Mundt, Carlos S. *Stars and Outer Space Made Easy.* Healdsburg, Cal.: Naturegraph Publishers, 1974.

Murchie, Guy. *Music of the Spheres.* New York: Dover, 1967.

Murray, Margaret A. *The Witch-Cult in Western Europe.* New York: Oxford University Press, 1971.

A National Plan for American Forestry. Letter from the Secretary of Agriculture in response to S. Res. 175 (72nd Congress). The Report of the Forest Service of the Agricultural Department on the Forest Problem of the United States. Vol. 2 (March 13, 1933). Washington, D.C.: U.S. Printing Office.

Neihardt, John G. *Black Elk Speaks.* New York: Pocket Books, 1972.

Neumann, Erich. *The Archetypal World of Henry Moore.* New York: Pantheon, 1959.

———. *The Great Mother.* Princeton, N.J.: Princeton University Press, 1972.

Nevens, William Barbour and Yapp, William Wodin. *Dairy Cattle Selection and Feeding.* New York: John Wiley and Sons, 1941.

Newman, James R. *The World of Mathematics.* Vols. 1 and 2. New York: Simon and Schuster, 1956.

Newton, Sir Isaac. *Opticks.* London: William and John Innys, 1721.

———. *Principia.* Translated by Andrew Motte. London: Daniel Adee, 1848.

Nietzsche, Friedrich. *Beyond Good and Evil.* New York: Random House, 1966.

————. *My Sister and I.* New York: Boar's Head Books, 1951.

Niles, Henry E. and M. C. H. *The Office Supervisor.* New York: John Wiley, 1935.

Nuclear Power Economics and the Environment. New York: The Scientists' Institute for Public Information, 1976.

O'Faolain, Julia, and Martines, Lauro, eds. *Not in God's Image.* New York: Harper & Row, 1973.

Paley, William. *Natural Theology.* Boston: Gould and Lincoln, 1866.

Panshin, A. J., Harrar, E. S., Baker, W. J., and Proctor, P. B. *Forest Products.* New York: McGraw-Hill, 1950.

Parkman, Francis. *The Oregon Trail.* New York: Grosset & Dunlap, 1927.

Parsons, Talcott. *Essays in Sociological Theory, Pure and Applied.* Chicago: Free Press, 1949.

Parsons, Talcott, and Bales, Robert F. *Family Socialization and Interaction Process.* Chicago, Free Press, 1955.

Pavlov, Ivan P. *Conditioned Reflexes.* Oxford: Oxford University Press, 1927.

————. *Lectures on Conditioned Reflexes.* New York: International Publishers, 1928.

Petersen, Karen, and Wilson, J. J. *Women Artists.* New York: Harper & Row, Colophon Books, 1976.

Petersen, W. E. *Dairy Science.* Philadelphia: Lippincott, 1939.

Plato. *The Republic of Plato.* Translated by Francis MacDonald Cornford. Oxford: Oxford University Press, 1945.

Podhajsky, Alois. *The Riding Teacher.* New York: Doubleday, 1973.

Post, Emily. *Etiquette.* New York: Funk & Wagnalls, 1960.

Power, Eileen. *Medieval Women.* Edited by M. M. Postan. New York: Cambridge University Press, 1975.

Pundel, J. Paul. *Histoire de l'operation Cesarienne.* Brussels: Presses Académiques Européenes, 1969.

Recent Prison Construction, 1950–1960. Washington, D.C.: U.S. Bureau of Prisons, 1961.

Reich, Wilhelm. *The Mass Psychology of Fascism.* New York: Farrar, Straus & Giroux, 1973.

Reid, Robert. *Marie Curie.* New York: New American Library, 1974.

Rich, Andrienne. *Of Woman Born.* New York: Norton, 1976.

Richards, Edward A., and Rubin, Edward B. *How to Select and Direct Office Staff.* New York: Harper, 1941.

Richards, M. C. *Centering in Pottery, Poetry and the Person.* Middletown, Conn.: Wesleyan University Press, 1964.

————. *The Crossing Point.* Middletown, Conn.: Wesleyan University Press, 1973.

Ricoeur, Paul. *The Symbolism of Evil.* Boston: Beacon, 1969.

Riegger, Hal. *Raku, Art and Technique.* New York: Van Nostrand Reinhold, 1970.

Roazen, Paul, ed. *Sigmund Freud.* Englewood Cliffs, N.J.: Prentice-Hall, 1973.

Robbins, Rossell Hope. *The Encyclopedia of Witchcraft and Demonology.* New York: Crown, 1959.

Rogers, Julia Ellen. *Trees.* Garden City, N.Y.: Doubleday, 1926.

Rogers, Katherine M. *The Troublesome Helpmate.* Seattle: University of Washington Press, 1966.

Rongy, Abraham J. *Childbirth, Yesterday and Today.* New York: Emerson Books, 1937.

Rousseau, Jean Jacques. *The First and Second Discourses.* Translated by Roger D. and Judith Masters. New York: St. Martin's Press, 1964.

Ruddick, Sara, and Danils, Pamela, eds. *Working It Out.* New York: Pantheon, 1977.

Ruether, Rosemary Radford. *Liberation Theology.* New York: Paulist Press, 1973.

Ruether, Rosemary Radford, ed. *Religion and Sexism.* New York: Simon and Schuster, 1974.

Ruitenbeek, Hendrik M. *Varieties of Classic Social Theory.* New York: Dutton, 1963.

Rush, Florence. "Freud and the Sexual Abuse of Children." *Chrysalis,* no. 1 (1977).

Russell, Diana, and Van de Ven, Nicole, eds. *The Proceedings of the International Tribunal on Crimes Against Women.* Millbrae, Cal.: Les Femmes, 1976.

Sasaki, Walker and Associates, *St. Louis Zoological Garden Development Program, 1962.*

Sauer, Carl O. *Agricultural Origins and Dispersals.* Cambridge, Mass.: MIT Press, 1969.

———. *Land and Life.* Berkeley: University of California Press, 1969.

Schopenhauer, Arthur. *The World as Will and Representation.* Translated by E. F. J. Payne. Vols. 1 and 2. New York: Dover, 1958.

Schroeer, Dietrich. *Physics and Its Fifth Dimension: Society.* Reading, Mass.: Addison-Wesley, 1972.

Scientific American. "Food and Agriculture." September 1976.

Sharkey, John. *Celtic Mysteries.* New York: Avon, 1975.

Shepherd, Jack. *The Forest Killers.* New York: Weybright and Talley, 1975.

Singer, Peter. *Animal Liberation.* New York: New York Review, 1975.

Slater, Philip. *Earthwalk.* New York: Doubleday, 1974.

Smith, Henry Nash. *Virgin Land.* Cambridge, Mass.: Harvard University Press, 1970.

Smith-Rosenberg, Carroll. "The Female World of Love and Ritual: Relations Between Women in Nineteenth Century America." *Signs*, vol. 1, no. 1

Spector, David A. *So You're Showing Your Horse*. New York: Arco, 1973.

Speert, Harold. *Obstetric and Gynecologic Milestones*. New York: Macmillan, 1958.

Spencer, Herbert R. *History of British Midwifery, 1650–1880*. London: John Bale Sons and Danielsson, 1927.

Speert, Harold, and Guttmacher, Alan. *Obstetric Practice*. New York: Landsberger Medical Books, 1956.

Stacks, John F. *Stripping*. San Francisco: Sierra Club, 1972.

Stanton, Elizabeth Cady. *Eighty Years and More: Reminiscences 1815–1897*. New York: Schocken, 1975.

Stanton, Theodore. *Reminiscences of Rosa Bonheur*. New York: Appleton, 1910.

Stern, Karl. *The Flight from Woman*. New York: Farrar, Straus & Giroux, Noonday, 1972.

Stone, Merlin. *When God Was a Woman*. New York: Dial Press, 1976.

Sullivan, J. W. N. *Isaac Newton, 1642–1727*. New York: Macmillan, 1938.

———. *The Limitations of Science*. New York: New American Library, 1957.

Tavard, George H. *Woman in Christian Tradition*. Notre Dame: University of Notre Dame Press, 1972.

Theiles, Carl R. *Men and Molecules*. New York: Dodd, Mead, 1962.

Thomas, William L., Jr., ed. *Man's Role in Changing the Face of the Earth*. Chicago: University of Chicago Press, 1956.

Tillyard, E. M. *The Elizabethan World Picture*. New York: Random House, Vintage Books, 1959.

Toulmin, Stephen. *The Philosophy of Science*. New York: Harper, 1960.

Toulmin, Stephen, and Goodfield, June. *The Architecture of Matter*. New York: Harper, 1963.

Trevor-Roper, H. R. *The European Witch-Craze*. New York: Harper & Row, 1967

Turnbull, Colin M. *The Forest People*. New York: Simon and Schuster, 1962.

Walsh, Mary Roth. *Doctors Wanted, No Women Need Apply*. New Haven, Conn.: Yale University Press, 1977.

Warner, Marina. *Alone of Her Sex: The Myth and the Cult of the Virgin Mary*. New York: Alfred A. Knopf, 1976.

Watson, James D. *The Double Helix*. New York: New American Library, 1968.

Weil, Simone. *First and Last Notebooks*. New York: Oxford University Press, 1970.

————. *Notebooks.* Vols. 1 and 2. New York: Putnam, 1956.

Weisheipl, James A. *The Development of Physical Theory in the Middle Ages.* Ann Arbor: University of Michigan Press, 1971.

Wendt, Herbert. *Before the Deluge.* Translated by Richard and Clara Winston. Garden City, N.Y.: Doubleday, 1968.

Westervelt, William D. *Hawaiian Legends of Volcanoes.* Rutland, Vt.; Charles E. Tuttle, 1966.

Westfall, Richard S. *Science and Religion in Seventeenth-Century England.* Ann Arbor: University of Michigan Press, 1973.

White, J. W. "Four Thousand Years of Obstetrics." *American Journal of Surgery,* vol. 2, no. 3 (March 1931).

Whitehead, Alfred North. *Concept of Nature.* New York: Cambridge University Press, 1971.

————. *Science and the Modern World.* New York: Free Press, 1967.

Wildenhain, Marguerite. *Pottery: Form and Expression.* New York: Reinhold, 1962.

William, Dorian. *Show Jumper.* New York: Arco, 1974.

Wittig, Monique. *The Lesbian Body.* New York: Morrow, 1975.

————. *Les Guerilleres.* New York: Avon, 1973.

Wollstonecraft, Mary. *Letters Written During a Short Residence in Sweden, Norway and Denmark.* Edited by Carol Poston. Lincoln: 1976.

Wright, Louis B., and Fowler, Elaine, eds. *The Moving Frontier.* New York: Delacorte, 1972.

Zaremba, Joseph. *Economics of the American Lumber Industry.* New York: Robert Speller and Sons, 1963.

Zim, Herbert S. *The Universe.* New York: William Morrow and Co., 1973.

Ziswiler, Vinzenz. *Extinct and Vanishing Animals.* London: English Universities Press, 1967.

Zivnuska, John A. *U.S. Timber Resources in a World Economy.* Baltimore: Resources for the Future, Inc., 1967.

ABOUT THE AUTHOR

SUSAN GRIFFIN is a well-known writer and social thinker. Her work, which includes *Woman and Nature: The Roaring Inside Her, Pornography and Silence,* and *A Chorus of Stones,* has been influential in several movements, shaping both ecological and feminist thought. *A Chorus of Stones,* nominated for a National Book Critics Circle Award, was a jury nominee for a Pulitzer Prize, and won the Bay Area Book Critics Award. A collection of her poetry published in 1987, *Unremembered Country,* won the California Commonwealth Prize for poetry. She has been the recipient of a MacArthur grant for Peace and International Cooperation, an NEA Fellowship, and she was awarded an Emmy for her play *Voices.* She lectures widely throughout the United States and Europe, and lives and teaches writing and the creative process privately in Berkeley, California. *The Eros of Everyday Life* was published September 1995. *What Her Body Thought: A Journey into the Shadows* was published in 1999. *Bending Home: Selected & New Poems, 1967–1998,* published by Copper Canyon Press in 1998, is a finalist for the Western States Art Federation Award for 1999.